ITALIAN COOKING
home style

PAULINE N. BARRESE

ACKNOWLEDGEMENTS go to my mother and sister Rose without whom . . .; to Elena Criscione of Ciminna, Sicily; and the other wonderful friends who have kindly offered some of these recipes.

———————————————

TO MY MOTHER SARINA,
   la bonna donnetta in cucina
   sembra a tutti una regina

———————————————

"In a region called Bengodi where they tied the vines with sausages and where one can buy a goose for a farthing and a gosling included, there is a mountain made of grated Parmesan cheese on which men worked all day making pasta and ravioli, cooking them in capon's sauce, and then rolling them down and who grabs most, eats most . . . "
                    —from Boccacio's *Decameron*

ITALIAN COOKING
home style

Editor: Grace Williams
Cover Photo: Ken Whitmore
Design: Josh Young
Book Assembly: Nancy Fisher
Typesetting: Grace Williams

ISBN Number 0-912656-19-0
Library of Congress Catalog
Card Number 74-82514
H. P. Books Number 19
© 1974 Printed in U.S.A. 9-74
H. P. Books, P. O. Box 5367
Tucson, AZ 85703

Classic Lasagne. See recipe on page 48.

Photo: Theodore R. Sills. Courtesy of National Macaroni Institute.

3

Sauce with Meatballs over spaghetti. See recipe on page 76.
Photo: Theodore R. Sills. Courtesy of National Macaroni Institute.

Macaroni with Sausage Eggplant Sauce. See recipe on page 57.
Photo: Theodore R. Sills. Courtesy of National Macaroni Institute.

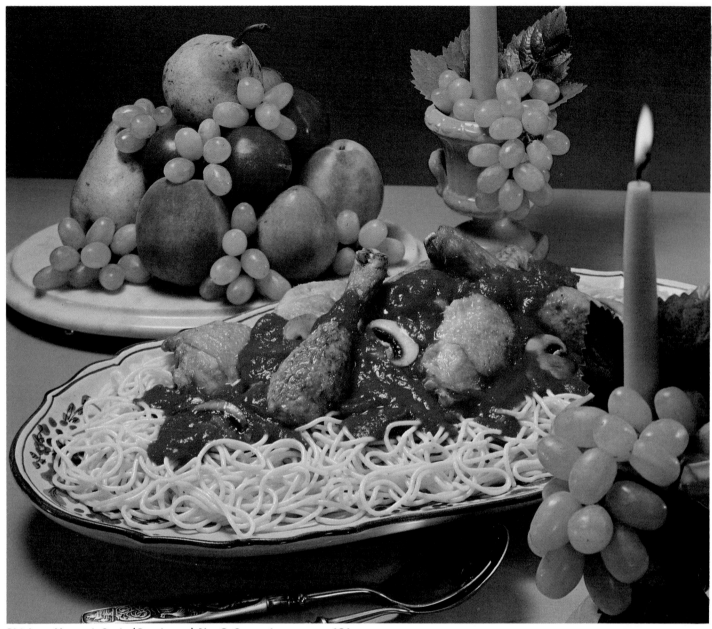

Chicken, Hunter's Style (Cacciatora) No. 2. See recipe on page 121.   Photo: Theodore R. Sills. Courtesy of National Macaroni Institute.

Beef Stew with White Wine. See recipe on page 96.
Photo courtesy of National Live Stock and Meat Board.

Baked Stuffed Rigatoni. See recipe on page 62.

Photo: Theodore R. Sills. Courtesy of National Macaroni Institute.

8

INTRODUCTION

This book actually was begun long before I decided it was high time to sit down and write it. The recipes compiled here are mostly my mother's, which lends them a kind of uniqueness.

My culinary interests budded at the age of ten when I took Saturday-morning cooking lessons at the Judson Clinic in Greenwich Village—an adventure that would never be complete until I cooked an entire meal for our family of nine.

One day (with the consent and supervision of my mother, of course) I went through with it, and albeit the compliments were very likely flattery, they were inspiring enough to further my engrossment with the skill.

Throughout the years, I hinged onto Mother's Sicilian expertness in preparing our meals (which differed slightly from our Northern Italian neighbors' who preferred more butter, fewer tomatoes, and subtler seasonings). Mother always had a passion for the kitchen, ever since her mother told her in their red-tiled *cucina* in Ciminna, Sicily that she made bread better than she—due to a discovery come upon one day when my mother put less salt in the dough. Her dream was to have five kitchens with ovens massive enough to hold all her creations. She couldn't wait to become a woman so her ardor for cookery would really be appreciated.

Mother's love for the kitchen was catching and I eventually came down with a "high cooking fever." I suppose it's only natural that I've inherited from her a keen appreciation of a genuine home-cooked meal attractively presented and enjoyed along with the leisurely conversation of family and friends. Perhaps to be followed by after-dinner *indovinelli* (guessing games) brought over from the "boot."

The mutual partaking of food stems from early life, when eating together symbolized kinship, perhaps one of the strongest ties of the ancients. In Mother's youth, the bond between Sicilian husband and wife was further represented by both eating from opposite ends of a long, oval platter.

Grabbing a morsel here and there outside the home is not really an ideal way to pass life. The habit of eating commercial foods is not only expensive but, in the long run, unhealthful as well.

There is simply no better eating than the meal prepared at home with love as the basic ingredient. The Italian woman appreciates this and it perhaps explains why her culinary skills and spirit have long been admired. She maintains that good home cooking should be encouraged no matter how hectic contemporary life proves to be.

Mother's own feelings for home cooking were instilled by a society which toiled close to the Italian earth: *contadini* (farmers) like my grandparents who survived on part of the yield from an allotted portion of a rich man's estate worked with only a few crude tools.

Holidays, then, as now, not only meant a homey meal, but a type of baking reserved for those special times. Several days before Christmas saw the town's womenfolk gathering to help each other prepare and bake quantities of their traditional Strufoli, Porcellate and Biscotti Regina with a fine pastry flour they called *maiorca*, later piling the cooled cookies in *cesti*, large round or square bamboo baskets. Requiring late hours, this was something they were unaccustomed to. But it could never mar that happy mood as they placed those goodies in white-hot brick ovens or in deep, bubbly olive oil.

That was an important part of a culinary heritage which Mother and millions of others like her from the North and the South of Italy swore they would uphold in this "promised land"—a transmigration of a kind of homespun spirit every day of the year.

Writing this book was indeed a delightful and interesting experience. I do sincerely hope its contents—an outcome of this mood and philosophy—will always prove likewise to you.

Pauline N. Barrese
Greenwich Village
September, 1974

OLIVES & OLIVE OIL

(*OLIVE E OLIO D'OLIVA*)

The Italian cook will always tell you how important olives are to her cuisine. Besides that, the oil expressed from them is 100% fuel for the body. She will astound you, perhaps, with the revelation that two tablespoons of olive oil hold more energy value than a quarter pound of beef steak. And that by making olive oil a habit in your salads and cooking, you are providing a form of concentrated energy to adults as well as growing children.

The use of olives and olive oil as food and cosmetics can be traced far back in Italian history. As early as 600 B.C. the Romans were planting the tree and putting its fruit to use. They and other early civilizations found that the olive was fit to be eaten after it was pickled: one of the most noteworthy nutritional discoveries of that time.

Horace, ancient Roman poet and follower of Epicurus, had mentioned in his *Satires*: "Sweet olive oil mixed with rich wine, fish brine or Byzantine pickles, blended with chopped herbs, boiled, sprinkled with saffron and allowed to stand is at last ready for the Venafran olives."

In daily Roman life the hands and scalp were habitually massaged, as well, with olive oil to soften the skin, make the hair grow and preserve its lively and shiny appearance.

Actually, the olive is one of the earth's oldest cultivated crops first grown as remotely as 3500 B.C. on the Greek island of Crete. It is the unceasing produce of an evergreen tree with dry, grayish-green leaves which seem to symbolize two dominant realities of the Italian: endurance as well as want. In contradiction to their appearance, however, they actually help to preserve necessary moisture in the tree's long roots which penetrate deeply into the earth. It takes an olive tree 11 years to mature and reach its growth of 20 to 30 feet. The Italian mountains and highlands cause the olive to be confined to the coasts; the shores of the Tyrrhenian Sea are an almost endless growth of olive trees where Tuscany produces the finest olive oil.

There is a false impression that all olive oil is more or less the same. Nevertheless, there is a great difference between one olive oil and another. There are hundreds of varieties of olives from which oil is crushed. The quality of the olive, the time of picking and the method of crushing determine the quality of the oil produced.

An olive picked too early, or green, gives a bitter and unpalatable oil. Olives picked too late give a greasy, flat and pungent oil that turns rancid quickly. The finest olive oil should be a brilliant light golden color, delicately fragrant and so delicious that you can drink it straight. Inferior olive oil has a pungent odor, leaves an unpleasant aftertaste and does not impart to the food or salad that delectable quality associated with the finest grades of olive oil.

It may very well be said that olive oil is the cream and butter of Italy as it usually replaces these milk products in cookery and table uses. It is, without a doubt, the most basic element of Italian cuisine.

Recommended Brands of Italian Olive Oil
Bertolli
Filippo Berio
Olio Sasso
Pope
Progresso

Photo: Josh Young

11

GRAPES & WINE
(UVA E VINO)

It has become quite a common proverb that in wine there is truth.

Pliny the Elder

Tonight with wine, drown care.

Horace

Away with you water, destruction of wine.

Catullus

Wine, The Pegasus of poets.

Pontanus

The grapevine was introduced to the Italians by the Greeks. They brought it to Sicily, and it transformed the colors and shapes of its ancient hills and valleys. From Sicily cultivation of "the vine" spread throughout all of Italy.

Later, the ancient Roman Horace offered some helpful and interesting comments on grapes and wine:

If a guest arrives unexpectedly, plunge a tough fowl into Falernian wine mixed with water; this will make it tender. Venusian grapes are suitable for preserving in jars; those from Alba are better for the smokehouse. I am in favor of serving these grapes with apples, caviar and white pepper finely mixed with black salt in neat little salt cellars.

Another Roman author, Pliny, gave accounts of 91 varieties of grapes in his writings, categorized 50 kinds of wine and elaborated on vine-training procedures.

Tilling of "the vine" is done upon the sun-drenched inclines of limestone hills and mountains. Italian vineyards once relied on rain for moisture, but now are mostly under irrigation. Among the grapes grown there are *Refosco, La-grain, Barbera Fresa, Nebbiolo* and *Moscatello Fino.*

There is much that goes into the making of good wine. Unless the fruit is mature when gathered, it must be ripened artificially by fire, steaming, sweating or freezing. If not ripe, the grape will produce a small amount of juice of excessive acidity. Utmost care must be taken to rid the grape of any dust that may taint the final product.

A wine in which all the sugar has been fermented away is called "dry." But in "sweet" wines, a considerable amount of sugar is left. An artificial "sparkling" wine is made by imbuing wine with carbonic acid gas.

Italy is noted for many wines such as *Lagrima Christi, Chianti, Madeira, Malaga* as well as those of *Asti* and *Montferrat.* Still another is *Marsala,* a light, sweet delicious wine which is an artificial production made of the local wines of Marsala, Sicily, fortified with *Aqua Vitae.* It was, of all things, first concocted by an Englishman named John Woodhouse who had established a wine trade in Marsala in 1773. To this day, *Marsala* is still highly favored the world over as an apéritif.

But whether used as a distinctive flavoring in cooking (where most of the alcohol evaporates), as an appetizer wine or accompaniment, wine is essential to Italian culinary repertoires. Veal cutlets with *Bardolino,* chicken cooked in *Marsala* or sesame seed cookies with a sunny cordial like *Moscato* are most charming ways to please the palate.

There is a wine for every food and every person. The following Wine Selection Guide is intended to be of some assistance to those with doubts about selecting wines to accompany certain foods. Color, chilling time and personally recommended brands of the different specialties are included.

If you have difficulty in obtaining some of these wines, your local wine dealer will probably be glad to order them.

Wine racks of standard sizes may be purchased at any good wine emporium. The durable honeycomb type with individual spaces for each bottle is ideal and can be made to measure.

STORING WINES

Place wine rack in a cellar with a constant temperature of 50°F. to 60°F. All bottles with corks should be stored lying down so the wine comes in contact with the cork which otherwise may dry out and allow seepage of air—an enemy of wine. Bottles without corks may be stored standing up.

Once opened, a dinner wine should be poured as soon as possible. If not entirely used, recap and place in the refrigerator where it will retain

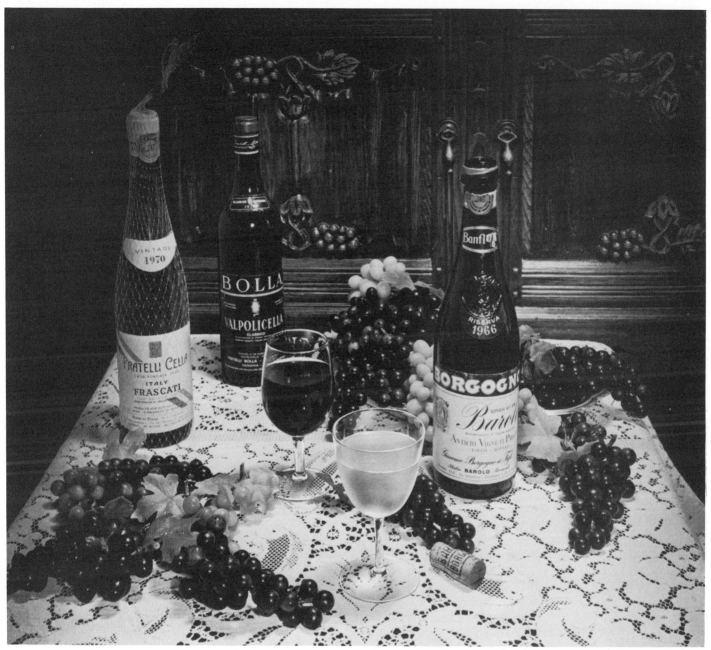

flavor about a week.

Recapped liqueurs, sherries, vermouth, Marsala and cordials do not need to be kept refrigerated.

SERVING WINES

Practically any glass you have in the cupboard can be used. Stem glasses add a touch of gaiety and should be used if available. Dessert and appetizer wines should be served in a three-ounce glass. Table wines should be served in a six-ounce glass filled only two-thirds full. Sparkling wines chill beautifully on their side in the refrigerator with temperatures not going below 40° F. They may be served in a stemmed wine glass about 5-1/2 inches tall with a bowl about 3-1/2 inches deep.

WHAT YOU WILL NEED FOR A PARTY

A bottle of table wine will serve six drinks. Plan to have one bottle for every three persons at the party.

A bottle of dessert wine contains eight servings (three ounces each).

A gallon of wine (bottle or jug) will serve 32 persons. A gallon of dessert wine will serve 42 persons (three ounces each).

13

WINE SELECTION GUIDE

COLOR & TYPE	NAME OF WINE (BRANDS)	PRONUNCIATION	SERVE WITH	CHILLING TIME
Appetizer Wines Golden-brown	**Sweet Vermouth** (Stock Italian) (California)	Vur-mooth'	Cheeses Snacks Appetizers Nuts	
White	**Dry Vermouth** (Stock Italian) (California)			1 hr.
White Dinner Wines	**Chianti** (Ruffino)	Kee-ahn'tee	Cheese, Clams, Fish, Omelets	
	Soave (Folonari)	So-ah'vay	Shrimp, Chicken, Roast, Mozzarella	1 hr.
	Frascati (Marino)	Fra-scot'tee	Pork	
Red Dinner Wines	**Barolo** (Borgogno)	Bah-roe'lo	Provolone, Duck, Steak	Room Temp.
	Chianti (Bertolli)	Kee-ahn'tee	Beef, Roast, Pizza, Spaghetti, Game	Room Temp.
	Zinfandel (California)	Zin'fan-dell	Chops, Cheeses, Red Meats, Spiced Dishes	Room Temp.
	Burgundy (California)			Room Temp. (Chill slightly when temperature is above 80° F.)
Light Red Dinner Wines	**Bardolino** (Folonari)	Bar-doe-lean'oh	Veal Mozzarella	Room Temp.
	Valpolicella (Folonari)	Val-po-lee-chel'lah	Lamb	Room Temp.
	Grignolino (Grignolino Riserva Cavour) (California)	Green-yo-lee'no	Liver	Room Temp.

WINE SELECTION GUIDE

COLOR & TYPE	NAME OF WINE (BRANDS)	PRONUNCIATION	SERVE WITH	CHILLING TIME
Dessert Wines	Marsala (sweet) (Florio)	Mahr-sah'lah	Pastry, Fruit, Puddings, Cookies	2 hours
	Sweet Sherry (Orvieto Abboccato) (Pertrurbani)		Fruit Bread Nuts Cheeses	1 hour or Room Temp.
	Moscato (Moscati Naturale d'Asti)	Mo-scah' toh	Cake Cookies	Room Temp.
Sparkling Wines	Asti Spumante (Cinzano)	Ah-stee' Spoo' mahn-tee	Appetizers Desserts	2–3 hours
	Lagrima Christi (M. & R.)	La-gree'mah Cree'stee	Appetizers Desserts	2–3 hours

OTHER POPULAR WINES

Red Wines
Freisa
Ciro di Calabria
Barbera
Faro
Chiaretta del Garda
Brolio
(Serve at room temperature.)

White Wines
Valtellina
Terlano
Orvieto
Est-est-est Montefiascone
Sansevero
Sherry
(Chill 1 hour.)

Dessert Wines
Malvasia
Greco di Girace
Vin Santo
(Chill 2 hours.)

Cordials
Anisette
Grappa
Creme de Menthe
Brandy
Maraschino
Galliano
Flora della Alpi
Mandorino
Blackberry
Creme de Mocca Caffe Sport
Strega
(Serve at room temperature.)

HERBS
(ERBI)

At least forty varieties of flavoring herbs are cultivated in European gardens. Yet, here in America, except for persons of foreign stock like Italians, few people grow herbs.

The Italian cook's garden, importantly close to the kitchen, almost always includes fresh basil, parsley, mint, garlic, fennel, rosemary, sage, thyme and onion, among others. But she is not daunted if soil and space are limited, as in the city. For she would, notwithstanding, manage to grow at least three or four herbs in a number of deep clay pots on her windowsills.

She obtains herb seedlings for her garden or pots from a local Italian vegetable market, though these can be purchased at a nursery as well.

But leaf herbs can also be grown from seeds bought at the five and dime store, a supermarket or nursery. These must be started in seed pans because some herbs have such small seeds. The seedlings are then put into well-drained pots. When large enough, they are transplanted to good garden soil. They don't require an excessive amount of care, but they do need full sunlight for at least six hours a day.

Easy accessibility of herbs is important to the Italian cook because she uses them daily in roast meats, stews, soups, stuffings, sauces, etc. She regards herbs as next to salad vegetables in significance because they heighten the enjoyment of her meals—and at a very low cost.

Sometimes, to have fresh herbs between seasons, she will transplant them in the fall from her garden to boxes or pots to be maintained indoors in a sunny window. More often, however, she will dry leaf herbs in the summer or autumn for winter use. She harvests them when the flower buds are forming. First washing the leaves the night before, she gathers them the following day as soon as the dew has evaporated but before the day becomes warm and begins to rob the leaves of their fragrant oil. They are then spread thinly on trays in a warm, airy place (not in an oven or strong sunlight) and turned daily.

Another way is to tie the sprays, after removing all imperfect leaves, and hang them in loose bunches in a sunny, airy room for a half hour, to be later put in a dark place to completely dry.

She will, then, remove the stems, finely crumble the leaves and store them in tight glass jars or stoppered bottles for ready use.

One of the most popular herbs in the Italian cuisine is fresh garlic cultivated from the earliest ages because of its warm and wholesome addition to food. Its juice is used in medicine as an antiseptic and occasionally in respiratory ailments.

It is in season all year and plump, firm, unbroken garlic is purchased one root at a time. It is stored in a cool, dry place. If placed in a jar, holes are made in top for ventilation.

To prepare, break the outer skin and remove the number of cloves needed. Use a garlic press or peel the clove of garlic by putting the clove between two pieces of paper towel. Crush the clove with the handle of a knife. Remove meat from the skin.

To mince, cut peeled garlic lengthwise not quite through. Then slice finely crosswise.

The Italian cook invites you to use the herbs mentioned here in your daily recipes, promising either a revelation or a temptation to combine some you may have never used together before.

Anise (*Anice*)—an herb of the carrot family. Its seed yields an oil used in liqueurs and as a flavoring in desserts.

Basil (*Basilico*)—a sweet annual herb of the mint family. Has an agreeable fragrance and taste. For seasoning soups, stews, fowl and meat.

Bay Leaf (*Foglio Di Alloro*)—a stiff grayish-green leaf of the bay tree, having a strong aroma. Used to flavor meat, fowl, sauces and olives.

Fennel (*Finocchio*)—a sweet perennial herb of the carrot family, grown mostly for its flavorful seeds used in sausages and cookies. Eaten in salads. Wild fennel is used in macaroni dishes.

Garlic (*Aglio*)—a pungent herb with a strong characteristic scent. Composed of small bulbs called "cloves." Used for adding taste to meats, fish, lamb, fowl, salads and sauces.

Marjoram (*Maggiorana*)—either of two genera of mints. Used for flavoring meat loaf, soups, veal, lamb and pork.

Mint (*Menta*)—bright green herb of the lilac family. Has an aromatic odor. Used for condiments and lends taste to vegetables, lamb and fowl.

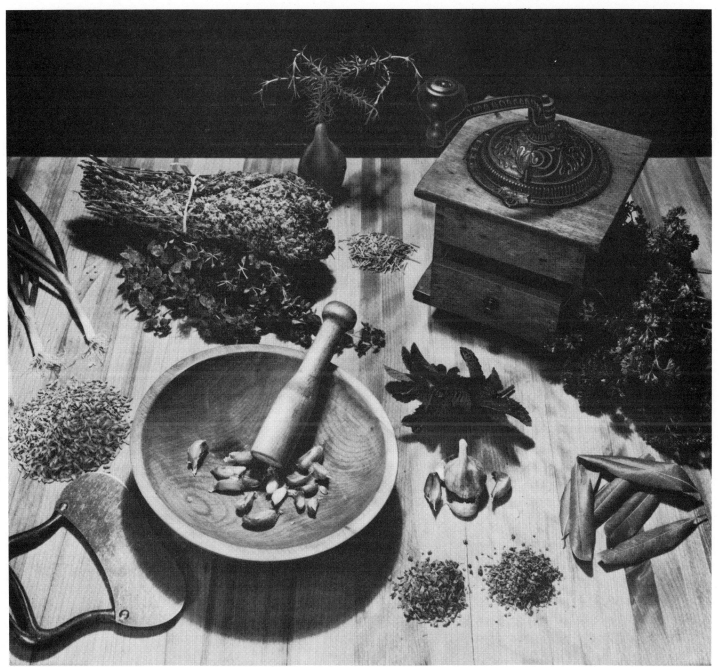

Important herbs for Italian dishes: onions, fresh and dried oregano, fresh and dried rosemary, parsley, bay leaf, dried marjoram, dried sweet basil, mint, garlic, and fennel.

Photo: Josh Young

Onion (*Cipolla*)—an edible bulb of sharp smell and taste. Used in most Italian dishes.

Oregano (*Orégano*)—gray-green leaves of a fragrant shrub. For flavoring pork dishes, sauces, mushrooms and beans.

Parsley (*Prezzemolo*)—a fragrant annual or biennial herb. Leaves are used to flavor soups, stews, etc. or as a garnish.

Rosemary (*Rosmarino*)—leaves of an evergreen shrub. Lends distinction to soups, lamb, eggs, meat and fish sauces.

Sage (*Salvia*)—a shrub-like mint with gray-green leaves. The leaves and flowering parts are used as tea and for flavoring meats and fowl.

Thyme (*Timo*)—an herb of half-shrubby plants with a mint-like aroma. Delicious in preparing stuffings, fish sauces, eggplant, beans, soups and meat dishes.

CHEESE

(*FORMAGGIO*)

In ancient times, the making of cheese was well known to the Romans, the earliest reference to it occurring around 1400 B.C. The milk of sheep and goats was used for making cheese as well as for drinking.

Cheese in its natural form is actually the curd of milk. In some types, this curd, after several procedures, is allowed to stand for a certain time, molded into a loaf and cured for a period ranging from a few weeks to two years. The longer the cure, the more sharpness it acquires.

In other kinds of cheese, molds are inoculated to give them their distinctive taste. Others are salt or brine processed which prevents mold and permits the cheese to cure from the outside in, while attaining its own characteristic flavor.

Italy's involvement in the sphere of cheese has been a very influential one both from the point of view of its production of cheese for the world and the distinctiveness of types and quality of the product. The Italian cook has gained special recognition of her skill with cheese. She will usually have at least six to seven cheeses handy for a variety of uses in her menus. For luncheon, she's apt to have some ready-grated Romano cheese to enhance a home-style Fresh Tomato Omelet and mozzarella cheese for that special Sunday dinner of Lasagne. Others likely to be found in her kitchen are among the best known: Gorgonzola, Parmesan, pecorino and provolone cheeses for uses that range from stuffing chilled celery sticks, salad dressings, and sprinkling pasta to sandwich making.

Weight watchers can find cheeses to suit their needs in the Italian cuisine. Ricotta, for example, is lower in calories than most other cheeses because it contains more moisture and less milk fat. Part-skim mozzarella also does not contain the calories that the whole-milk type does.

STORING CHEESE

Cheese keeps best in the refrigerator. How long it will keep depends on the kind of cheese and the wrapping.

Soft cheeses such as ricotta are highly perishable. Hard cheeses keep much longer than soft cheeses if protected from drying out. Approxi-mate storage times are given in this home storage guide for cheese:

Cheese Product	Recommendation for Storing
Fresh ricotta and other soft cheeses	Refrigerate, covered. Use within 3 to 5 days.
Hard varieties	Refrigerate tightly wrapped; will keep for several months unless mold develops.

Leave cheese in its original wrapper, if possible. Cover cut surfaces tightly with waxed paper, foil or plastic to protect the surface from drying out, or store the cheese in a tightly covered container. Store cheese that has a strong odor, such as Gorgonzola or provolone, in a tight container.

Any surface mold that develops on hard natural cheese should be trimmed off completely before the cheese is used. In mold-ripened cheeses such as Gorgonzola, the mold is an important part of the cheese and can be eaten.

Cheese that has dried out and become hard may be grated and stored in a tightly covered jar.

Freezing is not recommended for most cheeses because they become crumbly and mealy. Small pieces (one pound or less) not more than an inch thick of the following Italian varieties can be frozen satisfactorily: provolone, mozzarella, small quantities of Gorgonzola for salads or salad dressings, or other uses where a crumbly texture is acceptable. Wrap cheeses tightly, freeze quickly at 0° F. or below, and store no more than six months.

GRATING CHEESE

An electric blender is a most convenient appliance for grating cheese. However, a tall four-sided stainless steel hand grater is practical and most used by the Italian cook for grating hard and semi-soft cheeses. It allows you a choice of textures from very fine to coarse.

The four-sided hand grater, a wooden board, wax paper and a sharp, heavy-bladed knife are the tools you need for easy cutting and grating.

Begin by removing rind from cheese. For easier handling and grating of large pieces of cheese, place the wide flat side down on wooden board. With the palm of the left hand placed on the pointed end of the knife and the right hand holding the handle, press the blade firmly into the center of the cheese. With a rocking motion,

Italian cheeses: wedges of Romano, Fontina and Gorgonzola, ricotta in the small bowl, mozzarella and slices of Provolone.

press knife firmly down to obtain a clean cut.

Place wax paper on board to catch grated cheese. Take grater by the handle and hold upright on board. Holding cheese firmly in fingers and palm of hand, grate in an up-and-down motion until cheese is grated down to a smaller size. Use only the fingertips to hold the smaller piece and be careful not to scrape fingers. Grate, turning the cheese around when needed for a better grip. When cheese has dwindled to a very small piece, you simply place the piece between the thumb and top of grater and gently but firmly press down the length of grater until completely grated. Store in a tightly covered jar.

If you purchase cheese in an Italian specialty store, they may grate it for you free of charge, eliminating the need for home grating.

When serving grated cheese for soups and pasta, serve it in an attractive cheese server.

SUBSTITUTING ITALIAN CHEESES

For Italian recipes, Italian cheeses are highly recommended. However, if specific cheeses are not available in certain localities, other cheeses are good substitutes for them, as shown in the following chart.

Cheese	Substitute
Gorgonzola	Blue, Roquefort
Mozzarella	Muenster, Processed Gruyere
Parmesan	Pecorino
Provolone	Sharp Cheddar, Caciocavallo
Ricotta	Creamed Cottage Cheese (mild, with tiny soft curds)
Romano	Pecorino

There is no hard and fast rule about using Parmesan, Romano or pecorino cheeses; they can be mostly interchanged. Use is largely a matter of personal preference.

FAVORITE ITALIAN CHEESES

This glossary will serve to make clearer the characteristics of favorite Italian cheeses.

Bel Paese—a semi-soft cheese. It is light yellow and has a mild taste. A slicing type for every table use, for canapes, or for spreading on sandwiches.

Caciocavallo—a hard, slicing, yellow pungent cheese to serve with wine, bread or fruit. Similar to provolone. Can also be grated.

Fontina—warm ivory in color. The texture is fairly firm and the surface is broken here and there by tiny holes. A table cheese of extraordinary quality and a superb melting cheese with a special tang.

Gorgonzola—"the king of table cheeses." A pressed white cheese made from cow's milk. It is creamy and rich. When ripe, it acquires a bluish-green mold and resembles "blue" cheese. Excellent for spreading, fine for antipasto or cocktail tray, superb with wine.

Incannestrata—made from combined cow's and goat's milk. A sharp, yellowish-white Sicilian cheese sometimes containing black pepper. It is distinguished by braided basket wrapping; served with wine after dinner, also grated for hearty sauces.

Mozzarella—a fresh, smooth, creamy-white cheese. Very bland. May be sliced and cooked. Used in lasagne, omelets, various vegetable dishes, sandwiches or on pizza.

Mozzarella Affumicata—smoked mozzarella. A white slicing cheese.

Parmigiano (*Parmesan* or *Reggiano*)—a hard, dry, pressed skim-milk cheese made from pure cow's milk. Has a delicate, sweetish taste. Aged for two years or more. Good for grating. Made originally in the province of Parma, Italy. Some prefer a combination of Parmesan with pecorino. May be used on pasta, vegetable soups and dishes *au gratin*.

Pecorino—made from sheep's milk. It is whitish and medium-sharp. It is a semi-hard Roman grating and eating cheese. Fine for meat sauces, cacciatores and tomato dishes.

Provola—a semi-hard, yellowish-white cheese for slicing and grating. Not quite as sharp as provolone.

Provolone—made from pure, rich cow's milk. It is hard and yellow, but creamy, with a piquant taste. Can be sliced and grated. A provolone sandwich helps to make a delightful lunch. Serve in wedges for an appetizer.

Ricotta—a fresh cheese resembling cottage cheese. Made from skimmed, boiled milk. Has a low calorie content.

Romano—a sharp cheese with a yellowish-white interior and greenish-black surface. Aged for one year or more. Made from pure, rich sheep's milk. Used for grating.

Scamozza—a smooth, white, unsalted, oval cheese resembling mozzarella.

Stracchino—a light yellow, sharp slicing cheese made from goat's milk. Comes from Milan.

Photo courtesy of Manganaro's.

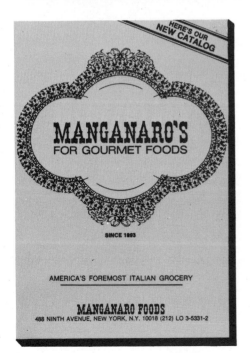

WHERE TO BUY ITALIAN FOODS

Wherever you may live, it's easy to order fine foods from Manganaro's—America's foremost Italian grocery. It is at 488 Ninth Avenue, New York, N.Y. 10018, telephone (212) LO 3-5331. Order by mail or by phone. Write for a free catalog.

Among items available are salamis, proscuitto, dry sausages, herbs, condiments, tomatoes, olive oil, cheeses, pastas, green noodles, Italian coffee and a variety of utensils and gadgets such as cheese graters, espresso makers and snail serving accessories.

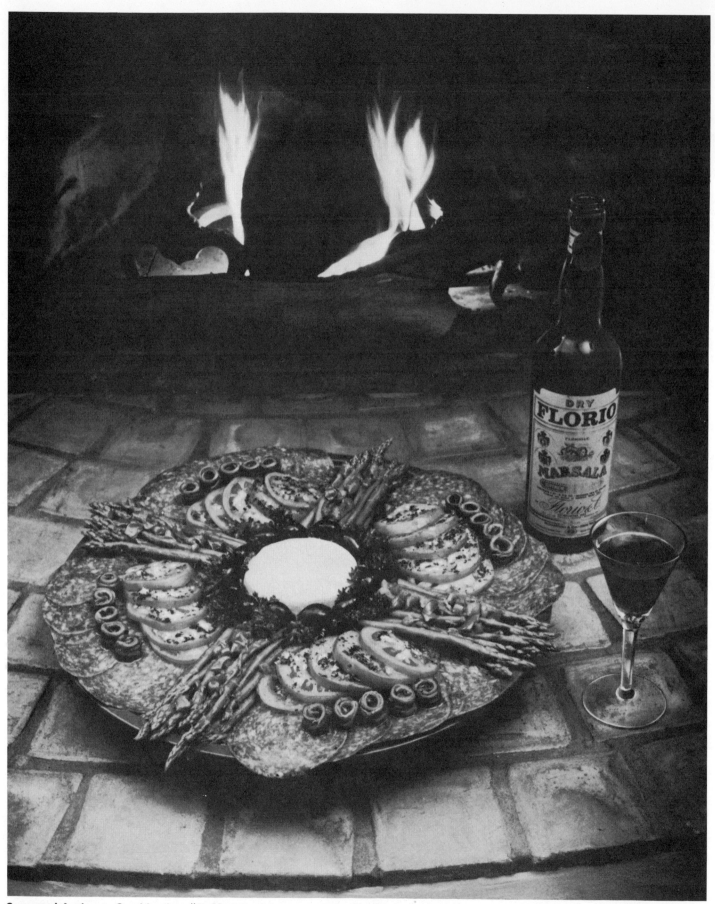

Suggested Antipasto Combination #5: Marinated Asparagus Tips, Genoa salami, Rolled Fillets of Anchovies with Capers, Bel Paese cheese in the center, Ripe Olives, Tomato Slices with Basil, and chilled Marsala. See page 25.

Photo: Josh Young

22

Buon appetito (good appetite) is uppermost in the mind of the Italian cook. When serving antipasto before a meal, she is careful not to serve so much that it dulls the appetite. If the occasion is a get-together that doesn't include a meal, the amounts may be increased.

Antipasto is meant to whet the appetite not only by way of the taste buds, but with visual appeal, as well, by presenting a colorful combination. One might serve something like Marinated Asparagus Tips that delightfully sting the tongue; crisp, cold celery sticks; or bright, firm tomato slices topped with attractive chopped green basil leaves fresh out of the flower pot.

The antipasto must complement the meal to follow. For example, don't serve too many anchovies or sardines if there is to be a fish supper. Or meat and cheese if, say, roast beef or a cheese dish is to follow.

It is customary for Italians to serve antipasto at a set dinner table before the meal. The setting includes medium-size antipasto plates onto which family or guests can place their choice from the food on attractive trays, platters and small bowls, or a lazy susan. Napkins, small plastic forks and spoons of bright hues and attractive appetizer wine glasses are also essential to the eye appeal and enjoyment of the appetizers. Colorful toothpicks help in dramatizing antipasto foods—like a red toothpick piercing a yellow cheese cube or a blue toothpick securing rolled Italian cold cuts.

The moment dinner begins with antipasto, the glasses are raised and the Italian toast *"Salute!"* (sa-loo-tay) (Good health!) is given with much gusto.

Antipasto may be served with any of these popular wines: chilled sweet vermouth, dry vermouth, dry sherry or Marsala.

ANTIPASTO TERMS

Anchovy Fillets (*Acciughe*)—a small herring-like fish found in the Mediterranean used for pickling, sauces, etc.

Capers (*Capperi*)—young, green, pickled berries used in relish, sauces, etc.

Caponatina—Sicilian-style appetizer containing eggplant, tomato sauce, capers, spices, olive oil, celery, olives and vinegar.

Cherry Peppers (*Peperoni Forte Rotondi*)—very hot, round red or green peppers in vinegar. Crushed red pepper seeds (*pepe forte*) are dried, ground cherry peppers and seeds used lightly as seasoning.

Fennel (*Finocchio*)—a type of celery with an anise taste. Used as antipasto, with macaroni and eaten in slices after dinner.

Giardiniera—a spicy, tangy vegetable salad.

Grissini—crisp, long, slender Italian bread sticks, usually eaten as antipasto.

Hot Red Pepper (*Peperone Forte Lungo*)—a slim, bright red cayenne pepper. May be pickled or dried. Has a hot, pungent flavor.

Peperoncini al'Aceto—small, tart green peppers in vinegar.

Pickled Sweet Red, Green and Yellow Peppers (*Peperoni Sottaceto*)—sweet peppers of various colors, cut in large sections and preserved in vinegar.

Sicilian Olives (*Olive Siciliani*)—sun-dried, ripe, black Sicilian olives prepared with olive oil, spices and herbs.

SALAMI

Casalinga Style—a flavorful domestic sausage. Pure pork ground in large chunks, seasoned with garlic and black pepper, cured in an age-old tradition and smoked by charred wood.

Citterio Brand—a finely ground pure pork, spiced lightly with garlic and black pepper.

Genoa Salami—a pure finely ground domestic pork, noted for its mildness, with just a touch of seasoning for flavor.

Salami Cotto—a domestic-style salami, chunky, generously seasoned pork in natural casing, to be sliced thin like cold cuts.

Sicilian Salami—finely ground pure pork, made after fashion popular in Southern Italy. Mildly seasoned with whole black peppers. Domestic.

Sopressata—slow-cured, marbled, highly-aromatic

Antipasto

pork with chewy texture in natural casing. Made with no garlic. Should be cut in 1/4-inch-thick slices to be eaten out-of-hand with bread.
Zampino—a boiled domestic salami, finely ground and mildly flavored with garlic.

ITALIAN HAMS, ETC.

Capocollo—a cold cut made from the pig's neck. Should be sliced thin.
Mortadella—a delicately prepared cold cut from Bologna, shaped like bologna, spiced with rare herbs and a touch of garlic. Serve on antipasto or cold-cut tray, makes tasty sandwiches.

Proscuitto—an exquisitely cured pressed ham. Its delicate flavor makes it a treat on all occasions. Should be sliced paper-thin.

DRY SAUSAGES

Cotechini—a style originating in Valle D'Aosta, Italy. Widely used to add flavor to lentil broth.
Pepperoni—a naturally cured sausage, reddish in color and hot, for those who enjoy sausage with a sharp and spicy flavor. Should be sliced thin.
Salsiccia Secca—a dry pork sausage. Should be sliced thin.

SUGGESTED ANTIPASTO COMBINATIONS

1
Pickled Beets
Mortadella
*Sardines with Green Olives
Caciocavallo Cheese
Sliced Pickled Cucumber
Finocchio
Well-Chilled Dry Sherry

2
Giardiniera
*Stuffed Eggs with Cheese
*White Beans with Oregano
*Shrimp with Tomato Mayonnaise
Grissini
Ripe Olives
Well-Chilled Dry Vermouth

3
*Caponatina
Sicilian Salami
Black Olives
*Stuffed Eggs with Pimiento
Grissini
Well-Chilled Dry Vermouth

4
*Marinated Artichoke Hearts
Provolone
Sardines
Black Queen Olives
Capocollo
Pimiento Strips
Grissini
Well-Chilled Sweet Vermouth with Lemon Peel

5
*Marinated Asparagus Tips
Genoa Salami
*Rolled Fillets of Anchovies with Capers
Bel Paese Cheese *or* Fontina Cheese
Ripe Olives
*Tomato Slices with Basil
Chilled Marsala

*Recipe included in this book. See index.

SARDE CON OLIVE VERDE
Sardines with Green Olives

6 canned sardines with oil
juice of 1/2 lemon

3 sliced stuffed green olives
freshly ground pepper to taste

Place sardines on platter. Add lemon juice to oil in sardine can. Mix. Pour over sardines. Arrange sliced olives on top. Sprinkle with pepper. Serves 3.

FETTI DI POMODORO CON BASILICO
Tomato Slices with Basil

4 medium-size tomatoes, sliced 1/4-inch thick
1 clove minced garlic

4 tsp. chopped fresh basil
olive oil

Arrange tomato slices on dish. Put garlic and 1 tsp. of basil on each tomato. Sprinkle lightly with olive oil. Serves 4.

UOVA IMBOTTITE CON PIMIENTO
Stuffed Eggs with Pimiento

6 eggs
1/2 small grated onion

French dressing
6 thin pimiento strips

Cook eggs until hard-boiled. Remove from stove and run cold water over them for easier removal of shells. Peel. When cool, slice eggs in half lengthwise. Remove yolks and mash in a bowl. Add grated onion and enough French dressing to moisten. Mix. Stuff eggs. Garnish centers with pimiento strips. Serves 6.

French Dressing:
1 1/2 cups olive oil
1/2 cup red wine vinegar

2 tsp. salt
1 tsp. finely ground pepper

Combine all ingredients and mix well. Place in a small bottle or jar. Shake well before using.

ROLLINI DI ACCIUGHE CON CAPPERI
Rolled Fillets of Anchovies with Capers

fillets of anchovies
capers

(amounts as desired)

Lay anchovy fillets flat. Place a caper on one end of each fillet and roll tightly. Arrange rolled anchovy fillets right side up on a platter.

GRISSINI CON PROSCUITTO
Bread Sticks with Italian Ham

grissini (bread sticks)
paper-thin proscuitto, cut into strips

(amounts as desired)

Wind one proscuitto strip around each bread stick.

CUORI DI CARCIOFI MARINATI
Marinated Artichoke Hearts

12 canned artichoke hearts (in brine)
1/4 cup olive oil
3 tbs. wine vinegar

1/4 tsp. dry parsley
salt and pepper to taste

Wash artichoke hearts. Drain. In a salad bowl, place artichoke hearts, olive oil, vinegar, parsley, salt and pepper. Toss. Marinate for 1 hour or more in refrigerator. Serves 4.

Broiled Stuffed Artichokes

CARCIOFI IMBOTTITI AL GRIGLIA
Broiled Stuffed Artichokes

3 globe artichokes
1 clove garlic
2 tbs. olive oil
1 cup coarse bread crumbs
3 tbs. chopped parsley

Dipping Sauce:
1/2 cup butter *or* margarine, melted
1/4 cup grated Parmesan cheese

1/4 cup grated Parmesan cheese
1/4 tsp. onion salt
1 tsp. lemon juice
1/4 cup olive oil

1 tsp. lemon juice
pepper to taste

Aioli Sauce
2 TBls Nonfat mayo
2 TBlsp hot mustard or
mustard seeds
1 tsp lemon juice
1 tsp chopped garlic
1 tsp miso
1/4 tsp black pepper
dash cayenne pepper

Wash artichokes and cut off prickly leaf tips. Trim stems. Add garlic and olive oil to boiling, salted water and drop artichokes into water. Cook for 30 to 40 minutes or until tender. Drain. When cool enough to handle, slice artichoke in half lengthwise and remove fuzzy choke. Fill each cavity with the combined bread crumbs, parsley, cheese, onion salt and lemon juice. Drizzle olive oil over each and place stuffed artichokes on broiler pan. Broil about 4 inches from heat for 3 to 5 minutes or until stuffing is golden brown.

Meanwhile, combine ingredients for Dipping Sauce and heat until blended. Serve hot artichokes with hot sauce. Serves 6. (**See photo above.**)

SPARAGI MARINATI
Marinated Asparagus Tips

2 lbs. fresh asparagus (or frozen asparagus tips
   cooked according to package directions)
2 tbs. finely chopped sweet red pepper (in vinegar)

1/4 cup olive oil
3 tbs. wine vinegar *or* lemon juice
salt and pepper to taste

Wash fresh asparagus well. Cut off tips. Cook tips in boiling, salted water until tender. Drain. Place in a salad bowl. Add sweet red pepper, olive oil, vinegar or lemon juice, salt and pepper. Mix well. Marinate for 1 hour or more in refrigerator. Serves 6.

MELONE CON PROSCUITTO
Melon with Italian Ham

1 large cantaloupe *or* honeydew melon
1/2 lb. proscuitto, cut paper-thin

Cut cantaloupe in half. Remove seeds and rind. Cut into cubes. Cut proscuitto into 1/2-inch-wide strips, long enough to wrap each cube. Secure with toothpicks. Chill. Serve with appetizer wine. Serves 5.

If desired, when serving, pass a pepper grinder or sprinkle with coarsely cracked pepper. Fresh pineapple fingers, green figs or persimmon may also be served in this manner.

SEDANO IMPANATO SAUTE
Sautéed Breaded Celery

1 medium bunch pascal celery (1 1/2 lbs.)
salted water to cover
2 eggs
1 1/2 cups fine bread crumbs
4 tsp. grated Romano *or* Parmesan cheese

2 tsp. finely chopped parsley
1/8 tsp. garlic powder
salt and pepper to taste
1/2 cup olive oil

Separate celery stalks. Scrub well with a brush. Trim off root and any blemishes. Remove strings. If too wide, cut in half. Cut into 3-inch pieces. In a covered, medium-size pot, cook celery in boiling, salted water to cover for 15–20 minutes or until tender. Drain.

In a shallow bowl, beat eggs. In a shallow dish, combine bread crumbs, cheese, parsley, garlic powder, salt and pepper. Dip celery pieces in egg. Dredge in bread crumb mixture.

Heat olive oil in a large skillet and sauté celery pieces over low flame until golden brown on both sides. Add more olive oil if needed. Drain on absorbent paper. Serve hot. Serves 5–6.

SEDANO IMBOTTITO CON GORGONZOLA
Celery Stuffed with Gorgonzola

8 tender pascal celery stalks
Gorgonzola cheese

Scrub celery stalks with a brush. Trim off root and any blemishes. Dry. Cut into 2-inch pieces. Chill. In a bowl, cream Gorgonzola cheese. Stuff celery sticks. Arrange on a serving platter. Serves 8.

CECI CON MAIONESE SENAPE
Chickpeas with Mustard Mayonnaise

canned chickpeas (garbanzos)
mayonnaise   (amounts as desired)
French mustard

Drain chickpeas. To every cup of mayonnaise add 1 tablespoon of French mustard. Moisten chickpeas with mixture. Place on serving platter.

VEGETALI MISTO
Mixed Vegetables

4 large red or green bell peppers
1/4 cup olive oil
1/4 lb. sliced fresh mushrooms
1 clove garlic, split

4 chopped fillets of anchovy
1 cup pitted, chopped ripe green olives
salt to taste (if desired)

Broil peppers as close to flame as possible. When black, place in a paper bag. Close. Let stand for 10 minutes. Then rub off skins. Cut into 1-inch strips. Discard seeds and fibers.

Heat olive oil in a medium-size skillet. Add peppers and mushrooms and cook over medium flame for 6 minutes. Add garlic, anchovies and olives. Mix. Cook 2 minutes longer. Season with salt, if desired. Serve hot with Italian bread. (This dish may be made ahead and reheated.) Serves 4.

CAPONATINA
Eggplant Relish

2 lb. unpeeled eggplant, cut into 1-inch cubes
1/2 cup olive oil
1 large chopped onion
1 cup chopped celery
3 1/2 oz. tomato paste
1 cup water

1 lb. green olives, salted and pitted
2 oz. jar of capers, unsalted and drained
salt and pepper to taste
1 heaping tsp. sugar
1/4 cup wine vinegar

Heat olive oil in a large skillet. Add onion and celery and cook until almost tender. Remove onion and celery and place in a bowl. In the same skillet, sauté eggplant until light brown. Remove. In same pan, over medium flame, place tomato paste and water. Stir until dissolved. Add olives, eggplant, capers, onion, celery, salt and pepper. Mix well. Bring to a boil over high flame. Lower flame. Simmer for 5 minutes. Then add sugar and vinegar. Stir and cook for 1/2 minute. Remove and allow to cool. Makes about 2 quarts. Sterilize jars before using. Cover tightly.

May be served immediately at room temperature or chilled. Keeps in refrigerator for as long as six weeks. May be used with meat, fowl or as antipasto.

OLIVE NERI SICILIANI
Black Olives Sicilian

1 lb. black Sicilian olives
2 bay leaves
pinch of crushed red pepper seeds

1 tsp. oregano
garlic powder to taste
5 tbs. olive oil

Wash olives well. Dry with absorbent paper. In a bowl, combine all ingredients. Place in a large sterilized jar and close tightly. May be used immediately. Keeps for several months in a cool place. Serve at room temperature.

OLIVE ALLA SICILIANA
Olives, Sicilian Style

1 lb. unripe green olives*
1 tsp. dry parsley
1/2 medium onion, sliced
1 tsp. oregano

1 tsp. salt
black pepper *or* crushed red pepper seeds to taste
1 crushed clove garlic
1/2 cup white vinegar

Crush olives. Remove pits. Place in a large jar filled with water. Change water daily for eight to twelve days until olives are ripe. Olives are ripe when they darken and the bitter taste disappears. Then drain. Place olives in a bowl. Add parsley, onion, oregano, salt, pepper, garlic and vinegar. Mix. Place in a large sterilized jar. Close tightly. May be used immediately. Keeps for a month to six weeks in a cool place. Serve at room temperature.

*If unripe olives are not available, ripe green olives preserved in salt may be used instead. Rinse in cool water for a few seconds. Drain. Crush olives and prepare as above, except for ripening process. Add a little salt, if desired.

MELENZANA SOTTO OLIO
Pickled Eggplant

5 lbs. small eggplants (about 5 inches long)
1 qt. wine vinegar
2 1/2 tbs. minced garlic
3/4 cup chopped celery with leaves

1 1/2 tbs. oregano
7 chopped hot red peppers
olive oil

Wash eggplants. Remove stems. Cut eggplants in half lengthwise. Slice halves lengthwise into thirds, 3/4 of the way through. In a colander, place them in layers. Sprinkle each layer with salt. Place a dish on top. Place a pot filled with water on the dish to allow bitter fluid to drain from eggplants. Let stand overnight. (It is advisable to place colander in sink.) If excess fluid remains, squeeze it out by hand.

Put vinegar in a medium-size enamel pot. (Do not use aluminum or stainless steel.) Bring to a boil and add eggplant gradually, being careful not to crowd the pot. Cook each batch for 1 minute or until vinegar boils again. Turn eggplant. Remove with slotted spoon. Bring vinegar to a boil again before adding more eggplant. As vinegar evaporates, add more to cover eggplant. Spread cooked eggplant out and let cool completely. Combine garlic, celery, oregano and hot red peppers.

In a sterilized quart jar, place a layer of vegetable mixture, then a layer of eggplants. Continue in this order until jar is full, pressing down ingredients with a wooden spoon. Fill jar with olive oil to cover. Shift ingredients slightly to allow oil to reach bottom. Repeat process in other jars until all ingredients are used. Cover tightly. Makes 2 quarts. If oil settles below top of mixture after a day, add more oil. Keep in cool, dry place. Let stand 1 month before using. Keeps 2 to 3 months.

Most children usually have their hand in the cookie jar. But when I was a child we didn't have one. Instead, Mother had a tall white enamel jar with a heavy lid brimming with wonderfully appetizing and pungent eggplant. Occasionally, when she wasn't looking, we'd sneak one or two and quickly eat them for fear of being discovered.

> To sterilize jars and lids, place clean jars and lids in a large kettle. Cover with water. Bring to a boil. Boil 15 minutes. Turn off heat. Leave jars and lids in water until needed. Remove jars and lids with a long-handled wooden spoon. Allow to dry at room temperature. Fill.

FAGIOLI CON OREGANO
White Beans with Oregano

2 cups dried white beans
salt to taste
olive oil

freshly ground pepper to taste
pinch of oregano

Wash the beans. In a medium-size heavy pot, cover with water and bring to a boil. Allow to soak for 1 hour. Bring to a boil again. Lower heat. Cover and cook at a moderate boil for 1 hour. Add salt. Cook for 1 hour more or until tender. Drain and cool. Taste beans for salt. If needed, add desired amount. Place in a serving bowl. Add enough olive oil to moisten, pepper and oregano. Toss. Serve at room temperature. Serves 6.

GAMBERI CON MAIONESE POMODORO
Shrimp with Tomato Mayonnaise

2 lbs. packaged frozen shrimp, thawed
1/4 cup dry white wine
1 bay leaf

pepper to taste
1 cup mayonnaise combined with 1 tbs. tomato
   catsup

Bring enough salted water to cover shrimp to a boil. Add shrimp. Lower flame. Simmer for 3 minutes. Drain. In a large saucepan, place shrimp, white wine, bay leaf and pepper. Mix. Cook over low flame for 3 minutes. Remove shrimp. Cool. Coat shrimp by dipping in mayonnaise mixture. Place on a serving platter. Serves 4–6.

UOVA AL TONNO
Eggs with Tuna

6 eggs
4 oz. tuna fish in olive oil (1/2 cup)
2 fillets of anchovy

1 tbs. minced fresh parsley
6 capers (unsalted)
mayonnaise

Cook eggs until hard-boiled. Run under cold water. Remove shells. When cool, cut in half lengthwise. Remove egg yolks and put through a sieve. Place in a medium-size bowl.

On a wooden board, chop tuna very finely. Then mix well with egg yolks. Mince the anchovies. Add anchovies and parsley to the tuna and egg mixture. Blend well. Stuff egg whites with mixture. Place on a platter and put a dollop of mayonnaise on each one and top with a caper. Serves 6.

POMODORI IMBOTTITI CON TONNO
Tomatoes Stuffed with Tuna

4 medium-size ripe tomatoes
7 oz. can tuna fish in olive oil, flaked
4 tsp. chopped capers (unsalted)
salt and pepper

mayonnaise to taste
4 slices of hard-boiled egg *or* 4 Rolled Fillets
     of Anchovies with Capers (p. 26)
crisp lettuce leaves

Wash tomatoes. Cut off tops. Scoop out pulp and chop finely. Invert tomatoes to drain. Sprinkle inside lightly with salt and pepper.

Combine tomato pulp, tuna fish, and capers. Add mayonnaise to taste. Stuff tomatoes with this filling. Top each tomato with either a slice of hard-boiled egg or a caper-rolled anchovy fillet. Keep refrigerated until needed. Serve each on a crisp lettuce leaf. Serves 4.

SPUMA DI TONNO
Tuna Foam

2 cups canned tuna fish in olive oil
2 cups cooked potatoes, boiled in jackets
1 tbs. butter
1 tbs. chopped parsley

1 cup mayonnaise
salt and pepper to taste
hard-boiled eggs
fillets of anchovy

Put tuna through a meat grinder twice (using fine cutter). Put peeled potatoes through grinder once. Add to tuna and mix well. Season with butter, parsley, mayonnaise, salt and pepper. Mix until blended. Grease a 1-quart mold with vegetable oil; then line mold with wax paper and grease it also. Put tuna-potato mixture in mold. Place in refrigerator to set for 1 hour. Unmold tuna onto a plate and spread with a thin layer of mayonnaise over top. Garnish with hard-boiled eggs cut in quarters with strips of anchovies over eggs. Serves 4—8.

COPPE DI ARAGOSTA
Lobster Cups

1 1/2 lbs. cooked lobster meat, in chunks
juice of 1 lemon
mayonnaise to moisten
drained capers

salt and pepper to taste
1 sliced hard-boiled egg
crisp lettuce leaves

Place lobster chunks in a bowl. Add lemon juice, salt and pepper. Moisten with mayonnaise and mix well. With crisp lettuce leaves, make lettuce cups. Place individual servings of lobster in cups. Sprinkle a few capers over each cup. Top with a slice of hard-boiled egg. Refrigerate until ready to serve. Serves 6.

CROSTINI DI MOZZARELLA ED ACCIUGHE
Mozzarella and Anchovies on Toast

slices of American white bread
thinly sliced mozzarella
fillets of anchovy
melted butter or margarine

(amounts as needed)

Cut out disks of bread with a round 2 3/4" cookie cutter. Place on a baking sheet. Place a slice of mozzarella on bread and 1/4 of an anchovy fillet on top. In a preheated oven at 350°F., cook until mozzarella becomes soft and well-heated. Place rounds on a serving platter. Drizzle each with hot, melted butter. Serve immediately.

CROSTINI DI GAMBERI
Shrimp on Toast

1 1/2 cups cooked fresh or frozen shrimp (3/4 lb.)
1/2 cup minced celery
1/4 cup chopped cooked green bell pepper
1/4 cup finely chopped black olives

8 slices American bread, without crusts
butter
fresh parsley sprigs

White Sauce:
1/2 cup butter or margarine
1/2 cup flour
1/2 tsp. salt

pinch of pepper
2 cups milk

Reserve 8 whole shrimp. On a wooden board, chop the rest of the shrimp into small pieces. Set aside.

Make white sauce: In a medium-size saucepan, melt butter over low flame. Add flour, salt and pepper. Stir till well-blended. Gradually add milk, stirring constantly until thickened. Then add chopped shrimp, celery, green pepper and olives. Heat thoroughly. Remove from flame.

Meanwhile, sauté bread in butter. Place four slices on a serving platter. Cover each with shrimp sauce. Then cover with the rest of the slices and top each one with two whole shrimp. Garnish with parsley. Serves 4.

UOVA FARCITE CON FORMAGGIO
Stuffed Eggs with Cheese

12 hard-boiled eggs, shelled and cooled
1/2 cup Gorgonzola *or* blue cheese
1/2 cup sour cream

1 tbs. vinegar *or* lemon juice
fresh parsley

Cut eggs in half lengthwise. Remove yolks and place in a bowl. Put egg whites on a platter and set aside. Add cheese to egg yolks and blend well. Add sour cream and vinegar or lemon juice. Mix well. Fill egg whites with mixture and place on platter. Garnish each egg half with a fresh parsley leaf. Serves 12.

VEGETALI IN ACETO
Marinated Vegetables

2 cans (3 or 4 oz. each) sliced mushrooms
14 oz. can artichoke hearts
7-1/4 oz. can baby carrots
2 tbs. chopped pimiento
2/3 cup white vinegar
2/3 cup olive oil *or* salad oil
1/4 cup minced onion
pinch of thyme

1/2 tsp. dry parsley *or* 1 tsp. finely chopped
    fresh parsley
1/4 tsp. dry basil *or* 1/2 tsp. finely chopped
    fresh basil
salt to taste (approximately 1 teaspoon)
1 tsp. sugar
1/4 tsp. finely minced garlic
ground black pepper to taste

Drain mushrooms, artichokes and carrots. Cut large artichokes in half. Place vegetables in a medium-size bowl. Add pimiento. Set aside. In a small saucepan, combine remaining ingredients. Bring to the boiling point. Cool slightly. Pour over vegetable mixture. Cover and refrigerate at least 12 hours. Serve as antipasto or salad or as an accompaniment to meat or poultry. Makes 1 quart.

OTHER ANTIPASTO FOODS

The following foods may be served as antipasto before dinner, a light meal, or components of a party spread. Recipes for these appear in other sections of this book. Please see the index.

Savory Stuffed Mushrooms
Sautéed Breaded Mushrooms
Deep-Fried Mozzarella Sticks
Cheese Fondue, Piedmont Style
Miniature Meatballs
Grilled Sweet or Hot Sausage
Fried Shrimp
Stuffed Shrimp with Italian Ham
Steamed Mussels with White Wine
Stuffed Clams
Snails, Sicilian Style
Squash with Vinegar

Roasted Peppers
Stuffed Artichokes Neapolitan
Roasted Artichokes
Green Salad Parmesan
Tossed Salad
Red Pepper Salad
Green Pepper Salad
Artichoke Salad
Eggplant and Pimiento Salad
Beef Salad
Fish Salads

Most everyone finds joy in a bowl of hot, bubbling soup. Besides being delicious and delightful, it can be a luncheon pick-me-up or a welcome relaxer following a hard day.

The making of soups is possibly one of the most ancient processes of cooking. And an art that the Italian cook would be least apt to abandon. If she is young, in all probability she's still listening to her mother's or grandmother's tales about the soups they simmered on their old Italian stone stoves fed with kindling wood. And before they've ended their accounts, she'll swear she can hear the sound of a *majolica* ladle against the copper kettles of charming, aromatic soup.

The Italian has always placed value on the cookery of soups for a variety of reasons. It's true that she cherishes the flavor and aroma. But nourishment stands out in her mind, and there is a great deal of it in soups, particularly in the egg and country vegetable types.

The Italian cook will call off, at the drop of a hat, the diversity of pastas she uses in her soups. This brings to mind an amusing story about the Bolognese father who once asked his six children what type of pasta they desired in their *zuppa*. When each one bellowed forth a different name, he had no choice but to put six different kinds into the broth and let them fish for their favorite.

Has this ever happened to you? If so, maybe it will solve a family argument sometime about which pasta to put in.

It's worthwhile making a flavorful, homey Italian soup because the compliments will be flown in via express by everyone, including perhaps neighbors taking a deep whiff outside your kitchen door.

PASTAS FOR SOUP

There is a great variety of pastas suitable for use in soups. Among these are **Tubettini**, **Stelline**, **Egg Alphabets** and **Folded Fine Egg Noodles** which are pictured on page 46.

Other soup pastas are:

Acini Di Pepe—tiny round or square pasta.

Ditalini—a smaller version of ditali, having a tubular form.

Fine Egg Noodles—similar to Folded Fine Egg Noodles, except not folded.

Pastina—tiny, round pasta (1/8 inch).

Tagliarini—very narrow noodles (1/8-inch wide), sometimes broken up for soup.

Vermicelli—very thin spaghetti sometimes broken up for soup.

SOME STOCK LINES

Leftover beef or chicken broth may be cooled and refrigerated in mason jars as a base for soups another day.

Whenever beef or chicken broth are not handy, bouillon cubes or canned consommé will do well to take their place.

To easily remove fat from broth, refrigerate until fat jells on surface and then remove.

BRODO DI MANZO
Beef Broth

2 lbs. shank beef	1 potato
4 beef soup bones	1 large onion
6 qts. water	1 large ripe tomato, cut up
2 stalks celery	3 sprigs parsley
1 large carrot	salt and pepper to taste

Place beef, bones and water in a large pot. Bring to a boil. Then lower flame. Skim fat off as it accumulates on top. Add celery, carrot, potato, onion, tomato, parsley, salt and pepper. Cover partially. Simmer for 2 hours. When done, skim fat from surface. Remove meat and bones. Strain. Beef broth may also be used as a base for other soups. Meat may be cubed for salad or sliced and served with any desired sauce. Serves 8.

BRODO DI POLLO ITALIANO
Chicken Broth, Italian Style

6 qts. water
4—5 lbs. soup chicken, quartered
2 large carrots
2 stalks celery, cut in half
1 large onion, cut in half
1 large ripe tomato, chopped *or* 2 heaping tbs.
    canned plum tomatoes

2 sprigs parsley
1 large potato
salt and pepper to taste
1/2 cup grated Romano cheese

In a large pot, put water, chicken, carrots, celery, onion, tomato, parsley, salt and pepper. Over high flame, bring to a boil. Cover partially. Lower flame and simmer for 1 1/2 hours. Then add potato. Continue cooking for 30 minutes or until chicken is tender. Remove chicken from pot. For clear soup, remove vegetables by straining. Or, if desired, vegetables may be chopped finely and served in the soup. Serve chicken as accompaniment to the soup. May also be served with cooked rice or soup pasta. Serve with grated Romano cheese. Serves 8.

In Mother's village, chickens were frequently raised for their eggs for consumption and small trade. Only a mature hen proving to be infertile would be utilized for making chicken broth.

SCAROLA IN BRODO
Escarole in Broth

Prepare Chicken Broth, Italian Style (*Brodo Di Pollo Italiano*). Strain vegetables and chicken from broth. Wash leaves of a 2-lb. head of escarole and cut leaves in half crosswise. Cook in salted, boiling water until almost tender. Drain. Add escarole to chicken broth and boil until tender. Do not add rice or pasta. Serve with grated Romano cheese. Serves 8.

BRODETTO DI MERLUZZO
Whiting Broth

2 lbs. fresh whiting
3 tbs. olive oil
1 clove minced garlic
1/2 cup canned plum tomatoes, mashed
2 1/2 cups water
1/2 cup dry white wine

2 tbs. fresh minced parsley
1 bay leaf
2 tbs. celery leaves
1/2 small onion, cut in half
salt and pepper to taste
lemon slices

Wash fish. Include fish head. Cut into 3-inch pieces. In a medium-size pot, sauté garlic in olive oil until golden. Add tomatoes. Cook for 5 minutes. Add water and bring to a boil over high flame. Add fish, wine, parsley, bay leaf, celery leaves, onion, salt and pepper. Bring to a full boil. Lower flame and cover. Simmer for 15—20 minutes or until fish is tender. Discard fish head. Remove whiting to platter. Strain broth. Press vegetables through strainer. Serve very hot. Remove bones and skin of whiting and serve fish separately with lemon slices. Serves 3.

Bean Soup. See recipe on following page.

Photo: Josh Young

ZUPPA DI SPARAGI E PISELLI
Asparagus and Pea Soup

10 oz. pkg. frozen asparagus spears, in 1-inch pieces
1 cup frozen peas
1 small chopped onion
2 tbs. olive oil

1/4 cup plum tomatoes
black pepper to taste
5 cups beef broth
1/4 cup grated Romano cheese

Heat olive oil in a medium-size pot. Add onion and cook over low flame until yellow. Add tomatoes and pepper. Cook for 8 minutes, stirring occasionally. Add beef broth, asparagus spears and peas. Cover partially. Allow to come to a boil over high flame. Lower flame. Simmer about 20 minutes or until vegetables are tender. Serve with grated Romano cheese. Serves 4.

ZUPPA DI FAGIOLI SECCHI
Bean Soup

1 cup dry Lima beans
2 1/2 qts. water
1 large chopped carrot
1 small chopped onion
2 tbs. canned plum tomatoes
2 cups broccoli, cut into bite-size pieces

1 clove minced garlic
1/2 tsp. dry parsley *or* 1 tbs. fresh chopped parsley
2 strips chopped bacon
salt and pepper to taste

Wash and soak beans overnight in water. In same water, bring to a boil. Lower flame. Cook, partially covered, at a moderate boil for 1 hour. Add carrot, onion, tomato, broccoli, garlic and parsley. Over high flame, bring to a boil. Lower flame. Cover partially and simmer for 20 minutes. Meanwhile, fry bacon until golden. Add bacon with drippings, salt, and pepper to beans. Continue cooking for 10 minutes. Serves 4.

MINESTRA DI LENTICCHIE E SALSICCIA
Lentil and Sausage Soup

1 cup lentils
1 3/4 qts. water
1 stalk chopped celery
1 large chopped carrot
3 tbs. mashed canned plum tomatoes
1 clove minced garlic

1 small chopped onion
1/2 lb. escarole, washed and cut into bite-size pieces
4 Italian sweet sausages
salt and pepper to taste

Rinse lentils and place in a large pot with water. Bring to a boil over high flame. Add celery, carrot, tomatoes, garlic and onion. Cover. Lower flame and simmer for 30 minutes. Add escarole to soup. Mix. Allow to come to a boil. Lower flame. Cover partially and cook for 20 minutes more. Remove casings from sausages, break the sausages up and fry thoroughly. Remove meat with a slotted spoon and add to soup. Continue cooking for 10 minutes. Season with salt and pepper. Serves 4.

ZUPPA SICILIANA DI PISELLI
Sicilian Split Pea Soup

2 cups split peas
3 qts. water
1 stalk chopped celery
1 large ripe chopped tomato, peeled
1 small chopped onion

1 large chopped carrot
1 clove minced garlic
1/4 cup olive oil
salt and pepper to taste
1/2 cup grated Romano cheese

Wash peas. Place in a large pot with water. Over high flame, bring to a boil. Add celery, tomato, onion, carrot, garlic, olive oil. Lower flame. Cover partially. Simmer for 1 hour or until tender. Season with salt and pepper. If desired, top individual servings with slices of toasted Sicilian bread. Sprinkle bread with grated Romano cheese. Serves 4–6.

This is Mother's favorite soup. Because meat was served only on special occasions in Ciminna, the legume became a main substitute, being rich in vitamins and minerals. Being organically grown made them even more beneficial.

ZUPPA DI BROCCOLI E LINGUINE
Broccoli and Linguine Soup

1 bunch broccoli
6 cups water
1 clove minced garlic
1 medium finely chopped tomato

1/4 lb. linguine, broken into 2-inch pieces
salt and pepper to taste
3 tbs. olive oil
1/3 cup grated Romano cheese

Clean and wash broccoli. Soak in cool, salted water for 15 minutes. Run under clear water. Cut into medium-size pieces. In a large pot place water, garlic and tomato. Over high flame, bring water to a boil. Add broccoli. Lower to medium flame. Cook for 10 minutes. Add linguine, salt and pepper. Cook for 15 minutes more or until tender, stirring occasionally. Add olive oil. Cook for 2 minutes more. Serve with grated Romano cheese. Serves 4–5.

ZUPPA DI ZUCCHINI
Squash Soup

4 medium Italian squash (zucchini)
1 qt. water
2 medium cubed potatoes
1 small chopped onion
1 clove minced garlic

1 tbs. fresh chopped parsley
2 tbs. olive oil
salt and pepper to taste
1/4 cup grated Parmesan cheese

Scrub squash well. Cut into 1-inch cubes. In a medium-size pot with 1 quart of boiling water, place potatoes, onion and garlic. Cover partially. Cook for 10 minutes over high flame. Lower flame. Add squash, parsley, olive oil, salt and pepper. Continue cooking for 12–15 minutes or until vegetables are tender. Serve with grated Parmesan cheese. Serves 4.

ZUPPA DI POLLO E TACCHINO CON POLPETTINI
Chicken Turkey Soup with Meatballs

4 qts. water
1 turkey neck and giblets
1 large onion, cut in half
1 stalk celery, cut in half
1 ripe chopped tomato

2 medium carrots
3 sprigs parsley
salt and pepper to taste
2 chicken drumsticks
1/4 cup grated Parmesan cheese

Meatballs:
3/4 lb. ground beef
2 eggs
3 tbs. grated Romano cheese
1/2 tsp. dry parsley *or* 1 tbs. fresh minced
    parsley

2 tbs. milk
1/4 cup fine bread crumbs
1/2 small minced onion
salt and pepper to taste

In a bowl, combine meatball ingredients well. Form mixture into round balls about the size of marbles. Cover and refrigerate.

Place turkey neck, giblets and drumsticks in a large pot with cold water. Over high flame, bring to a boil. Lower flame. Cover partially. Skim fat as it accumulates on top. When water is clear, add carrots, onion, celery, tomato, parsley, salt and pepper. Simmer for 1 hour 20 minutes. Strain vegetables and meat from soup. Add tiny meatballs to soup. Over high flame, bring to a boil. Lower flame. Cover partially. Simmer for 25 minutes. Serve with grated Parmesan cheese. Serves 6–8.

MINESTRA RICCA DI VONGOLE
Rich Clam Chowder

4 qts. water
1/2 cup dry red kidney beans
1/2 cup dry chickpeas (garbanzos)
1/4 cup canned plum tomatoes, mashed
2 tbs. olive oil
1 medium chopped onion
1 clove minced garlic
3 chopped cabbage leaves
1 sprig fresh minced parsley *or* 1 tsp. dry
    parsley
1 fresh sweet red pepper, diced

1/4 lb. string beans, cut into 1/2-inch pieces
1 large diced carrot
1 stalk diced celery
salt
crushed red pepper seeds *or* black pepper
    to taste
pinch of thyme
1/2 tsp. oregano
3 diced potatoes
2 tbs. cornstarch
10 oz. can whole baby clams, with juice

In a large pot, soak red beans and chickpeas overnight in 4 quarts of water. In the same water, allow to come to a boil. Cover partially. Lower flame so that liquid boils moderately. Cook for 45 minutes. Add tomatoes, olive oil, onion, garlic, cabbage, parsley, red pepper, string beans, carrot, celery, thyme and oregano. Allow to boil over high flame. Lower flame. Cover partially. Continue cooking for 15 minutes. Add potatoes. Cook 30 minutes more. Put cornstarch in a small bowl. Gradually add 1 cup of soup from pot to cornstarch. Stir until starch dissolves. Return to pot. Stir for a few minutes or until soup thickens slightly. Then add clams with clam juice. Cook until well heated. Season with salt and crushed red pepper seeds or black pepper. Serve hot. Serves 8.

MINESTRA DI BOMBOLINE DI PATATE
Potato Dumpling Soup

1/2 lb. potatoes
2 tbs. butter *or* margarine
1/4 cup grated Parmesan cheese
1 egg yolk
2 sprinkles of nutmeg

dash of salt
2 tbs. flour
olive oil for deep frying
1/4 cup grated Parmesan cheese
1 qt. chicken broth *or* beef broth

Scrub potatoes. Boil in skins until tender. Peel and mash until smooth. Combine with butter, 1/4 cup grated cheese, egg yolk, nutmeg, salt and flour. Allow to cool. On a board, knead potato mixture until ingredients are well blended. Sprinkle a little flour on board and roll potato mixture in long cords. Cut and shape into balls the size of an olive.

In a skillet, fry potato balls in hot olive oil until they are golden. (Use enough oil so the potato balls will float.) Drain on absorbent paper. Place balls on bottoms of soup dishes. Sprinkle with grated Parmesan cheese (1 tbs. to each dish). Then pour hot chicken broth or beef broth over them. Serves 4.

ZUPPA DI PISELLI E PATATE
Pea and Potato Soup

2 medium diced potatoes
2 chopped scallions
3 tbs. olive oil
2 cups frozen peas

1 clove minced garlic
1/2 tsp. dry parsley *or* 1 tbs. fresh minced
    parsley
4 cups beef broth
pepper to taste

In a medium-size pot sauté potatoes and scallions in hot olive oil for 5 minutes. Add peas, garlic and parsley. Cook for 2 minutes, stirring frequently. Add beef broth and pepper. Bring to a boil over high flame. Lower flame and cover partially. Simmer for 20 minutes or until vegetables are tender. Serves 3–4.

ZUPPA VEGETALE
Vegetable Soup

10 oz. fresh asparagus spears, cut in 1-inch pieces
8 small artichokes
3 tbs. olive oil
1 small chopped onion
1/2 large chopped fresh tomato

1 1/4 cups cubed potatoes
1 tsp. dry parsley *or* 1 tbs. fresh minced parsley
4 cups boiling water
salt and pepper to taste
1/4 cup grated Romano cheese

Strip artichokes of stalks and leaves, keeping the hearts. Wash. Slice in quarters. Soak in cool water with 1 tsp. salt for 10 minutes. Drain.

Heat olive oil in a large pot. Add onion and cook over low flame until yellow. Add tomato. Cook for 5 minutes. Add artichoke hearts, potatoes, parsley, water, salt and pepper. Bring to a boil. Cover partially and lower flame. Simmer for 15 minutes. Add asparagus. Cover tightly. Cook for 10 minutes or until vegetables are tender. Serve with grated Romano cheese. Serves 4.

STRACCIATELLA
Egg Soup

2 lightly beaten eggs
4 tsp. flour
pinch of salt

sprinkle of nutmeg
3 tbs. grated Parmesan cheese
1 1/2 qts. chicken broth or beef broth, boiling

In a bowl, combine flour, salt, nutmeg and cheese. Add eggs and form a paste. Then sieve slowly through a strainer into boiling chicken broth or beef broth. Stir constantly with a fork until eggs set. Serves 5–6.

CREMA IN BRODO
Cream in Broth

8 cups chicken broth
4 eggs
1/4 cup light cream

4 tsp. lemon juice
1/4 cup grated Parmesan cheese
croutons

In a medium-size bowl, place eggs, cream and lemon juice. Beat very well. In a medium-size pot, bring chicken broth to a boil. Remove from heat. Pour egg mixture into broth. Beat vigorously with a wire whisk so that eggs will not curdle and broth becomes creamy. Allow 2 cups per person. Serve with grated Parmesan cheese and fried bread croutons. Serves 4.

Croutons:

Allow 1 slice of bread per person. Remove crusts and cut into 1-inch cubes. Sauté in hot butter until golden brown.

PALLOTTOLINE DI RISO IN BRODO
Rice Dumplings in Broth

4 cups hot chicken broth, fat removed
2 cups milk
7 tbs. raw rice
pinch of salt
2 tbs. butter
2 tbs. grated Parmesan cheese

1 beaten egg
dash of pepper
flour
butter or olive oil (for sautéing)
1/4 cup grated Parmesan cheese

In a heavy, medium-size aluminum saucepan, place milk, rice, salt and butter. Cook over low heat, stirring frequently, until rice has absorbed milk. Remove from heat and mix in 2 tbs. grated Parmesan cheese and beaten egg. Mix quickly so the egg will not curdle. Add pepper. Form mixture into balls the size of a cherry. Dredge them in flour.

In a medium-size skillet, sauté dumplings in hot butter or olive oil until golden brown. Drain on absorbent paper. Place dumplings in bottoms of four soup dishes. Pour 1 cup of hot chicken broth in each and serve with grated Parmesan cheese. Serves 4.

ZUPPA DI FUNGHI
Cream of Mushroom Soup

1/2 lb. fresh mushrooms
3 tbs. butter *or* margarine
3 tbs. flour
4 cups hot chicken broth

1 cup milk
salt and pepper to taste
1 beaten egg yolk

Wash and chop mushrooms. In a medium-size pot over low flame, melt butter. Add mushrooms and cook for 5 minutes. Add flour and stir until well-blended. Gradually add chicken broth. Stir until thick. Add milk, salt and pepper. Heat. Before removing from flame, add egg yolk and stir well. Serves 4–5.

ZUPPA DI CECI
Chickpea Soup

1 lb. 4 oz. can chickpeas, undrained
3 tbs. olive oil
1/2 small chopped onion
1 medium chopped tomato, peeled and de-seeded
   or 2 tbs. mashed canned plum tomatoes

1 clove minced garlic
3 cups water
salt and pepper to taste
2 finely chopped strips of bacon

Heat olive oil in a medium-size pot. Add onion and cook over low flame until yellow. Add tomato. Stir. Cook for 3 minutes. Add undrained chickpeas, garlic, water, salt and pepper. Over high flame, bring to a boil. Lower flame. Cover partially and simmer for 20 minutes. Fry bacon until crisp. Drain. Add to soup. Continue cooking for 5 minutes. Serves 4.

ZUPPA DEL PARADISO
Paradise Soup

3 stiffly beaten egg whites
3 slightly beaten egg yolks
3 tbs. fine dry bread crumbs
3 tbs. grated Parmesan cheese

2 sprinkles of nutmeg
2 qts. chicken broth
1/2 cup grated Parmesan cheese

In a bowl, combine egg yolks, bread crumbs, 3 tbs. grated cheese, and nutmeg. Fold egg whites into mixture. Then drop mixture a teaspoonful at a time into boiling chicken broth, stirring constantly with a fork until eggs set. Serve with grated Parmesan cheese. Serves 6.

ZUPPA DI CIPOLLE
Onion Soup

2 cups boiling water
1 tbs. crushed aniseed
3 tbs. butter
3 medium finely sliced onions

2 tbs. flour
4 cups hot beef broth
pepper to taste

In a small saucepan, cook crushed aniseed for 5 minutes in 2 cups of boiling water. Strain. Combine liquid with beef broth.

In a medium-size pot cook onions in hot butter over low flame until light brown. Add flour. Stir until well-blended. Then gradually add hot beef broth and water, stirring continuously. Sprinkle with pepper. Over high flame, bring to a boil. Lower flame. Cover partially and simmer for 10 minutes. Serves 4–5. Has a very delicate and different flavor!

ZUPPA DI RISO E SALSICCIA
Rice and Sausage Soup

1/4 cup raw rice
1 1/2 quarts chicken broth
1 Italian sweet sausage, without casing and
    broken up

1/2 cup sliced turnips
1/2 cup shredded cabbage
2 tbs. butter
1/4 cup grated Parmesan cheese

In a small saucepan with water to cover, boil turnips and cabbage until half tender. Drain well. Melt butter in a small skillet and sauté turnips and cabbage until tender and golden. Meanwhile, boil rice until half done. Drain.

In a medium-size pot, place chicken broth, turnips, cabbage, rice and sausage. Allow to come to a boil over high flame. Cover partially and simmer, over low flame, for about 25–30 minutes. Skim fat from top as it accumulates. Serve with grated Parmesan cheese. Serves 4.

DADETTI DI RICOTTA IN BRODO
Italian Cheese Cubes in Broth

2/3 lb. ricotta, sieved *or* sieved, creamed, mild
    cottage cheese with tiny, soft curds
2 large eggs
5 tbs. grated Parmesan cheese
pinch of nutmeg

salt and pepper to taste
1/2 tbs. fresh finely chopped parsley
1 qt. hot chicken broth
grated Parmesan cheese

In a bowl, beat eggs slightly. Add 5 tbs. grated Parmesan cheese, nutmeg, salt, pepper and parsley. Beat till well combined. Add sieved ricotta and mix well.

Grease a shallow baking pan (11" x 7") and pour mixture into it. Spread it evenly. Place the shallow pan into another pan filled with enough water to keep the top one afloat. Bake in a preheated oven at 375°F. for 30 minutes or until set. When done, unmold ricotta mixture and place on wax paper. Allow to cool. Cut into 3/4-inch cubes. Place in individual dishes. Cover with boiling chicken broth. Serve with grated Parmesan cheese. Serves 4.

PASTA & RICE

4

Thousands of years ago, man was crushing, between two millstones, a seed that grew concealed at the end of a tall, yellow stalk. It was wheat, which eventually became the most important cereal crop grown by the Romans who raised both smooth and bearded varieties. It was later used to make pasta after Marco Polo returned from China with macaroni which was destined to become a mainstay in the Italian diet.

Today, however, machines with steel rollers have taken the place of those two stones, increasing production of the many varieties of pasta.

Pasta may be made from either durum wheat semolina (the gluten part of durum wheat), farina (the hard part of hard wheat kernels), wheat flour or from a mixture of these. Semolina and farina contain less starch than wheat flour and hold their shape well after cooking. The best quality of pasta is obtained from semolina. When evenly ground it has the best flavor as well as the most food value.

The Italian cook, nonetheless, will tell you she sometimes prefers to make her own pasta, declaring that it is much lighter than the commercial kind. Her homemade pasta may include lasagne, ravioli, fettucelle, linguine, gnocchi and manicotti, among others.

The photograph on page 46 shows some of the most popular kinds of pasta. The list below is a guide to some other types not shown in the photograph.

Cannelloni—large ribbed tubular pasta cut obliquely, resembling manicotti rigati.
Ditali—a tubular pasta about 1/4-inch in diameter and 1/2-inch long.
Fettucelle—long, plain noodles (1/4-inch wide).
Linguine—flat, narrow spaghetti (1/8-inch wide).
Mezzani—a curved, tubular pasta about 1 inch long and 1/4-inch in diameter.
Ravioli—freshly made pasta in small squares filled with chopped meat, spinach, chicken, or ricotta.
Spaghettini—very thin spaghetti.
Tubetti—a larger version of tubettini.
Ziti—a tubular pasta about 3 inches long and 1/2-inch in diameter.

COOKING PASTA

Consult package directions for amount of salt because different brands suggest different amounts. Add salt to recommended amount of water and bring to a *rapid boil.* If desired, add 1 teaspoon of olive oil or corn oil to prevent pasta from sticking. Add pasta slowly enough so the water continues to boil. Gently ease the unbroken strands into the pot with a long-handled fork (or use a long-handled wooden spoon for smaller varieties). Cook uncovered. Stir occasionally to keep the pasta distributed in the boiling water so it will all cook evenly. When done, drain immediately in a colander and serve as soon as possible. Rinsing is not recommended unless the recipe requires cooling the pasta for easier handling.

FREEZING COOKED PASTA CASSEROLES

A casserole made with a pasta product, sauce, and meat, cheese, fish or vegetables may be frozen for future use. Freeze individual portions in plastic freezer containers of appropriate size. To serve, thaw and turn each portion into individual casseroles. Bake, uncovered, in a 375° oven for 20 to 25 minutes or until piping hot (or heat in top of double boiler over hot water).

THE ETIQUETTE OF SPAGHETTI EATING

One wonders why there should be any question about how to eat such a popular and frequently enjoyed food as spaghetti. And yet, the question is asked, the doubt still remains: "What is the proper way to eat spaghetti?"

Ask an Italian. Surely the native of the country which has enjoyed spaghetti longer than any other will give you a quick and definite answer. Or better yet, ask for a demonstration. With a gentle but sure grip on the fork, holding it almost upright in the manner of holding a pencil, he sends the tines speeding into the very center of the platter of spaghetti. And starts twirling the fork immediately. In the wink of an eye the fork is wrapped with a generous mouthful of the slender strands. And the next thing you know the fork is lifted, then it's empty and on its way back to the steaming spaghetti. It is one continuous

Photo: Theodore R. Sills.
Courtesy of National Macaroni Institute.

TYPES OF PASTA

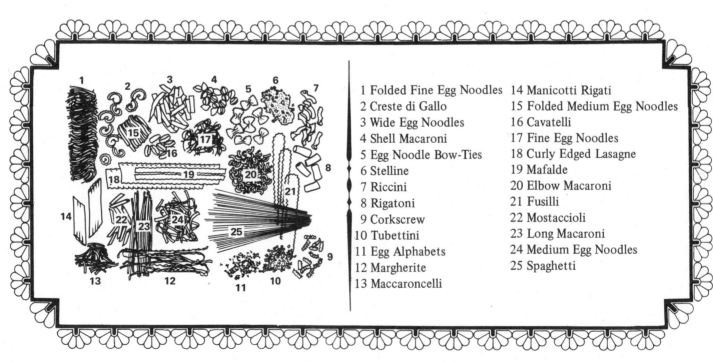

1 Folded Fine Egg Noodles
2 Creste di Gallo
3 Wide Egg Noodles
4 Shell Macaroni
5 Egg Noodle Bow-Ties
6 Stelline
7 Riccini
8 Rigatoni
9 Corkscrew
10 Tubettini
11 Egg Alphabets
12 Margherite
13 Maccaroncelli

14 Manicotti Rigati
15 Folded Medium Egg Noodles
16 Cavatelli
17 Fine Egg Noodles
18 Curly Edged Lasagne
19 Mafalde
20 Elbow Macaroni
21 Fusilli
22 Mostaccioli
23 Long Macaroni
24 Medium Egg Noodles
25 Spaghetti

movement, deft and graceful, from start to finish. Yes, do ask an Italian what is the best way to eat spaghetti and most likely he'll answer, "With gusto!"

"PASTA" OR "MACARONI"?

The words "pasta" and "macaroni" are often interchanged because they are generic terms describing macaroni, spaghetti and egg noodle products.

There are various legends about macaroni that have amused people for centuries. The "Legend of an Epicure" is a particularly charming one about how macaroni got its name. A wealthy nobleman of Palermo (or was it a thirteenth century king?) who was noted for his love of fine food possessed a cook with a marvelous inventive genius. One day this talented cook devised the farinaceous tubes with which we are familiar today—and served them with rich sauce and grated Parmesan cheese in a large china bowl. The first mouthful caused the illustrious epicure to shout, "*Cari!*" or in idiomatic English, "The darlings!" With the second mouthful, he emphasized his statement, exclaiming, "*Ma Cari!*" ("Ah, but what darlings!"). And as the flavor of the dish grew upon him his enthusiasm rose to even greater heights, and he cried out with joyful emotions, "*Ma Caroni!*" ("Ah, but dearest darlings!"). In paying this supreme tribute to his cook's discovery, the nobleman bestowed the name by which this admirable preparation is known today—"Macaroni!"

Recommended Brands of Pasta
Ronzoni
Buitoni (Pasta Romana)
La Rosa

LASAGNE IMBOTTITE
Lasagne

Meat Sauce:

4 medium pork chops, browned and chopped
1 lb. ground beef, browned
2 tbs. chopped onion
1/4 cup olive oil
7 oz. can tomato paste

4 cups hot water
2 lbs. 3 oz. can plum tomatoes, mashed
2 whole cloves garlic
1/2 tsp. dry basil *or* 3 or 4 fresh basil leaves, minced
salt and pepper to taste

1 lb. broad curly-edged noodles (lasagne) or wide egg noodles

Stuffing:

1 1/2 lbs. ricotta
1 tsp. dry parsley *or* 1 tbs. fresh minced parsley
1 lightly beaten egg
pinch of salt

pepper to taste
1/2 lb. mozzarella, in 1/4-inch cubes
1 cup grated Romano cheese

1/2 cup grated Romano cheese (for serving)

Step 1: Heat olive oil in a large saucepan. Add onion and cook over low flame until yellow. Add tomato paste and water. Stir until blended. Then add plum tomatoes, garlic, basil, salt and pepper. Over high flame, bring to a boil. Lower flame. Cover partially and simmer for 30 minutes, stirring occasionally. Add browned meat, using slotted spoon in order to drain off excess fat. Simmer for 35 minutes more. Remove garlic.

Step 2: Cook noodles in 6 quarts of rapidly boiling, salted water until medium-cooked (*al dente*). Drain. Run under cool water for better handling. Drain once more.

(**Continued on following page.**)

Step 3: Combine ricotta, parsley, egg, salt and pepper. Coat bottom of a 10"x14"x2" baking dish with some meat sauce. Place in layers: some noodles, meat sauce, mozzarella, dollops of ricotta mixture here and there, meat sauce and grated Romano cheese (in this order). Repeat process until all ingredients have been used. Cook in a preheated oven at 375°F. for 25 minutes or until crisp and brown. When done, remove from oven and let sit for 10 minutes. Then cut portions with a spatula. Serve with grated Romano cheese. Serves 10.

LASAGNE CLASSICO
Classic Lasagne

Sauce:

1 medium chopped onion	1/2 cup water
2 cloves crushed garlic	salt to taste
4 tbs. olive oil	1/2 tsp. dry basil
1 lb. 12 oz. can tomatoes	1/2 tsp. oregano
two 6 oz. cans tomato paste	1/8 tsp. crushed red pepper seeds

Meatballs:

1 lb. ground beef chuck	1/2 cup fine dry bread crumbs
1/2 lb. lean ground pork	freshly grated Parmesan cheese
1/4 cup chopped parsley	salt and pepper to taste
2 eggs	

1 lb. curly-edged noodles (lasagne) *or* wide egg noodles (about 8 cups)

Filling:

1 lb. ricotta *or* mild creamed cottage cheese with tiny soft curds (sieved)	1/2 lb. mozzarella cheese, sliced

Heat 2 tbs. of the oil in a large saucepan and sauté onion and garlic over low flame until lightly brown. Add tomatoes, tomato paste, 1/2 cup water, salt, basil, oregano and crushed red pepper seeds. Simmer, covered, for 1 hour.

In a large bowl, mix together beef, pork, parsley, eggs, bread crumbs, 2 tbs. grated Parmesan cheese, salt and pepper. Shape into 1/2-inch meatballs. Heat remaining 2 tbs. oil in a large skillet and sauté meatballs over low flame until browned. Add to sauce and simmer 15 minutes.

Meanwhile, in 6 quarts of rapidly boiling salted water, gradually add lasagne so that water continues to boil. Cook for 20 minutes or until tender. Drain.

Place in layers in a 13"x9"x2-1/4" roasting pan: sauce with meatballs, lasagne, dollops of ricotta and Parmesan cheese. Repeat layers in this order until all ingredients are used. Top with mozzarella slices. Bake in a preheated oven at 375°F. for 25 minutes or until crisp and brown. Remove from oven and let sit for 10 minutes. Cut portions with a spatula. Serves 8. **(See color photo on p. 3.)**

SPAGHETTI CON SALSA DI GAMBERI
Spaghetti with Shrimp Sauce

1 lb. medium-size shrimp (in shells)	4 minced fresh basil leaves
1/4 cup olive oil	1 clove minced garlic
2 tbs. chopped onion	salt and crushed red pepper seeds to taste
2 lb. 3 oz. can plum tomatoes, mashed	pinch of thyme

1 lb. spaghetti   1/4 cup grated Romano cheese

Shell, devein and wash shrimp. In a medium-size saucepan, cook onion in hot olive oil over low flame until yellow. Add tomatoes, basil, garlic, salt, crushed red pepper seeds and thyme. Over high flame, bring to a boil. Lower flame. Cover partially and simmer for 30 minutes, stirring occasionally. Add shrimp. Cook for 5–6 minutes more.

Cook spaghetti in 6 quarts of rapidly boiling, salted water for 15–20 minutes or until tender. Drain. Place in a large platter. Pour hot shrimp mixture over spaghetti. Serve with grated Romano cheese. Serves 4.

SPAGHETTI CON SALSA DI CARNE
Spaghetti with Meat Sauce

1 lb. spaghetti

Meat Sauce:

1/4 cup olive oil	salt and pepper to taste
1 small chopped onion	2 tbs. butter
2 lb. 3 oz. can plum tomatoes, mashed	1/2 lb. ground lean beef
1 sprig chopped fresh parsley *or* 1 tsp. dry	3 medium sliced mushrooms
parsley	1/4 cup red wine
sprinkle of nutmeg	1/4 cup grated Parmesan cheese
1/2 tsp. basil	

Heat olive oil in a medium-size saucepan. Add onion and cook, over low flame, until yellow. Add tomatoes, parsley, nutmeg, basil, salt and pepper. Mix. Over high flame, bring to a boil. Lower flame. Cover partially and simmer for 30 minutes, stirring occasionally.

Meanwhile, in a skillet with hot butter, cook meat until light brown. Then add meat, mushrooms and wine to sauce. Continue to simmer for 30 minutes more.

Cook spaghetti in 6 quarts of rapidly boiling, salted water for 15–20 minutes or until tender. Drain. Place in a large platter. Pour meat sauce over spaghetti. Serve with grated Parmesan cheese. Serves 4.

It is a custom among many Southern Italians to enjoy pasta with meat sauce on Thursday evenings. It springs from being forbidden, by religious law, to eat meat on Friday; therefore meat is enjoyed the previous day. Although this law has now been abolished, the practice still continues.

SPAGHETTI CON CAVOLO
Spaghetti with Cabbage

3/4 lb. spaghetti, broken into 3-inch pieces	salt and pepper to taste
1 head cabbage (2 lbs.)	1/4 to 1/2 cup grated Romano *or* Parmesan
1/4 cup olive oil	cheese
1 small chopped onion	

Wash cabbage. Remove core. Cut into bite-size pieces. In a large saucepan cook onion in hot olive oil over low flame until slightly yellow. Add cabbage, salt and pepper. Stir. Cover and steam for 30 minutes or until tender, stirring occasionally. If necessary, add a small amount of hot water.

Cook spaghetti in 5 quarts of rapidly boiling, salted water for 15 minutes or until tender. Do not drain completely; leave spaghetti slightly moist. Turn onto platter. Add cabbage mixture. Toss well. Serve with grated Romano or Parmesan cheese. Serves 4–6.

SPAGHETTI CON VITELLA E PEPERONI
Spaghetti with Veal and Peppers

1 lb. spaghetti
2 lbs. boneless veal shoulder, cut in strips
flour
1/4 cup butter *or* margarine
1/3 cup olive oil
4 medium green peppers, cut in strips
2 small sliced onions

4 cloves minced garlic
two 1 lb. 3 oz. cans plum tomatoes
two 8 oz. cans tomato sauce
1 1/2 tsp. dry basil
1/4 to 1/2 tsp. oregano
salt and freshly ground pepper to taste

Coat veal strips with flour. Heat butter and oil in a large skillet and cook strips over low flame until brown. Remove meat. In same pan, sauté green peppers and onion about 5 minutes. Return meat to pan. Add garlic, tomatoes, sauce, basil, oregano, salt and pepper. Cover and simmer for one hour, stirring occasionally.

In 6 quarts of rapidly boiling salted water, cook spaghetti for about 20 minutes or until tender. Drain. Turn onto large platter. Top with veal and peppers. Serves 8. **(See photo on opposite page.)**

SPAGHETTI CON POLLO E FUNGHI ALLA CORTINA
Spaghetti with Chicken and Mushrooms Cortina

1 lb. spaghetti
1 lb. fresh mushrooms
5 tbs. butter *or* margarine (divided)
2 cups diced, cooked chicken
3 chicken bouillon cubes

2 cups boiling water
1 cup heavy cream
3 tbs. flour
3/4 cup grated Romano *or* Parmesan cheese
1/16 tsp. ground white pepper

Rinse, pat dry and slice fresh mushrooms (makes about 5 cups). In a large skillet heat 2 tbs. of the butter. Add the mushrooms and sauté for 5 minutes. Add chicken. Cook until heated. Set aside. Dissolve bouillon cubes in boiling water. Stir in cream. Set aside. In a large saucepan heat remaining 3 tbs. of butter. Stir in flour; blend well. Gradually mix in bouillon and cream mixture. Cook and stir over low flame until slightly thickened. Stir in cheese and white pepper. Add reserved mushrooms and chicken. Heat only until hot.

Meanwhile, cook spaghetti in 6 quarts of rapidly boiling salted water for 15–20 minutes or until tender. Drain. Place in a large platter. Pour hot chicken and mushroom sauce over spaghetti. Serves 6. **(See photo on opposite page.)**

SPAGHETTI AGLIO E OLIO
Spaghetti with Oil and Garlic

1 lb. spaghetti, cooked and drained
1/2 cup olive oil
2 cloves minced garlic

1/4 cup fresh minced parsley
black pepper to taste
1/4 cup grated pecorino *or* Parmesan cheese

In a small saucepan, place olive oil, garlic, parsley and pepper. Allow to cook over low flame for a minute and a half. Then remove from heat. Pour oil, garlic and parsley mixture over hot spaghetti in a platter. Mix. Serve with grated pecorino or Parmesan cheese. Serves 4.

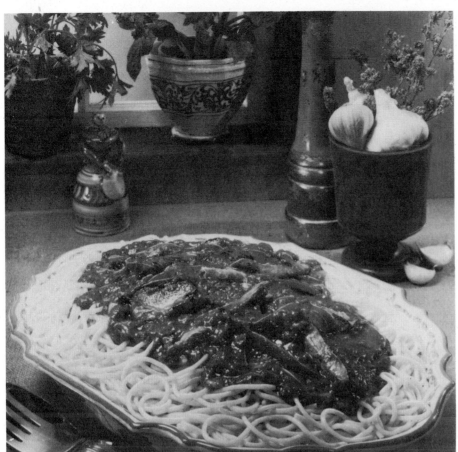

Spaghetti with Veal and Peppers.
See recipe on opposite page.

Photo: Theodore R. Sills.
Courtesy of National Macaroni Institute.

Spaghetti with Chicken and Mushrooms Cortina.
See recipe on opposite page.

Photo: Lewis/Neale, Inc.
Courtesy of American Mushroom Institute.

CONCHIGLIE CON SPAGHETTI ALLA MARINARA
Scallops in Marinara Sauce with Spaghetti

1 lb. spaghetti

1 lb. sea scallops

1/4 cup olive oil

1 clove minced garlic

1/2 cup chopped onion

8 oz. can tomato sauce

1 lb. 1 oz. can Italian plum tomatoes, mashed

1 tsp. dry parsley

salt and pepper to taste

1 tsp. sugar

1/4 tsp. thyme

4 tsp. fresh chopped parsley

1/4 cup grated Parmesan cheese

Wash scallops well. Drain. Heat olive oil in a large pot. Add garlic and onion and cook over low flame until yellow. Add tomato sauce, plum tomatoes, dry parsley, salt, pepper, sugar and thyme. Bring to a boil over high flame. Lower flame. Cover partially and simmer for 30 minutes, stirring occasionally. Add scallops. Simmer uncovered 5 minutes longer or until scallops are tender.

Cook spaghetti in 6 quarts of rapidly boiling, salted water for 15 minutes or until tender. Drain. Toss scallops and sauce with spaghetti. Serve in individual dishes. Sprinkle with fresh parsley. Serve with grated Parmesan cheese. Serves 4.

SPAGHETTI CON CARCIOFI E GRANCHIO MARINARA
Spaghetti with Artichokes and Crab Marinara

1 lb. spaghetti

two 6 oz. jars marinated artichoke hearts, cut into bite-size pieces

two 9 oz. pkgs. frozen precooked king crab meat, thawed

3 tbs. olive oil

1/2 small onion, chopped

two 8 oz. cans tomato sauce

pepper to taste

garlic salt to taste

6 tbs. melted butter

1/4 cup grated Parmesan cheese

In 6 quarts of boiling, salted water, cook spaghetti for 15—20 minutes or until tender. Drain. Place on a large platter. Meanwhile, combine artichoke hearts and crab meat in a medium-size saucepan. Heat. Arrange over spaghetti.

Meanwhile, heat olive oil in a small saucepan. Add onion and cook until yellow. Add tomato sauce and pepper. Heat. Then pour hot sauce over half of spaghetti. In another small pan, add garlic salt to hot melted butter. Pour over other half of spaghetti. Serve with grated Parmesan cheese. Serves 4.

TIMBALLO DI SPAGHETTI
Timbale of Spaghetti

2 tbs. olive oil

2 tbs. flour

1 cup canned plum tomatoes, drained & mashed

3/4 cup grated Parmesan cheese

pinch of salt

pinch of black and white pepper

1 lb. spaghetti

3 eggs, separated

In a large skillet mix olive oil and flour until well blended. Gradually add tomatoes, stirring until it comes to a boil. Lower flame and simmer for 2 to 3 minutes. Add grated cheese, salt and pepper. Remove from flame and set aside.

Meanwhile, break spaghetti in half and cook until medium cooked (*al dente*). Drain. Combine with tomato mixture.

In a bowl, beat egg yolks until pale yellow in color and add to macaroni. Mix well. Then beat egg whites stiff and fold into macaroni mixture. Put into a greased 2 quart casserole and bake in a preheated oven at 350°F. until golden brown. Serves 4.

SPAGHETTINI ALLA SICILIANA
Spaghettini Sicilian Style

1 lb. spaghettini *or* linguine
2 oz. can fillets of anchovies, cut up
1/4 cup olive oil
1 clove minced garlic

7 oz. can tomato paste
2 1/2 cups hot water
pinch of pepper

Heat olive oil in a small saucepan. Add garlic and cook about a half a minute. Add tomato paste and water. Stir until dissolved. Add pepper. Cover partially. Simmer for 25 minutes, stirring occasionally. Add anchovies. Cook and stir until dissolved.

Topping:
1 tbs. olive oil
1 cup fine dry bread crumbs
1 tsp. sugar

In a small skillet with slightly warm olive oil, cook bread crumbs over very low flame, stirring constantly for about 10 minutes or until golden brown. Place in a small bowl. Add sugar. Mix well.

Cook spaghettini in 6 quarts of rapidly boiling water with 1/2 tsp. of salt (little salt is required because anchovy sauce is salty) for about 13 minutes or until tender. Drain. Place in a platter. Pour hot anchovy sauce over spaghettini. Sprinkle individual portions with bread crumbs. Serves 4.

Some Sicilians favor grated cheese over this dish, but we prefer sprinkling a bread crumb topping because of the salty anchovy-flavored sauce.

SPAGHETTINI CON SALSA DI SALSICCIA FORTE
Spaghettini with Hot Sausage Sauce

1 1/2 lbs. spaghettini *or* spaghetti
1 lb. Italian hot sausage, cut in chunks
1/4 cup hot water
1/2 lb. medium mushrooms, sliced
3/4 cup shredded carrot
1 medium onion, sliced
1/2 cup chopped celery
1/4 cup chopped parsley
2 lbs. ground beef chuck

28 oz. can plum tomatoes
two 6 oz. cans tomato paste
1 cup dry red wine
1 bay leaf
salt to taste
1 tsp. dry basil leaves
pepper (optional)
1/2 cup grated Parmesan cheese (if desired)

In a tightly covered Dutch oven or kettle, cook sausage in water 10 minutes, stirring occasionally. Remove sausage with slotted spoon. In same kettle, sauté mushrooms, carrots, onion, celery and parsley in sausage drippings until tender. Remove vegetables and add beef to pan. Cook, stirring frequently, until browned and all liquids are cooked down. Remove any excess fat. Return sausage and vegetables to pan. Add tomatoes, tomato paste, wine, bay leaf, salt, basil, and pepper if desired.

(Continued on following page.)

Cover and simmer for 30 minutes. Uncover and simmer 1 1/2 hours, stirring occasionally.

Meanwhile, in 6 to 9 quarts of rapidly boiling salted water, gradually add spaghettini so that water continues to boil. Cook for about 13 minutes or until tender. Drain. Place on a large platter. Top with sausage sauce. Serve with grated Parmesan cheese, if desired. Serves 12. **(See photo below.)**

Spaghettini with Hot Sausage Sauce. See recipe on page 53.

Photo: Theodore R. Sills.
Courtesy of National Macaroni Institute.

LINGUINE CON PESTO ALLA GENOVESE
Linguine with Herb Sauce Genoa Style

1 lb. linguine *or* spaghettini
2 large cloves of garlic
1/2 cup fresh basil leaves
1 tbs. melted butter
2 fresh mint leaves

pepper to taste
4 tbs. olive oil
meat of 1 walnut
1/4 cup grated Parmesan cheese

In a mortar with pestle, pound together garlic, basil leaves, butter, mint leaves and pepper until very fine. Add olive oil gradually while pounding until very smooth. Then pound in walnut well. Or, on a wooden board, with a sharp knife chop all ingredients until extremely fine. Place in a bowl. Add olive oil gradually and continue same process with a wooden spoon.

Cook linguine in 6 quarts of rapidly boiling, salted water for 11 minutes or until tender. Drain. Turn onto a large platter. Add herb mixture (*pesto*). Mix well. Serve with grated Parmesan cheese. Serves 4.

LINGUINE CON SALSA DI POMODORO E VERDURE
Linguine with Tomato Sauce and Vegetables

1 lb. linguine (pasta) *or* spaghettini
9 tbs. olive oil
1 small chopped onion
1 large diced carrot
1 qt. plum tomatoes, mashed
1 tsp. dry basil *or* 3 fresh torn basil leaves

1 whole clove garlic
salt and pepper to taste
1 cup diced unpeeled eggplant
1 1/2 tbs. pine nuts
4 tsp. capers
freshly ground pepper (optional)

Heat 5 tbs. olive oil in a medium-size saucepan. Add onion and carrot and cook over medium flame until golden. Add plum tomatoes, basil, garlic, salt and pepper. Allow to come to a boil. Lower flame. Cover partially and simmer for 30 minutes, stirring occasionally. In a small skillet, brown eggplant and pine nuts in remaining 1/4 cup of olive oil. Remove with slotted spoon. Add to sauce. Cook for about 3 minutes. Remove garlic.

Meanwhile, cook linguine in 6 quarts of rapidly boiling, salted water for 11 minutes or until tender. Drain. Turn onto large platter. Pour hot sauce over linguine. Top with capers and freshly ground black pepper. Serves 4.

MAFALDE CON SALSA DI SGOMBRO
Mafalde with Mackerel Sauce

1 lb. mafalde (pasta) *or* medium-wide noodles
2 lbs. fresh mackerel
3 tbs. olive oil
1 tbs. chopped onion
2 lbs. 3 oz. can plum tomatoes, mashed
1 clove minced garlic

4 fresh basil leaves *or* 3/4 tsp. dry basil
pinch of oregano
salt and pepper to taste
flour and fine cracker crumbs
1/4 cup olive oil
1/4 cup grated Romano cheese

Heat 3 tbs. olive oil in a large saucepan. Add onion and cook over low flame until yellow. Add tomatoes, garlic, basil, oregano, salt and pepper. Over high flame, bring to a boil. Lower flame. Cover partially and simmer for 20 minutes, stirring occasionally.

Meanwhile, clean and wash mackerel. Dry and cut each in half. Dredge in fine cracker crumbs

(Continued on following page.)

and flour. Heat 1/4 cup olive oil in a large skillet and fry fish until golden. Then add mackerel to sauce. Simmer for 15 minutes more.

In 6 quarts of rapidly boiling, salted water, cook mafalde for 12–15 minutes or until tender. Drain. Place on a platter. Remove mackerel from sauce. Pour hot sauce over mafalde. Serve with grated Romano cheese. Serve fish as an accompaniment. Serves 4.

Fresh mackerel is highly recommended for best flavor, the season for it being April to November. But if the fresh type is unobtainable, frozen mackerel fillets may be substituted.

MAFALDE AL FORNO
Baked Mafalde

1 lb. mafalde (pasta) *or* medium-wide noodles
6 thinly sliced hard-boiled eggs
8 oz. thinly-sliced mozzarella

1/4 cup grated incannestrata *or* Romano cheese
1/2 cup grated incannestrata *or* Romano cheese
   (for serving)

Sauce:

1/4 cup olive oil
1 small chopped onion
3 1/2 oz. tomato paste
2 lbs. 3 oz. can plum tomatoes, mashed
3 cups hot water

1 clove minced garlic
1 bay leaf
1/2 tsp. dry basil *or* 3 or 4 fresh chopped basil
   leaves
salt and pepper to taste

Heat olive oil in a medium-size saucepan. Add onion and cook over low flame until yellow. Add tomato paste and water. Stir until dissolved. Add plum tomatoes, garlic, bay leaf, basil, salt and pepper. Bring to a boil over high flame. Lower flame. Cover partially and simmer for 1 hour. Stir occasionally. When done, remove bay leaf.

In 6 quarts of rapidly boiling, salted water, cook mafalde for 10 minutes or until medium-cooked or firm (*al dente*). Drain. Run under cool water for better handling. Drain once more.

Coat bottom of a 10"x14"x2" baking dish with a little sauce. Place in layers (in this order): some mafalde, sauce, eggs, mozzarella, sauce, ending with grated cheese. Repeat process until all ingredients are used. Bake in a preheated oven at 375°F. for 25 minutes or until brown. Remove from oven. Let sit for 10 minutes before serving. Serve with grated incannestrata cheese or Romano cheese. Serves 4–5.

For variety, Mother surprised Father and us, one day, with this different pasta casserole containing hard-boiled egg and cheese stuffing. We often include this dish in a Sunday dinner.

PASTA CON SALSA DI SALSICCIA E MELANZANE
Macaroni with Sausage Eggplant Sauce

1 lb. elbow macaroni (about 4 cups)
1 large eggplant (about 2 lbs.)
3/4 lb. Italian hot sausage
3/4 lb. Italian sweet sausage
1/3 cup water
1 tbs. olive oil
1/2 cup chopped onion

2 large cloves crushed garlic
28 oz. can plum tomatoes
two 8 oz. cans tomato sauce
1 tsp. crushed dry basil
salt and freshly ground black pepper to taste
1/2 cup grated Parmesan cheese (if desired)

Peel the eggplant and cut into 1/2-inch cubes. Set aside. Remove casings and break sausages into chunks. In Dutch oven or kettle, cook sausage in 1/3 cup water over medium-low flame for 10 minutes, tightly covered. Stir occasionally. Drain off water. Over low flame, sauté sausage until lightly browned. Remove sausage from Dutch oven. Add olive oil and heat. Stir in onion and garlic. Sauté until lightly browned. Add sausage, eggplant, tomatoes, tomato sauce and basil. Simmer covered for 45 minutes, stirring occasionally. Uncover and simmer 15 minutes more. Season sauce to taste with salt and pepper.

About 15 minutes before sauce is done, in 6 quarts of rapidly boiling salted water, gradually add macaroni so that water continues to boil. Cook for 15 minutes or until tender. Drain. Place macaroni in a large platter. Top with sausage-eggplant sauce. Serve with Parmesan cheese. Serves 8. (See color photo on page 5.)

MACCHERONI CON VEGETALI VERDI ALLA SICILIANA
Macaroni with Green Vegetables, Sicilian

2 cups elbow macaroni (short type)
3 tbs. olive oil
1 small chopped onion
1 cup cold water
1 3/4 cups frozen asparagus spears, cut into
    1-inch pieces

1 cup frozen zucchini (Italian squash)
1 1/2 cup frozen peas
salt to taste
freshly ground pepper to taste
1/4 cup grated Romano cheese

Cut larger slices of zucchini into quarters, smaller slices in half.

In a medium-size saucepan, heat olive oil. Add onion and sauté until yellow. Add water. Bring to a boil over high flame. Add asparagus spears and let come to a boil again. Lower flame. Cover. Simmer for 5 minutes. Add zucchini and peas. Over high flame, bring to a boil again. Lower flame, cover and simmer for 5–7 minutes or until vegetables are tender. Season with salt and freshly ground pepper. Mix.

Meanwhile, cook short elbow macaroni in 3 quarts of rapidly boiling, salted water for 15 minutes or until tender. Drain. Place macaroni and vegetable mixture in a large bowl. Mix. Serve with grated Romano cheese. Serves 4.

CONCHIGLIE CON CAVOLFIORE
Sea Shells with Cauliflower

1 medium head cauliflower
1 lb. conchiglie (medium-size sea shell pasta)
4 tbs. olive oil
1 small chopped onion

2 oz. can fillets of anchovy, cut up
1 clove minced garlic
pinch of pepper
1/4—1/2 cup grated Parmesan *or* Romano cheese

Remove leaves and core from cauliflower. Wash. Cut cauliflower into large pieces. In a pot with boiling, lightly salted water, cook cauliflower until tender. Drain, but reserve water. Cut cauliflower into small pieces.

Heat olive oil in a large saucepan. Add onion and cook over low flame until golden. Add anchovies, garlic and pepper. Stir until anchovies dissolve. Add cauliflower. Mix until cauliflower is well-coated. Simmer for 5 minutes, stirring occasionally.

About five minutes before making anchovy sauce, start cooking conchiglie in rapidly boiling water reserved from cooking cauliflower for 15 minutes or until tender. Do not drain completely; leave conchiglie slightly moist. Place in a large bowl. Add hot cauliflower mixture. Mix. Serve with grated Parmesan or Romano cheese. Serves 4—6.

MEZZANI AL FORNO
Baked Mezzani with Meat and White Sauce

1 lb. mezzani (pasta) *or* ziti
7 oz. ground beef
1/4 lb. sliced Italian sweet sausage
4 tbs. butter (divided)
1 tbs. chopped parsley
2 eggs

salt and pepper to taste
2 tbs. flour
2 cups milk
fine dry bread crumbs
2 tbs. grated Parmesan cheese

In a medium-size skillet, brown ground beef in 1 tbs. of butter. Place in a bowl. Add parsley, eggs, salt and pepper. Mix well.

Meanwhile, prepare a white sauce: Melt 2 tbs. of butter in a small saucepan over low flame. Add flour and blend until smooth. Add milk gradually and stir constantly until sauce thickens. If it becomes too thick, add a small amount of milk.

Fry sausage slices for about 2 minutes over low flame in a large skillet. Set aside. Cook mezzani in 6 quarts of rapidly boiling, salted water for 10—12 minutes or until *al dente*. Drain. Season with remaining butter (1 tbs.) and cheese, mixing well.

Then in a buttered 3-quart casserole, place a layer of mezzani. Distribute half the amount of beef and sausage on top. Add another layer of mezzani and the remainder of the meats. Cover with white sauce. Sprinkle top with fine dry bread crumbs and dot with butter. Bake in a preheated oven at 350°F. until golden brown. Serves 4.

MEZZANI CON FORMAGGIO AL FORNO
Baked Mezzani with Cheese

1/2 lb. mezzani (pasta) *or* ziti
2 large sliced tomatoes
1/4 lb. sliced mozzarella

Cheese Sauce:

2 tbs. butter *or* margarine
2 tbs. flour
salt and pepper to taste
1 tsp. dry basil
1/4 tsp. thyme

1/2 small grated onion
1/2 tsp. dry mustard
pinch of cayenne
2 cups milk
1 cup grated Cheddar cheese

Cook mezzani in 6 quarts of rapidly boiling, salted water for 10—12 minutes or until tender. Drain.

Meanwhile, in a small saucepan, melt butter over low flame. Remove from heat. Add flour, salt and pepper. Stir until smooth and well-blended. Add basil, thyme, onion, mustard and cayenne. Place over low flame. Add milk gradually. Stir until thick. Add Cheddar cheese. Stir until melted.

Place half of the mezzani in a buttered 2-quart baking dish. Add half the cheese sauce. Arrange half the tomato slices on top. Add other half of the pasta, sliced mozzarella and remainder of cheese sauce, ending with tomato slices. Bake in a preheated oven at 375°F. for 25 minutes. Serves 3—4.

DITALI CON FAGIOLI E BROCCOLI
Ditali with Beans and Broccoli

2 cups ditali (pasta) *or* short elbow macaroni
1 lb. 4 oz. can cannellini (white kidney beans),
    with liquid
1/4 cup olive oil
1 small finely chopped onion

2 tbs. tomato sauce
1 clove minced garlic
1 3/4 cups broccoli, cut into 1-inch pieces
salt and pepper to taste

In a medium-size saucepan, over low flame, cook onion in hot olive oil until golden. Add tomato sauce, garlic, undrained cannellini, broccoli, salt and pepper. Over high flame, bring to a boil. Lower flame. Cover. Steam for 10—15 minutes or until broccoli is tender.

Meanwhile, cook ditali in 3 quarts of rapidly boiling, salted water for 12—15 minutes or until tender. Drain well. Add ditali to broccoli mixture. Mix. Cook for 5 minutes longer. Serves 3—4.

FUSILLI A FILETTO DI POMODORO
Fusilli with Fillet of Tomato

3 cups diced onions
1/4 cup butter *or* margarine
1 cup diced proscuitto

35 oz. can plum tomatoes*
salt and pepper to taste
1 lb. fusilli *or* spaghetti

In a Dutch oven or large heavy saucepan, sauté onions in butter over low heat until golden. Add proscuitto. Cook 10 minutes. Stir in tomatoes and mash. Simmer covered for 15 minutes. Uncover and cook 20 minutes longer, stirring occasionally. Season with salt and pepper.

In 6 quarts of rapidly boiling salted water, gradually add fusilli so that water continues to boil. Cook until tender. Drain. Place in a large platter and cover with sauce. Serves 8.

*Or use 2 lbs. fresh plum tomatoes, peeled and diced (and seeded, if desired). When fresh tomatoes are used, cook sauce covered for half an hour, adding water if necessary. (**See photo on opposite page.**)

ZITI AL FORNO
Baked Ziti

1 lb. ground beef chuck
1/2 lb. lean ground pork
1/3 cup seasoned dry bread crumbs
salt and pepper
1 egg
1 tbs. grated Parmesan cheese
1 medium eggplant, pared and diced (about 1 lb.)
1/2 cup olive oil
35 oz. can Italian plum tomatoes
6 oz. can tomato paste
1 clove pressed garlic

1 tsp. sugar
salt to taste
1/2 tsp. basil
1/2 tsp. oregano
1/4 tsp. crushed red pepper seeds
1 lb. ziti *or* elbow macaroni
Parmesan cheese
1 lb. ricotta
1/2 lb. sliced mozzarella
2 cups medium white sauce*

Have butcher grind chuck and pork together to mix well and then separate into 1 lb. and 1/2 lb. portions. Mix together 1 lb. of meat with bread crumbs, 1/2 tsp. salt, pepper, egg and 1 tbs. grated Parmesan cheese. Shape into 1/2-inch meatballs. Set aside.

In a large saucepan, sauté eggplant in olive oil until lightly browned, adding more oil if necessary. Remove. In same pan, brown meatballs. Remove. Next, brown the 1/2 lb. of meat. Add tomatoes, tomato paste, garlic, sugar, salt, basil, oregano and red pepper. Simmer covered 1/2 hour. Uncover and simmer 1/2 hour longer, stirring occasionally. Add eggplant and meatballs.

Meanwhile, in 6 quarts of rapidly boiling, salted water, gradually add ziti so that water continues to boil. Cook until tender. Drain.

In buttered 5-quart baking dish, make a layer using half the ziti, half the tomato sauce, then sprinkle with Parmesan cheese. Top with dollops of ricotta, mozzarella slices and white sauce; sprinkle with Parmesan. Cover with remaining ziti, tomato sauce and a final sprinkle of Parmesan. Bake in a preheated oven at 375°F. for 25 minutes or until bubbling hot. Serves 8.

Medium White Sauce:
In a saucepan, blend 1/4 cup flour with 1/4 cup melted butter until smooth with a wooden spoon. Gradually stir in 2 cups milk, 1 tsp. salt, dash of pepper and 1 tbs. minced onion. Bring to a boil, stirring constantly. Boil gently for 1 minute. Makes 2 cups. (**See photo on opposite page.**)

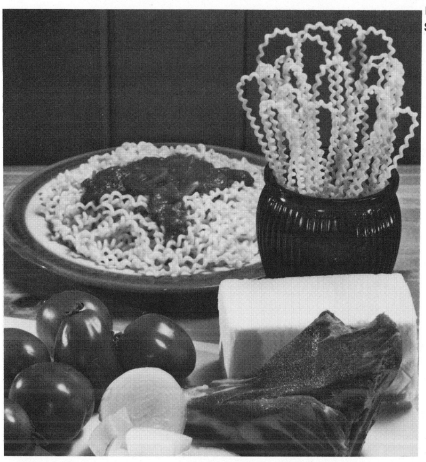

Fusilli with Fillet of Tomato.
See recipe on opposite page.

Baked Ziti. See recipe on opposite page.

RIGATONI RIPIENI AL FORNO
Baked Stuffed Rigatoni

8 oz. rigatoni (pasta) (about 60)	1/2 tsp. sugar
5 slices diced bacon	salt to taste
3/4 cup chopped onion	2 cloves crushed garlic
3/4 cup chopped celery	8 parsley sprigs
3/4 cup finely diced carrot	1/2 tsp. thyme leaves
two 28 oz. cans tomatoes in tomato purée	1 bay leaf
two 10-1/2-oz. cans condensed beef broth	2 cups water

Cook bacon for about 2 minutes in a large saucepan or Dutch oven. Add onion, celery and carrot. Cook until onion is tender. Stir in tomatoes in tomato purée, condensed beef broth, sugar, salt, garlic, parsley, thyme, bay leaf and water. Simmer uncovered for 2 hours, stirring occasionally. If sauce becomes too thick, add a little hot water during cooking. Strain sauce through a sieve or force through a food mill. Add enough water to make 6 cups of sauce.

In 3 quarts of rapidly boiling, salted water, gradually add rigatoni so that water continues to boil. Cook until tender. Drain. Then rinse with cold water and drain again. Spread rigatoni out on a tray.

Filling:

2 tbs. olive oil	2 beaten eggs
3/4 cup chopped onion	1/2 cup dry bread crumbs
1 clove minced garlic	3 tbs. chopped parsley
2 lbs. ground beef *or* pork sausage	salt and pepper to taste

Heat olive oil in a large skillet. Add onion and garlic and cook over low heat until golden. Raise to medium flame. Add beef and cook, stirring constantly, just until lightly browned. (If using sausage, omit olive oil and place sausage in skillet. Break it up into small pieces. Cook, stirring constantly, until lightly browned. Pour off excess fat from skillet. Add onion and garlic and cook until golden.) Remove meat mixture from heat. Place in a large bowl and cool slightly. Then blend in eggs, bread crumbs and parsley. Season with salt and pepper. Stuff rigatoni with meat mixture.

Arrange stuffed rigatoni in a shallow 3-quart casserole. Pour sauce over rigatoni. Bake uncovered in a preheated oven at 350°F. for 30 minutes, spooning sauce over top occasionally. Serves 8–10. **(See color photo on page 8.)**

TAGLIATELLE AL' ALFREDO
Noodles Alfredo

1 lb. medium egg noodles (about 8 cups)	1/2 cup heavy cream (at room temperature)
1/2 lb. sweet butter, softened	freshly ground pepper (optional)
2 cups grated Parmesan cheese	

In 6 quarts of rapidly boiling salted water, gradually add noodles so that water continues to boil. Cook until tender. Drain.

Place butter in a hot 2-quart casserole. Add noodles and toss gently. Add cheese and toss again. Pour in cream. Toss. Sprinkle with freshly ground pepper, if desired. Serves 6–8.

MANICOTTI CON RIEMPIMENTO DI CARNE E VEGETALE
Manicotti with Meat-Vegetable Filling

8 oz. manicotti rigati noodles or cannelloni (16 noodles)

Sauce:
Italian Tomato Sauce (p. 75)
1/2 lb. sliced fresh mushrooms
1 tbs. olive oil

Filling:

1/2 lb. fresh mushrooms	1/3 cup grated Parmesan cheese
1/2 cup chopped onion	2 beaten eggs
3 tbs. olive oil	2 tbs. heavy *or* light cream
1 small minced clove garlic	1/2 tsp. crumbled marjoram leaves
10 oz. pkg. frozen chopped spinach, thawed	salt and ground black pepper to taste
1 1/2 cups ground beef, cooked	

To make filling: Rinse, pat dry and chop mushrooms. In a large skillet, heat olive oil. Add onion, garlic and the mushrooms. Sauté 5 minutes over low flame.

Meanwhile, squeeze as much liquid as possible from spinach. Add to mushroom mixture. Sauté over high heat, stirring constantly until mixture begins to stick to pan. Put into a large bowl. Add the meat, grated cheese, eggs, cream, marjoram, salt and black pepper. Set aside.

Meanwhile, follow directions for Italian Tomato Sauce. Sauté the sliced mushrooms in a medium-size skillet with 1 tbs. olive oil for five minutes. Add mushrooms when sauce is done.

In 6 quarts of rapidly boiling, salted water, cook manicotti for 6 minutes (do not overcook). Immediately drop into cold water to prevent further cooking. Drain.

Gently fill each manicotti with meat mixture. Coat bottom of a 10"x14"x2" baking pan with sauce. Arrange stuffed noodles in pan, side by side. Spoon remaining sauce over all. Cover pan with aluminum foil, sealing edges tightly. Bake in a preheated oven at 375°F. for 40 minutes. Serve at once. Serves 6.

FETTUCELLE
Italian Egg Noodles

3 1/2 cups sifted flour	1 tbs. olive oil
3 medium eggs, beaten	pinch of salt
2 eggshells full of water	

Place 3 1/4 cups of flour on a board. Make a well in it. Add eggs, water, olive oil and salt. Blend by rubbing mixture between palms of hands. Add remaining flour gradually, kneading meanwhile until dough is very smooth. Flour board, if too sticky. Place in a bowl. Cover. Let stand for 1 hour. Divide dough into two sections.

Roll out sections until paper-thin. Allow dough to stand for 12 minutes. Sprinkle each sheet lightly with flour, spreading flour over sheet with hand. Then keep flapping dough over until three inches wide. With a sharp knife, cut dough crosswise into strips 1/4-inch wide. Toss the shreds apart. Cut to desired length. Dry for 5 minutes on clean, dry towel. If all noodles are not to be used, let dry very well. Then store in a tightly closed container.

In 8 quarts of rapidly boiling water, cook fettucelle for 10 minutes or until tender. Drain. Serve with any desired sauce for pasta. Serve with 1/2 cup grated Romano or Parmesan cheese. Serves 5—6.

BUDINO DI TAGLIATELLE
Egg Noodle Pudding*

1 lb. tagliatelle (medium egg noodles)
3 oz. butter
1/2 cup heavy cream
1/2 cup grated Parmesan cheese

1/4 cup grated Gruyere cheese
3 eggs, separated
very fine bread crumbs
butter

In 6 quarts of rapidly boiling, salted water, cook noodles for about 10 minutes or until firm but not hard (*al dente*). Drain. Place in a large platter. Add butter and mix until it melts. Add heavy cream and cheeses, mixing well. Beat egg yolks until frothy. Add to mixture. In a large bowl, beat egg whites until stiff. Fold noodles into egg whites.

Place in a buttered 2-quart casserole. Sprinkle with fine bread crumbs. Dot with butter. Bake in a preheated oven at 350°F. until top is golden and crusty. Serves 4–5.

*The word *budino* literally means "pudding." This dish is not a pudding in the real sense, but it sets like one when baked, hence the name.

FETTUCELLE CON RICOTTA
Fettucelle with Italian Cheese

1 lb. fettucelle (pasta) *or* spaghetti
1/2 lb. ricotta *or* mild creamed cottage cheese
   with tiny, soft curds

1/4 cup milk
freshly ground pepper to taste (optional)
1/4 cup grated pecorino *or* Parmesan cheese

Cook fettucelle in 6 quarts of rapidly boiling, salted water for 10–12 minutes or until tender. Drain.

If using creamed cottage cheese, put it through a fine sieve. In a small saucepan, blend ricotta and milk until smooth. Cook over low flame until warm. Pour over hot fettucelle. Serve with pepper, if desired, and grated pecorino or Parmesan cheese. Serves 4.

FETTUCINE ALLA ROMANA
Noodles with Butter, Roman Style

1 lb. fettucine (pasta)
8 tbs. butter (1/2 cup)
1 1/2 tbs. grated Parmesan cheese

pepper to taste
1/4 cup grated Parmesan cheese

Cook fettucine in 6 quarts of rapidly boiling, salted water for 9–13 minutes or until tender. Drain. In a large platter, place butter, 1 1/2 tbs. of cheese and pepper. Add fettucine. Mix until butter melts. Serve with grated Parmesan cheese. Serves 4.

Fettucine are ingrained in the Roman soul. At home or in the hundreds of *trattorie* (restaurants) dotting the ancient city, Romans eat them late into the night.

TAGLIATELLE VERDE CON SALSA DI PROSCUITTO
Green Noodles with Italian Ham Sauce

1 lb. green noodles* *or* plain noodles
1 tbs. chopped onion
2 tbs. butter
1 stalk diced celery
1 diced carrot

3 finely chopped strips proscuitto *or* Virginia ham
6 oz. can tomato paste
3 cups hot water
salt to taste
1/4 cup grated Parmesan cheese

Heat butter in a medium-size saucepan. Add onion, celery and carrot. Cook until tender. Add proscuitto. Continue cooking until golden brown. Add tomato paste, hot water and salt. Stir until tomato paste dissolves. Bring to a boil over high flame. Lower flame. Cover partially and simmer for 35 minutes. Stir occasionally. If using Virginia ham, add pepper to taste, if desired.

Cook green noodles in 6 quarts of rapidly boiling, salted water for about 15 minutes or until tender. Drain. Place in a platter. Pour hot proscuitto sauce over noodles. Serve with grated Parmesan cheese. Serves 4.

*Green noodles are made with sieved, cooked spinach and beaten eggs added to a plain noodle dough.

GNOCCHI DI PATATE TUSCANA
Potato Dumplings, Tuscany Style

2 lbs. mature potatoes
1 slightly beaten egg
3/4 tsp. olive oil
pinch of salt

3 1/4 cups flour
Italian Tomato Sauce *or* melted butter
1/4 cup grated Romano *or* Parmesan cheese

Scrub potatoes. Boil them in their skins until tender. Drain, peel and put through a ricer or mash until extremely smooth. When cool, combine with egg, olive oil and salt. Gradually add flour. Then knead thoroughly until very smooth.

Take pieces of potato dough and roll into ropelike strips (the width of a finger) under palm of hand. Cut into 1-inch pieces or you can thin each piece by pressing with the thumb in a flipping motion away from you.

Into 5 quarts of rapidly boiling, salted water, drop pieces of potato dough (*gnocchi*), about 2 dozen at a time. After gnocchi rise to the surface, cook for 3 minutes longer. Remove with slotted spoon. Transfer to heated platter. Place in individual dishes and serve with hot Italian Tomato Sauce (page 75) or hot melted butter. Serve with grated Romano or Parmesan cheese. Serves 4.

This gnocchi recipe was given to me by a Tuscan neighbor. Many Northern Italians prefer a Butter Sauce or Pesto with their gnocchi. I decided to include our own Tomato Sauce, for those who favor it instead. The leftover sauce may be refrigerated and used another time for two servings of pasta and rice, to flavor vegetable soups or to top a plain meat loaf. Another excellent use is to make Eggs in Tomato Sauce which is found in chapter nine.

POLENTA CON RAGU
Corn Meal with Sauce

2 cups yellow corn meal
8 cups water
1 1/2 tsp. salt

1 tsp. butter
Sauce with Meatballs (p. 76)
1/2 cup grated Parmesan cheese

Make Sauce with Meatballs.

Boil water with salt and butter in a heavy aluminum or stainless steel pot. (Corn meal will stick in any other kind of pot.) Add corn meal very gradually, stirring constantly to prevent lumps. Cook over very low flame for 50 minutes, stirring frequently. Add 2 finely chopped meatballs and 2 tbs. sauce to corn meal. Stir. Cook for 10 minutes more. Spoon polenta out into individual dishes and pour hot sauce over it. Serve with grated Parmesan cheese. Serve meatballs as an accompaniment. Serves 6.

MANICOTTI
Pasta Muffs

6 medium eggs
1 tbs. butter *or* margarine
pinch of salt

2 cups water
2 cups flour
1/2 tsp. butter (for pan)

Allow butter or margarine to become soft at room temperature. In a bowl, cream the butter. Add eggs and beat. Then add salt and water. Add flour gradually. Beat until smooth. In a 6 1/4-inch cast-iron skillet coated with hot melted butter, pour 2 tbs. of batter and tip and swirl pan to cover bottom with a thin layer. Over very low flame, cook on both sides until set and slightly brown on edges. It is necessary to butter the pan only once. Repeat process until all of the batter is used. Makes about 32.

Note: Cooked but unfilled manicotti may be prepared ahead, cooled, wrapped and frozen for future use.

Filling:
2 1/2 lbs. drained ricotta *or* mild creamed
    cottage cheese with tiny soft curds, sieved

1/2 lb. shredded mozzarella
pinch of salt

Sauce:
1/4 cup olive oil
1 small chopped onion
7 oz. can tomato paste
4 cups hot water
2 lbs. 3 oz. can plum tomatoes, mashed
20 oz. can plum tomatoes, mashed

2 or 3 torn leaves of fresh basil *or* 1/2 tsp.
    dry basil
1 sprig chopped fresh parsley
1 whole clove garlic
salt to taste
pepper to taste

1/2 cup grated Parmesan *or* Romano cheese (for serving)

In a large saucepan heat olive oil. Add onion and cook over low flame until yellow. Add tomato paste and water. Stir until dissolved. Then add tomatoes, basil, parsley, garlic, salt and pepper. Over high flame, let come to a boil. Lower flame. Cover partially and simmer for 1 hour, stirring occasionally. Remove garlic.

Mix filling ingredients well. Then place 2 heaping tbs. of filling in center of each disk of dough, folding edges over on either side so they overlap to hold filling in. On the bottoms of two baking pans 10"x14"x2", pour enough sauce to coat heavily. Place manicotti in pans, side by side in one layer, with the overlapped side down. Spoon remaining sauce over manicotti. Bake in a preheated oven at 375°F. for 25–30 minutes. Serve with grated Parmesan or Romano cheese. Serves 8–10.

Sometimes homemade manicotti noodles are made with rolled-out dough cut to size, dried and boiled. The crepe method above, I feel, is a much easier one and also produces a lighter product.

RAVIOLI

Filling:

3/4 lb. cooked ground beef
1/4 lb. cooked ground pork
2 eggs
1 lb. fresh or frozen spinach, cooked, finely chopped, and well drained

1/4 cup grated Romano cheese
1 small minced onion
salt and pepper to taste

Prepare this filling before making dough. In a bowl, combine all ingredients. Refrigerate.

Sauce:

Follow directions for Italian Tomato Sauce (p. 75).

For Serving:

1/2 cup grated Romano cheese

Dough:

1/3 cup cream of farina
3 cups sifted flour
pinch of salt

1 egg
1 cup cold water

On a board, combine cream of farina, flour and salt. Make a well. Add egg. Blend by rubbing between palms of hands. Add water gradually. Work in the same manner. If dough gets too sticky, add a little flour to board. Knead until smooth. Place dough in a bowl. Cover. Let stand for 30 minutes. Divide dough into two parts. Roll out until paper-thin. Cover first sheet with a towel to prevent drying out while rolling out second sheet.

Place heaping teaspoonfuls of filling about 1 inch apart on half of one sheet of dough, leaving one inch on all outside edges. Flap the remaining side over filling. To make cutting the ravioli easier, press dough down with fingers between individual fillings. Then cut out ravioli with a ravioli cutter or knife, halfway between the fillings, leaving enough dough on all sides to prevent stuffing from falling out. Press edges down well. Continue same process on other sheet of dough. Spread ravioli out on a tablecloth that has been lightly sprinkled with corn meal. Let ravioli stand for 2 hours.

In 8 quarts of rapidly boiling, salted water, cook ravioli for 25 minutes or until tender. Drain well. Place ravioli on individual dishes. Pour hot Italian Tomato Sauce over them. Serve with grated Romano cheese. Makes 5 or 6 dozen. Serves 6.

NOTE: If desired, ravioli may be prepared and frozen days ahead. In pastry boxes, place sheets of wax paper. Sprinkle with corn meal. Place a layer of ravioli. Sprinkle with corn meal. Cover with a sheet of wax paper. Continue process with other layers, ending with wax paper. Tie box. Wrap tightly in a plastic or aluminum wrap. Place in freezer. Thaw completely before cooking.

RICE

Rice is a more modern product in Italy than pasta. Its appearance there may be attributed to the Arab conquerors of ancient Sicily. In medieval times the Fifth Duke of Milan became so interested in rice that he sent twelve sacks of it to be grown at Ferrara, a region conducive to rice cultivation because it stands in the marshy delta of the Po. Today Milan is famous for its trade in rice as well as for its *risotto*, and other Northern regions, as well, prefer rice to pasta.

Actually, rice is one of the world's greatest crops, providing food for one half of the human population. It is a popular cereal for a number of reasons. Besides being easily digestible and attaining greater food value when combined with complementary nutriments, it is one of those rare foods that can be reheated without spoiling its flavor. Delectable leftover *risotto* may be easily heated by placing it in a double boiler over boiling water.

Because rice is a bland food, it waits to be used in a variety of combinations which lend it an infinite variety of tastes. And the Italian does this uniquely in excellent ways with meat, cheese, tomato sauce and vegetables, bringing interest as well as economy to the menu.

RISOTTO CON SALSICCIA
Italian Rice with Sausage

2 cups raw long-grain rice
3 Italian sweet sausages
1 large chopped onion
8 cups chicken stock

black pepper to taste
1 small chopped tomato
1 tsp. dry parsley *or* 1 tbs. fresh minced parsley
1/2 cup grated Parmesan cheese

Remove casings from sausages. Crumble sausages. In a large saucepan over low flame, cook until brown. Add the onion and cook until yellow. Add rice, stirring constantly until well-coated. Add 2 cups of the stock, pepper, tomato and parsley. Stir. Cover and cook until liquid is absorbed. Add remaining broth as it becomes absorbed by rice, covering with a lid each time. Simmer for 25 minutes or until tender. Serve with grated Parmesan cheese. Serves 4—6.

RISOTTO ALLA MILANESE
Rice Milanese

2 cups raw long-grain rice
6 tbs. butter
1 large finely sliced onion
2 tbs. beef marrow (optional)
1/4 tsp. saffron

2 tsp. dry parsley *or* 2 tbs. fresh minced parsley
1/4 cup dry white wine
8 cups chicken stock
8 tbs. grated Parmesan cheese

To remove beef marrow, use a thin knife to scoop out of bone.

Melt butter in a large saucepan. Add onions and marrow and cook, over low flame, until onions are yellow. Add rice. Stir until coated with butter. Add saffron, parsley, white wine and 2 cups of chicken stock. Stir. Cover. Cook until stock is absorbed. Add remaining broth as it becomes absorbed by rice, replacing lid each time. After 15 minutes of cooking, add grated cheese. Mix. Continue cooking, covered, for 10 minutes or until rice is tender. Serves 4—6.

ARANCINI IMBOTTITI
Stuffed Orange Balls

2 cups raw long-grain rice
2 tbs. butter
4 eggs, separated
1/2 cup grated Romano cheese

salt and pepper to taste
1 cup fine bread crumbs
corn oil for deep frying

Cook rice until firm (not tender). Drain. Put in a large platter. Add butter and cheese. Mix and spread out to cool. When cool, add egg yolks, salt and pepper. Mix well. Set aside.

Filling:

2 tbs. olive oil
1/4 lb. ground beef
1/4 small minced onion
1/8 tsp. garlic salt

black pepper to taste
1/2 cup frozen peas
1/2 cup tomato sauce

Heat olive oil in a skillet. Add meat and cook until it loses its red color. Add onion. Cook until onion is yellow. Then add garlic salt, pepper, frozen peas and tomato sauce. Cover. Simmer for 7 minutes. Remove from skillet and allow to cool.

To make Stuffed Orange Balls: Put 1 heaping tablespoonful of rice in palm of hand. Flatten slightly. Then place 1 teaspoonful of filling in center of rice. Add another heaping tablespoonful of rice on top. Pack well and form into a ball. Continue making balls until all ingredients have been used.

In a dish, beat egg whites until frothy. Dip rice balls in egg whites. Then roll in bread crumbs. In hot corn oil, fry until golden brown on all sides. Use enough fat so the balls float and do not fry so many at one time that they crowd the pan. Drain on absorbent paper. Serve hot or cold. Makes 16.

TORTA DI RISO CON RICOTTA
Italian Cheese Rice Pie

1/2 lb. raw long-grain rice
3/4 lb. ricotta
1/4 lb. mozzarella, cut into 1/4-inch cubes

1/2 lb. grated Romano cheese
1 cup tomato sauce

Boil rice in lightly salted water until almost tender. Drain. Place in a greased 2-quart casserole. Add ricotta, then mozzarella cubes. Sprinkle with grated cheese. Cover with sauce. Bake in a pre-heated oven at 375°F. for 35 minutes. Serves 4.

RISOTTO ALLA CREMA
Italian Rice with Cream

2 cups raw long-grain rice
2 egg yolks (at room temperature)
2 tbs. light cream

1/4 lb. butter (softened at room temperature)
1 cup grated Parmesan cheese

In a large saucepan, cook rice in boiling, salted water until *al dente* (firm). Drain. Set aside and keep warm.

In a large bowl, beat egg yolks with cream. Add hot rice and butter. Mix well. Add cheese and mix again. Serve immediately. Serves 4–6.

RISOTTO CON PISELLI E FUNGHI
Italian Rice with Peas and Mushrooms

1 lb. raw long-grain rice
2 tbs. olive oil
1 strip diced bacon
1 clove minced garlic
1/2 tsp. dry parsley *or* 1 tbs. fresh minced parsley
salt and pepper to taste
small amount of butter

1/2 lb. sliced mushrooms
1 cup frozen peas
1/4 cup hot water
6 tbs. butter
1 small chopped onion
2 qts. chicken broth
1/4 cup grated Parmesan cheese

Heat olive oil in a small saucepan. Add bacon, garlic and parsley seasoned with pepper and cook over low flame until bacon is slightly brown. Add peas. Stir until peas are well-coated. Add hot water. Cover. Cook until peas are tender. If water evaporates before peas are done, add a very small amount of hot water.

In a medium-size skillet with a small amount of melted butter, sauté mushrooms for 5 minutes, stirring frequently. Add to peas. Taste for salt. If needed, season with a little salt. Set aside.

Melt 6 tbs. of butter in a large saucepan and sauté onion over low flame until yellow. Add rice and stir until rice is well-coated. Add 2 cups of broth. Stir. Cover and cook until broth is absorbed. Add remaining broth as it becomes absorbed, covering each time. Simmer for 25 minutes or until rice is tender. Add pea and mushroom mixture. Mix well. Serve with grated Parmesan cheese. Serves 4–6. **(See photo on opposite page.)**

RISO CON RICOTTA
Rice with Italian Cheese

1 lb. raw long-grain rice
1/2 lb. ricotta
1/4 cup milk

1/4 cup grated Romano cheese
black pepper to taste (optional)

Boil rice in salted water until tender. Drain.

In a small saucepan, mix ricotta and milk until smooth. Add pepper, if desired. Cook over low flame until well-heated. Pour over hot rice. Mix well. Serve with grated Romano cheese. Serves 4–6.

Italian Rice with Peas and Mushrooms.
See recipe on opposite page.

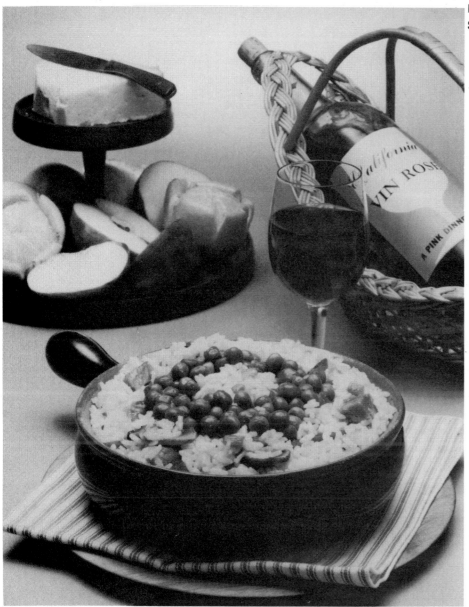

Photo courtesy of the Wine Institute.

RISOTTO CON ZUCCHINI
Italian Rice with Zucchini

4 medium zucchini (Italian squash)
3 tbs. olive oil
1 finely sliced medium onion
2 tomatoes, peeled and chopped
2 cups raw long-grain rice

salt and pepper to taste
5 cups chicken broth
2 tbs. butter
4 tbs. grated Parmesan cheese

Wash zucchini well. Remove stem and blossom ends. Cut into 1/2-inch cubes.

In a large saucepan with hot olive oil, over low flame, cook onion until yellow. Add tomatoes and zucchini and cook till browning begins. Add rice, salt, pepper and 2 1/2 cups broth. Cover and simmer until broth is absorbed. Add remaining broth. Cover and cook for 25 minutes or until tender. If rice becomes too dry while cooking, add a small amount of hot chicken stock. When done, remove from flame. Add butter and cheese. Mix well. Serves 4–6.

RISO DELLA SIGNORA NINA
Nina's Baked Rice

2 cups raw long-grain rice
2 tbs. olive oil
1 lb. ground beef

salt and pepper to taste
1 beaten egg

Sauce:

1 tbs. sausage fat *or* bacon fat
1 tbs. olive oil
1/3 cup chopped onion
2 lb. 3 oz. can of plum tomatoes, mashed

1 large crushed clove of garlic
1 tsp. dry basil *or* 2 or 3 fresh basil leaves, torn
salt and pepper to taste

Boil rice in salted water until tender. Drain. In a skillet with hot olive oil, cook beef seasoned with salt and pepper until light brown.

Heat sausage or bacon fat and olive oil in a medium-size saucepan. Add onion and cook until yellow. Add plum tomatoes, garlic, basil, salt and pepper. Cover partially. Simmer for 15 minutes over low flame. Add lightly browned meat. Continue cooking 15 minutes more. Remove garlic.

Coat bottom of a 2-quart baking dish with 1/2 cup of sauce. Set aside 1 3/4 cups of rice. Mix remaining rice with balance of sauce and place in dish. Spread remainder of rice on top. Brush egg over surface. Bake in a preheated oven at 425°F. until golden. Serves 4—6.

RISO ALLA PARMIGIANA
Rice, Parmesan Style

1 cup raw long-grain rice
1/4 tsp. salt
butter
1 cup grated Parmesan cheese

pepper to taste
3/4 cup milk
very fine bread crumbs

Boil rice until *al dente* (firm, but not hard) with 1/4 teaspoon of salt in the water. Drain.

In a greased 2-quart baking dish, place half of the rice in a layer. Dot with butter. Sprinkle with half the grated cheese and pepper. Add balance of rice, dots of butter, some pepper and remaining cheese. Cover top lightly with bread crumbs. Pour milk over rice.

Bake in a preheated oven at 350°F. for 20 minutes. Serves 2—3.

SAUCES

The tomato is an essential ingredient in many Italian sauces, especially the Southern types. The tomato's history is so interesting that I felt I'd like to share it with you.

A little over three centuries ago a peculiar "red fruit" was found growing in the Andes in Peru. It was later transported to Europe, but was only utilized as a decoration. No one dared to consume it, being given such names as "the love apple" and "the poisonous, forbidden fruit."

Cultivated in certain places only as a colorful ornament and object of curiosity, it had already been used as a food by ancient people in Mexico who called it *tomatl*, providing its present name.

By the eighteenth century the tomato was being eaten in small sections of Europe, including Italy which later introduced the tomato to Americans who had also regarded it as an attractive but poisonous ornament.

But after 1800, there was a change of heart. People began to eat it and relish its taste. The plum tomato and some larger varieties eventually became highly favored, particularly for making sauces.

In this chapter you will find tomato bases in fish, fowl and meat sauces to serve over pasta and rice as well as other types to add savor to blandly prepared vegetables, fish and meats.

In making sauces, always use a wooden spoon for stirring to avoid a metallic taste.

With the right Italian sauce, boiled beef, boiled whiting, salmon, asparagus and other dishes take on surprisingly delightsome and interesting characteristics.

Recommended Brands of Italian Canned Tomato Products
Contadina
Pastene
Progresso
Rinaldi

SALSA DI PEPERONI
Green Pepper Sauce

4 Italian green peppers
1/2 cup olive oil
1 tbs. butter

1 clove minced garlic
salt to taste
8 oz. can tomato sauce

Wash peppers. Remove seeds and stems. Dry with absorbent paper. Cut into fourths. Heat them in a medium-size saucepan with 1/4 cup hot olive oil over low flame. This will make it easy to skin the peppers.

Heat butter and remaining 1/4 cup olive oil in another saucepan. Add garlic and cook over low flame until golden. Then add peppers and salt. When tender, add tomato sauce. Cook until heated through. May be used on boiled meats. Makes enough for 4 portions.

SALSA PICCANTE
Piquant Sauce

2 anchovy fillets
1 tsp. capers (in vinegar)
1 sprig fresh parsley

1/2 cup olive oil
pepper to taste
juice of 1 small lemon

Chop anchovies, capers and parsley until fine. Place in a bowl. Add olive oil, pepper and lemon juice. Mix well. May be used on boiled fish. Makes 3/4 cup or enough for 4 portions.

SALSA VERDE
Green Sauce

2 anchovy fillets
1 tsp. capers (in vinegar)
1/2 small onion
1/4 clove garlic

1 sprig fresh parsley
3 fresh basil leaves
juice of 1 small lemon
1/2 cup olive oil

Chop anchovies, capers, onion, garlic, parsley and basil until fine. Place in a bowl. Add lemon juice and olive oil. Stir until well-blended. May be used on any boiled meat or fish. Makes 3/4 cup or enough for 4 portions.

SALSA D'ACCIUGHE
Anchovy Sauce

1/3 cup olive oil
1 clove whole garlic

2 oz. can fillets of anchovy, chopped (with oil)
dash of pepper

Heat olive oil in a small saucepan. Add garlic and cook over low flame until golden. Remove garlic. Add anchovies with their oil. Stir constantly for 2 minutes until dissolved. Add pepper. Mix.

May be used on 1 lb. of spaghetti or pasta boiled with only a very small amount of salt because Anchovy Sauce is salty. Serves 4.

SALSA DI TONNO
Tuna Fish Sauce

1/4 cup olive oil
1 clove minced garlic
1 sprig chopped fresh parsley
a few capers (unsalted)

1 small can tuna fish
pepper to taste
15 oz. can tomato sauce

In a small saucepan with hot olive oil, cook garlic over low flame until golden. Add parsley, capers, tuna fish, pepper and tomato sauce. Cook until well heated.

May be used on spaghetti or other types of pasta. Serves 4.

SALSA DI POMODORO ITALIANO
Italian Tomato Sauce   *gramma Esset's recipe*

1/4 cup olive oil
1 small chopped onion
3 tbs. tomato paste
3 cups hot water
dash oregano

2 lbs. 3 oz. can plum tomatoes, mashed
1 clove minced garlic
1/2 tsp. dry basil *or* 3 torn basil leaves
salt and pepper to taste
sugar to taste

Heat olive oil in a medium-size saucepan. Add onion and cook over low flame until yellow. Add tomato paste and water. Stir until dissolved. Then add tomatoes, garlic, basil, salt and pepper. Cover partially. Over high flame, bring to a boil. Lower flame and simmer for 1 hour, stirring occasionally. May be used on any type of pasta or rice. Serves 6.

SALSA DI PREZZEMOLO E UOVA
Fresh Parsley and Egg Sauce

1/4 lb. fresh parsley (Italian, if available)
1 clove garlic
2 tbs. fine dry bread crumbs
a small amount of milk

2 tbs. white vinegar
2 tbs. olive oil
2 minced hard-boiled eggs
salt and pepper to taste

Wash parsley. Remove leaves from stems. Chop parsley leaves with garlic until extremely fine. Moisten bread crumbs with a small amount of milk. Place parsley mixture and bread crumbs in a small bowl. Add vinegar and olive oil alternately in small amounts, mixing very well. Add minced hard-boiled eggs, salt and pepper. Mix and let stand in refrigerator until ready to use.

May be used on slices of cold veal roast or cold boiled fish.

SALSA CON POLLO E FUNGHI
Chicken and Mushroom Sauce

3/4 cup olive oil
4 chicken drumsticks
1 small chopped onion
6 oz. can tomato paste
4 cups hot water

2 lbs. 3 oz. can plum tomatoes, mashed
1 whole clove garlic
1 tsp. dry basil *or* 1 tbs. chopped fresh parsley
1/4 lb. sliced fresh mushrooms
salt and pepper to taste

Heat 1/2 cup of olive oil in a medium-size skillet and brown chicken drumsticks.

Heat remaining olive oil in a large saucepan. Add onion and cook over low flame until yellow. Add tomato paste and hot water. Stir until dissolved. Add plum tomatoes, garlic, basil, drumsticks, salt and pepper. Over high flame, let come to a boil. Lower flame. Cover partially and simmer for 45 minutes. Add sliced mushrooms. Simmer for 15 minutes more, stirring occasionally. Discard garlic. Remove meat from drumsticks. Shred. Return meat to sauce. May be used on any desired pasta. Serves 6.

SALSA MARINARA
Sauce Mariner Style

2 lbs. 3 oz. can plum tomatoes
1/4 cup olive oil
1 large clove minced garlic *or* 2 medium cloves
    minced garlic
4 or 5 finely chopped basil leaves

1/2 tsp. oregano
salt to taste
black pepper *or* crushed red pepper seeds
    to taste

Mash plum tomatoes well with fork. In a medium-size saucepan, place olive oil, garlic, tomatoes, basil, oregano, salt and pepper. Cover partially. Over low flame, simmer for 30 minutes, stirring occasionally. May be used on any type of pasta. Serves 4.

RAGU CON POLPETTI
Sauce with Meatballs

Meatballs:
1 lb. ground beef
2 eggs
1 small clove minced garlic
1/2 cup bread crumbs
2 tbs. grated Romano cheese

1 tsp. dry parsley *or* 1 tbs. chopped fresh
    parsley
2 tbs. milk
salt and pepper to taste
3 tbs. olive oil

Sauce:
1/2 lb. pork skin (rolled and tied)
3 tbs. olive oil
1/2 small chopped onion
6 oz. can tomato paste
3 cups hot water

3 cups canned plum tomatoes, mashed
1 clove minced garlic
1/2 tsp. dry basil
salt and pepper to taste
1/2 lb. neck of lamb, cut in half

Cover pork skin with boiling water and allow to soak 5 minutes to soften it. Drain.

In a bowl, combine beef, eggs, garlic, bread crumbs, cheese, parsley, milk, salt and pepper. Mix well. Form into 12 or more balls. Heat 3 tbs. olive oil in a large skillet and cook meatballs in oil until brown.

Heat 3 tbs. olive oil in a large saucepan. Add onion and cook over low flame until yellow. Add tomato paste and water. Stir until dissolved. Add plum tomatoes, garlic, basil, salt and pepper. Over high flame, bring to a boil. Add lamb and pork skin. Cover partially. Lower flame and simmer for 1 hour. Stir occasionally. Add meatballs. Continue cooking for 20 minutes more. Serves 6.

Use sauce on any pasta. Serve meat as an accompaniment. **(See color photo on page 4.)**

SALSA BESCIAMELLA
White Sauce

8 tbs. butter
1 tbs. flour
1 cup hot beef broth

1 tbs. lemon juice
1 beaten egg yolk
white pepper

In a small saucepan, melt 4 tbs. butter over low flame. Add flour, stirring with a wooden spoon until well blended. Then add hot broth gradually, stirring constantly until a smooth and somewhat thick sauce is obtained. Add remaining butter, lemon juice and pepper. Remove from heat. Add egg yolk slowly, stirring all the time.

May be used on cooked asparagus, cauliflower, fava beans, green cabbage, carrots, spinach and kohlrabi. Makes about 1 cup.

SALSA DI POLLO E PISELLI
Chicken and Pea Sauce

3 lb. chicken
3 lbs. fresh plum tomatoes
1/2 cup boiling water
1/2 cup olive oil
1/4 small chopped onion
1 clove garlic (whole)

1 sprig chopped fresh basil
1/2 tsp. oregano
salt and pepper to taste
4 tbs. dry sherry
1 cup frozen peas

Wash and chop tomatoes. In a large pot with 1/2 cup boiling water, place tomatoes. Cover and cook over low flame for 10 minutes. Put through sieve.

Have chicken cut into serving portions. Wash. Dry with absorbent paper. In a large skillet with hot olive oil, place chicken. Sprinkle with salt and pepper. Fry over medium flame until brown. Remove from pan and set aside.

In the same oil, cook onion over low flame until yellow. Add tomatoes, garlic, basil, oregano, salt, pepper and sherry. When it starts to simmer, add chicken. Cover partially. Cook over low flame for 30 minutes, stirring occasionally. Then add peas. Cook for 15 minutes more or until tender. Remove garlic.

Serve sauce on any desired pasta and serve chicken as an accompaniment. Serves 4.

ENTREES

6

FISH IS GOOD ANY DAY

You can have an Italian fish festival any day of the week. That's exactly what the occasion becomes when fish lovers get together and everyone digs into a home-cooked meal of all kinds of delicious dishes such as Spaghetti with Anchovy Sauce, Steamed Mussels, and Tuna Sicilian Style along with a crisp, green salad.

In ancient times, man caught fish with the help of numerous devices, one of which was a stone gorge about an inch in length with a groove in the middle for a line. After stone, bone was used. Now, there are not only many improved methods of catching fish, but also ways of preparing it, including the Italian style. Fish must always be purchased fresh and in the right season for best quality and taste, and should never be overcooked which dries and toughens it.

Italy is surrounded by bodies of water and consequently is supplied with an abundance of sealife. Tunny fisheries were established there by the Phoenicians and salted tunny was esteemed by the Romans.

In Sicily, where the sea is warm, tuna and sardine fisheries are extensive and much fish exportation exists. About a half-century ago, donkies and horses were still laden with sparkling fish to be taken to an open market in Ciminna, Sicily. It was called *Scaro* (Scah-róh), literally meaning "a bargain place," where the townsfolk would soon come to buy the fresh, diversified bounty.

It's only natural that Italians have a fine understanding of this resource, whether it be boiled, baked, broiled or fried—or in salads which will be found in the salad section of this book.

Fish is rich in mineral salts—and is good any day. If properly cooked, it can be welcome even on Sunday.

IF YOU ARE FISHING FOR SUGGESTIONS

To wash fish—Do not use running water. Dip in salted cold water and pat "damp dry" with absorbent paper.

Fresh fish and shellfish are done when the flesh becomes opaque or solid in appearance. Slice it open to check. Do not overcook.

To squeeze juice easily from lemons, run under warm water, then roll on table with pressure under palm of hand. If a small amount of juice is required, pierce fruit deeply with fork and squeeze. This keeps the rest of the fruit fresh for another time.

Dry salt cod is prepared by packing in dry salt after cleaning. It can be freshened by soaking in cold water for at least 48 hours, changing the water when it becomes cloudy. This process removes the salt and makes it tender.

TONNO SAUTE CON L'ACETO
Sautéed Fresh Tuna with Vinegar

2 lbs. fresh tuna fish
3 tbs. flour
1/2 cup olive oil
2/3 cup wine vinegar

1 clove minced garlic
4 chopped fresh mint leaves *or* 4 dry mint
    leaves
salt and pepper to taste

Have tuna sliced about 1 inch thick. Wash. Dry with absorbent paper. Roll in flour. In a large skillet with hot olive oil, cook fish over medium flame until golden brown on both sides. Meanwhile, combine vinegar, garlic, mint, salt and pepper. Remove tuna from heat. Pour vinegar mixture over tuna. Keep covered for 2 minutes. Serves 4–5.

TONNO AL GRIGLIA
Grilled Tuna

3 fresh tuna steaks (1 1/2 lbs.)
2 tbs. olive oil
salt and pepper to taste

1 tsp. dry parsley *or* 1 tbs. fresh minced parsley
juice of 1 lemon

Wash and dry tuna. Brush tuna steaks on both sides with olive oil. Sprinkle with salt and pepper. Preheat broiler at 550°F. at least 10 minutes. Place fish in broiling pan 2 inches from heat. Broil until a rich golden brown color and tender on both sides. (For 1/2-inch-thick steaks, broil 3 minutes on each side. For 1-inch-thick steaks, broil 4 minutes on one side and 5 minutes on the other.) Place on a platter. Sprinkle with parsley. Serve with lemon juice. Serves 3.

TONNO ALLA SICILIANA
Tuna Sicilian Style

1 lb. fresh tuna
1/4 cup olive oil
1 medium chopped onion
1 cup canned plum tomatoes, mashed

1 tbs. minced fresh basil *or* 1/2 tsp. dry basil
pinch of marjoram
salt and pepper to taste

Have tuna cut into 4-inch pieces about 1 inch thick. Wash tuna. Dry. Heat olive oil in a large skillet. Add tuna and cook over medium flame until light brown on both sides. Remove from skillet. Set aside and keep warm. In oil remaining in skillet, cook onion over low flame until yellow. Add tomatoes, basil, marjoram, salt and pepper. Allow to simmer for 6 minutes. Add tuna. Cover. Simmer over low flame for 20 minutes or until tender and brown on both sides. Stir and turn occasionally. Remove to platter. Pour hot tomato sauce over slices. Serves 2.

FILETTI DI SOGLIOLE A LA PIZZAIOLA
Fillets of Sole, Pizzaiola Style

1 lb. fresh or frozen fillets of sole
1/4 cup olive oil

4 1/2 tbs. bread crumbs
1 tbs. grated Romano cheese

Sauce:
1/4 cup olive oil
1 tbs. minced onion
1/2 cup canned plum tomatoes, mashed
salt and pepper to taste

1 clove minced garlic
1/2 tsp. oregano
1 sprig fresh chopped parsley

Wash and dry fish. Coat bottom of a shallow 7"x11" baking pan with olive oil. Sprinkle with 2 tbs. of bread crumbs. Arrange fish on top. In a small bowl combine sauce ingredients. Pour over fish. Combine balance of bread crumbs with olive oil and grated cheese. Sprinkle on top. Bake in preheated oven at 375°F. for 25 minutes or until tender. Serves 3–4.

BACCALA INDORATO FRITTO CON OLIVE
Fried Golden Cod with Olives

2 lbs. soaked salt codfish *or* fresh or frozen
   cod fillets
1/3 cup fine cracker crumbs
pepper to taste

3/4 cup olive oil
20 Greek olives *or* ripe olives
juice of 1 large lemon

If soaked salt codfish is not available, soak dry salt codfish in cold water for 48 hours or until soft, changing water when it becomes cloudy. Remove. Wash in clear, cool water. Dry. Cut fish into 3-inch pieces. Dredge in combined cracker crumbs and pepper. Heat olive oil in a large skillet. Add fish and fry, over medium flame, until golden brown. Add olives. If using fresh or frozen cod fillets, add salt to taste. Cook for 5 minutes. Serve with lemon juice. Serves 4.

BACCALA ALLA FIORENTINA
Salt Codfish, Florentine Style

2 lbs. soaked salt codfish *or* fresh or frozen
   cod fillets
1/2 cup flour
2/3 cup olive oil
2 whole cloves garlic

pepper to taste
8 oz. can tomato sauce
1 tsp. unsalted capers
pinch of rosemary

If soaked salt codfish is not available, soak dry salt codfish for 48 hours, changing water when it becomes cloudy. Remove. Wash in clear, cool water. Dry. Cut into pieces the size of the palm of the hand. Roll in flour.

Heat olive oil in a large skillet. Add garlic and cook over low flame until golden brown. Discard garlic. Put codfish in pan and fry over medium flame until golden brown and tender on both sides. Sprinkle with pepper. If using fresh or frozen cod fillets, add salt to taste. Then pour tomato sauce combined with capers and rosemary over pieces. Cook until well-heated. Serve hot. Serves 4.

BACCALA ALLA BOLOGNESE
Salt Codfish, Bologna Style

2 lbs. soaked salt codfish *or* fresh or frozen cod
   fillets
2 cloves finely chopped garlic
2 tsp. finely chopped fresh parsley

2/3 cup olive oil
butter
pepper to taste
juice of 1 large lemon

If soaked salt codfish is not available, soak dry salt codfish for 48 hours, changing water when it becomes cloudy. Remove and wash in clear, cool water. Dry with absorbent paper. Cut into 4-inch pieces. Spread garlic and parsley over each piece. Then season with pepper and dot with butter. If using fresh or frozen cod fillets, add salt to taste.

Heat olive oil in a large skillet. Add fish and cook over medium flame until golden brown and tender on both sides. Place in a platter and serve with lemon juice. Serves 4.

BACCALA ALL' LUCANIA
Salt Codfish, Lucania Style

2 lbs. soaked salt codfish *or* fresh or frozen
   cod fillets
2 cups fresh bread crumbs (a day old)
1 clove finely chopped garlic
1 tbs. oregano

2 or 3 sweet peppers in vinegar (chopped and
   sprinkled with a pinch of salt)
1/4 cup olive oil
1/4 cup water

If soaked salt codfish is not available, soak dry salt codfish in cold water for 48 hours or until soft, changing water when it becomes cloudy. Remove. Wash in clear, cool water. Dry. Cut fish in 4- or 5-inch pieces.

In a medium-size bowl, combine fresh bread crumbs, garlic and oregano. Place a layer of fish in a 2-quart casserole. If using fresh or frozen cod fillets, add salt to taste. Sprinkle fish with 2/3 cup of bread crumb mixture. Top this with another layer of fish and sprinkle with another 2/3 cup of bread crumbs and pickled sweet peppers. Top with remaining bread crumbs and drizzle with olive oil.

Pouring into each corner of the casserole, cover bottom with 1/4 cup water. Bake in a pre-heated oven at 350°F. for 1 hour or until tender. (Bake about 30 minutes if using fresh or frozen fillets.) Serves 4.

CALAMAI AFFOGATI
Steamed Squid

2 lbs. fresh or frozen squid
1 cup canned plum tomatoes, mashed
1/2 tsp. dry parsley *or* 1 tbs. fresh minced parsley
1 large clove minced garlic

1 tbs. fresh minced basil *or* 1/2 tsp. dry basil
3 tbs. olive oil
salt to taste
1/3 tsp. crushed red pepper seeds

Clean squid and cut them crosswise into 1-inch pieces. Wash well. After last rinse, place squid dripping with water in a large saucepan. Then add tomatoes, parsley, garlic, basil, olive oil, salt and crushed red pepper seeds. Mix. Over high flame, bring to a boil. Lower flame. Cover. Steam for 30 minutes or until tender, stirring occasionally. Serves 3–4.

CALAMAI IMBOTTITI CON SALSA DI POMODORO
Stuffed Squid with Tomato Sauce

2 lbs. fresh or frozen squid
olive oil

Stuffing:
1 cup bread crumbs
3 cloves minced garlic
1 tbs. grated Romano cheese
1 tbs. minced parsley
salt and pepper to taste

1 tbs. raisins
1 chopped hard-boiled egg
1 tsp. pine nuts (optional)
1 tbs. olive oil

Sauce:

1 tbs. olive oil

1 diced onion

3 cloves minced garlic

1 cup tomato paste

1 cup water

salt and pepper to taste

Clean and wash squid. Mix all stuffing ingredients together. Fill squid 3/4 full and fasten well with toothpicks.

Heat olive oil in a large skillet and fry squid over medium flame until light brown, not fully cooked. Set aside.

Meanwhile, cook sauce. Heat olive oil in a large saucepan. Add onion and garlic and cook over low flame until golden. Add tomato paste, water, salt and pepper. Cover partially. Cook slowly for 30 minutes, stirring occasionally. Then place stuffed squid in sauce and simmer covered another 30 minutes. In case too much evaporation occurs, add some hot water. Remove toothpicks. Serves 5.

SPIGOLA AL FORNO
Baked Striped Bass

3 lbs. striped bass

1 large clove slivered garlic

1 tsp. oregano

1 tbs. fresh chopped parsley *or* 1 tsp. dry parsley

salt and pepper to taste

1 tbs. bread crumbs

1/4 cup olive oil

juice of 1 large lemon

Have fish cleaned and leave whole. Wash. Dry with absorbent paper. Make two slantwise slashes in fish 2 1/2 inches long and 1/2 inch deep. Insert garlic in slashes. Sprinkle fish with oregano, parsley, salt and pepper.

Line a shallow 7"x11" baking dish with aluminum foil. Sprinkle with bread crumbs and half of the olive oil. Place striped bass in dish. Pour remainder of olive oil and the lemon juice on top of fish. Bake in a preheated oven at 375° for 35 minutes or until tender. Baste occasionally. Serves 4.

FILETTI DI PASSERINO IMPANATI SAUTE
Sautéed Breaded Fillets of Flounder

1 lb. fresh or frozen fillets of flounder

1 beaten egg

1/2 cup fine bread crumbs

1/2 tsp. dry parsley

1/2 tbs. grated Romano cheese

salt and pepper to taste

1/2 cup olive oil

If fillets are large, cut each one in two. Wash. Dry with absorbent paper. Dip fish in egg. Then roll in bread crumbs combined with parsley, grated cheese, salt and pepper. Heat olive oil in a medium-size skillet. Add fillets and cook until golden brown on both sides. Serves 3.

LUMACHE ALLA SICILIANA
Snails, Sicilian Style

1 lb. live snails
2 lbs. fresh chopped tomatoes
1 cup water
3 tbs. olive oil

1 tbs. chopped onion
1 clove minced garlic
1/4 tsp. oregano
salt and pepper to taste

Wash snails well until water comes off clear. Keep snails in a pot with enough cold water to cover them until they emerge from shells. Rub rim of pot with salt to prevent snails from crawling out. Cover with a heavy lid.

Place tomatoes and water in a medium-size saucepan. Simmer for 10 minutes. Sieve. In a large saucepan with hot olive oil, cook onion over low flame until yellow. Add tomatoes, garlic, oregano, salt and pepper. Simmer 10 minutes. Add snails. Continue cooking, partially covered, for 30 minutes, stirring occasionally. Serve with toothpicks or a two-pronged snail fork to extract snail meat. Serves 2–3.

Snails have changed the course of history. A Roman legionnaire hunting snails one day discovered a secret passageway leading under the walls and into Carthage, resulting in the fall of that city.

The Romans considered snails such a delicacy that they traveled to distant places for better varieties.

ANGUILLE SAUTE
Sautéed Eels

1 lb. thick eels
1/4 cup flour
salt to taste
1/4 tsp. crushed red pepper seeds

1 bay leaf, crumbled
1/4 cup olive oil
juice of 1 lemon

Have eels skinned and cleaned. Wash. Cut into 3-inch pieces. Dry. Dredge pieces in flour combined with salt, pepper and bay leaf. In a medium-size skillet, sauté fish in hot olive oil until golden brown on both sides. Serve with lemon juice. Serves 2–3.

On Christmas Eve, many Italians serve sautéed or baked eel as a main dish. Broccoli, artichokes and other fresh vegetables accompany the fish feast as do black olives and anchovies. On this night candles are lighted and the "Urn of Fate" filled with wrapped packages is brought out. The mother draws first and other family members follow and continue to draw, grab-bag style, until the package with their name is drawn.

FILETTI DI PESCE SAPORITI
Savory Haddock Fillets

1 1/2 lbs. fresh or frozen haddock fillets
dry bread crumbs
3 tbs. olive oil

Topping:

1 1/4 cups fresh bread crumbs
1 clove minced garlic
1/4 tsp. thyme
3 tbs. olive oil
1 tbs. minced scallions

2 tbs. grated pecorino *or* Romano cheese
celery salt and pepper to taste
paprika
juice of 1 lemon

Wash haddock. Dry. Cut into 4-inch pieces. Combine fresh bread crumbs, garlic, thyme, 3 tbs. olive oil, scallions, cheese, celery salt and pepper.

Line a shallow 14" round baking pan with aluminum foil. Coat with 3 tbs. olive oil. Sprinkle lightly with dry bread crumbs. Place haddock pieces in pan. Place bread topping on each piece. Sprinkle with paprika and pour lemon juice over each. Bake in a preheated oven at 375° for 25 minutes, or until tender. Serves 4.

INVOLTINI DI PESCE
Rolled Haddock Fillets

5 fresh or frozen fillets of haddock (1/4 lb. each)
1 1/2 tbs. butter *or* margarine
2 tbs. chopped onion
1 clove minced garlic
1 cup small toasted bread cubes
1 1/2 tsp. grated lemon rind

1 tbs. lemon juice
1 tbs. chopped fresh parsley
1 tbs. grated Parmesan cheese
salt and pepper to taste
2 tbs. milk *or* water
3 tbs. butter *or* olive oil

Wash fillets. Dry. In a small saucepan with 1 1/2 tbs. of hot, melted butter, cook garlic and onion until yellow. Add bread cubes, lemon rind, juice, parsley, cheese, salt, milk or water. Mix well. Put some stuffing on each haddock fillet. Then roll each and fasten with toothpicks so stuffing will not fall out. Sprinkle with salt and pepper.

Melt 2 tbs. butter in a shallow 7"x11" baking pan (or use olive oil, if desired). Place stuffed fillets in pan. Dot with 1 tbs. of butter or drizzle with same amount of olive oil. In a preheated 350° oven, bake for 20–30 minutes or until tender. Serves 4.

PESCE LESSO
Boiled Fish

2 lbs. whole fish, slices or fillets*
3 qts. boiling, salted water
1/2 small onion
2 cloves

1 stalk celery, cut in half
1 carrot
2 sprigs parsley
3 lemon slices

In a large pot with 3 quarts of boiling, salted water, add onion, cloves, celery, carrot, parsley and lemon slices. Allow to boil for 15 minutes. Add 2 pounds of washed fish which has been placed in cheesecloth and tied and put in a wire basket (or fish may be placed in a heat-proof plate, wrapped in cheesecloth and tied). Cover and simmer. Simmer 6—10 minutes per pound for whole fish, depending upon thickness. Allow 10—20 minutes for slices or fillets.

When fish is cooked, lift from pot and carefully remove from cheesecloth. Turn onto a platter. Serve with any preferred sauce for boiled fish. Garnish with boiled beets, boiled potatoes and finely sliced hard-boiled eggs. Serve hot. Serves 4.

Strain vegetables from fish stock. Discard vegetables. Save stock to use in making fish soup or chowder.

*Some fish suitable for boiling: mackerel, salmon, haddock, whiting, flounder, etc. Lean fish give best results because they do not fall apart.

SGOMBERI IN UMIDO
Mackerel Stew

2 lbs. fresh or frozen fillets of mackerel	1 sprig chopped parsley
4 tbs. butter	1 clove minced garlic
2 tbs. olive oil	2 fresh basil leaves, torn in bits
1 1/4 lbs. chopped fresh ripe tomatoes	salt and pepper to taste

Clean and wash fish. In a large skillet with hot butter and olive oil, cook tomatoes, parsley, garlic, basil, salt and pepper for 5 minutes. Arrange mackerel fillets in a layer in the skillet. Cook on one side for 10 minutes. Then turn carefully. Cook for another 10 minutes or until fish is tender. Serve with sauce. Serves 4.

STOCCO AGHIOTTA AL CALABRESE
Stockfish Stew, Calabrian Style

1 lb. soaked stockfish*	10 green olives
1/4 cup olive oil	1 tbs. seedless raisins
3 medium potatoes, cut in eighths	1 tbs. chopped fresh parsley
1 qt. warm water	1/2 tsp. crushed red pepper seeds
1 stalk celery, cut into 4-inch pieces	salt to taste

Wash fish and cut into 1-1/2-inch pieces. In a large pot with olive oil, cook potatoes over high flame for 5 minutes, stirring occasionally. Add water and bring to a boil. Add fish, celery, olives, raisins, parsley, red pepper seeds and salt. Cover partially. Lower flame. Let simmer for 25 minutes or until fish is tender, stirring occasionally. Serves 3—4.

*Fish such as cod or haddock cured by splitting and drying without salt.

This delicious stew was my Calabrian father's frequent request. It became imbedded in Mother's cooking repertory after they were married.

Cioppino

CIOPPINO

1/4 cup olive oil
1 large chopped onion
1 clove crushed garlic
2 tbs. chopped parsley
1/2 cup chopped celery
2 tbs. chopped green pepper
4 tomatoes, peeled and coarsely chopped
6 oz. can tomato paste
salt to taste
1 tsp. paprika
2/3 cup dry sherry

4 cups water
1/4 tsp. basil
pinch of rosemary
1/2 tsp. oregano
1 tsp. Worcestershire sauce
2 lobster tails, cut into 1-inch pieces
1/2 lb. medium-size fresh shrimp
6 to 12 scallops
3 crab legs, cut in halves
1 lb. white fish, cut into bite-size pieces

Heat olive oil in a large kettle. Sauté onion, garlic, parsley, celery and green pepper until golden. Add tomatoes, tomato paste, salt, paprika and sherry. Simmer, over low flame, for 15—20 minutes, stirring occasionally. Add water and remaining seasonings. Cook slowly for 45—60 minutes. Fifteen minutes before serving, add chunks of raw white fish. Ten minutes before serving, add shell fish. Cook over low heat just until fish are done. Serves 6.

Serve with Italian garlic bread and a green salad. Makes a perfect dish for an informal supper. **(See photo above.)**

NOTE: Clams and oysters can be added in season.

POLPETTE DI MERLUZZO
Fish Balls

1 1/4 lbs. fresh fillets of cod
1 lb. potatoes
3 beaten eggs
pinch of nutmeg
salt and pepper to taste

2 tbs. fresh chopped parsley
about 1/2 cup milk
bread crumbs
olive oil
lemon slices & parsley sprigs

Wash fillets and boil them in a small amount of water until tender. Drain well. Chop finely. Boil potatoes in jackets. When cooked, remove skins and put potatoes through a ricer, or mash until smooth. In a large bowl, combine fish, potatoes, eggs, nutmeg, salt, pepper and parsley. Add milk in small amounts to hold this mixture together. The type of potatoes used will determine whether you will need all of the amount given. Mix slowly until mixture just holds together. Form balls. Roll in bread crumbs and fry in a large skillet with hot olive oil until golden brown. Drain on absorbent paper. Serve garnished with lemon slices and sprigs of parsley. Or, if preferred, with a tomato sauce. Serves 4–5.

SARDE BECCAFICO
Stuffed Sardines

2 lbs. fresh sardines
fine bread crumbs
6 tbs. olive oil

Stuffing:

1 cup bread crumbs
1 tbs. fresh minced parsley *or* 1 tsp. dry parsley
1 large clove minced garlic
1/4 tsp. oregano

2 tbs. grated Romano cheese
salt and pepper to taste
olive oil to moisten
salt

Clean and slit sardines down centers and remove bones. Wash. Dry with absorbent paper. Dredge outside of fish with bread crumbs. Combine stuffing ingredients. On the bottom of a shallow 14" round baking pan, pour 6 tbs. of olive oil. Fill sardines with stuffing. Close and pat lightly. Place sardines in pan. Season with salt. Drizzle with olive oil. Bake in a preheated oven at 375°F. for 25 minutes or until sardines are tender. Serves 6.

SARDE IN TEGAME
Pan-Fried Sardines

1 lb. fresh sardines
1/2 cup wine vinegar
1 beaten egg
3 1/2 tbs. flour

1/4 tsp. thyme
celery salt and pepper to taste
1/3 cup olive oil
1 whole clove garlic

Clean and slit sardines down centers. Remove bones. Wash. Spread open. In a bowl, marinate in wine vinegar for 1 hour. Dry. Dip sardines in egg. Dredge in combined flour, thyme, celery salt and pepper. In a large skillet with hot olive oil, cook garlic over low flame until brown. Discard garlic. Then fry sardines over medium flame until golden brown on both sides. Serves 3.

SCUNGILLI
Boiled Conchs with Tomato Sauce

1 1/2 lbs. boiled conchs
1/4 cup olive oil
1 small chopped onion
6 oz. can tomato paste
3 cups water

1 clove minced garlic
salt to taste
pinch of crushed red pepper seeds
1/2 tsp. oregano

Purchase already-boiled conchs. Remove hard outer cover. Clean. Cut into 1/2-inch pieces. In a large saucepan with hot olive oil, cook onion over low flame until yellow. Add tomato paste, water, garlic, salt, red pepper seeds and oregano. Stir until paste dissolves. Cover partially and simmer for 15 minutes. Add conchs. Cook covered partially for another 30 minutes or until tender. Serves 3–4.

TROTE IN VINO BIANCO
Trout in White Wine

4 trout (1/2 lb. cach)
2 cups water
2 cups dry Marsala
salt
3 peppercorns
1 bay leaf

1 small sliced onion
3 or 4 slices carrot
1 sprig celery leaves
1 sprig parsley
2 lemon slices
3 tbs. olive oil

In a large skillet, simmer together water, Marsala, salt, peppercorns, bay leaf, onion, carrot, celery leaves, parsley, lemon and olive oil. Place trout in simmering liquid. Cover pan and poach (without boiling) for about 10 minutes. Serve with Green Sauce (p. 74). Serves 4.

GAMBERI FRITTI
Fried Shrimp

2 lbs. fresh or frozen medium shrimp
2 eggs
salt and pepper to taste
1 cup bread crumbs

1 clove minced garlic
1 sprig finely chopped parsley
3/4 cup olive oil
lemon slices (optional)

Shell and de-vein fresh shrimp. Wash. Drain well. In a bowl, beat eggs with salt and pepper. In another bowl, combine bread crumbs, garlic and parsley. Dip shrimp in eggs, then roll in bread crumb mixture. Heat olive oil in a skillet and fry shrimp until golden brown on both sides. If desired, serve with lemon slices. Serves 4.

Perhaps in all the history of hangover cures, no stranger recommendation exists than ancient Roman satirist Horace's of "fried shrimp and African snails forming," he claimed, "an excellent stimulus."

Certainly, there are many who will differ with him on that!

GAMBERI MARINARA
Shrimp with Marinara Sauce

2 lbs. fresh or frozen shrimp
1/2 cup olive oil
1 clove minced garlic
2 lbs. 3 oz. can plum tomatoes, mashed

1 tbs. fresh minced basil *or* 1 tsp. dry basil
pinch of oregano
2 tbs. dry white wine
salt and pepper to taste

Shell and de-vein fresh shrimp. Wash. Drain well. Dry. In a medium-size saucepan, cook garlic in 1/4 cup hot olive oil, over low flame, until light brown. Add tomatoes, basil, oregano, wine, salt and pepper. Cover partially. Simmer for 30 minutes. In a large skillet, heat remaining olive oil. Sauté shrimp for 3 minutes. Discard the oil and add shrimp to sauce. Simmer for 3 minutes. Serves 4.

GAMBERI RIPIENI CON PROSCUITTO
Stuffed Shrimp with Italian Ham

1 lb. fresh jumbo shrimp

Filling:
1/2 cup bread crumbs
1 clove minced garlic
1 tsp. minced fresh parsley
1/2 tsp. oregano
1 tbs. grated Romano cheese

1 slice minced proscuitto
3 tbs. olive oil
salt to taste
pinch of cayenne
1 cup cold water

In a bowl, mix bread crumbs, garlic, parsley, oregano, cheese, proscuitto, olive oil, salt and cayenne.

Do not remove shells or tails from shrimp. De-vein, wash and drain. Make a slit in shrimp deep enough for it to lie flat, shell sides down. Fill each with stuffing. On the bottom of a 14" round baking pan, pour 1 cup of cold water or enough to coat it. Place shrimp in pan. Bake in a preheated oven at 375°F. for 25 minutes or until tender. Serves 3.

COZZI AFFOGATI CON VINO BIANCO
Steamed Mussels with White Wine

3–4 dozen small mussels
2 sprigs finely chopped parsley
1 bay leaf
1 large clove minced garlic

salt and freshly ground pepper to taste
1/4 cup dry white wine
1/4 cup water

Scrub and rinse tightly-closed mussels thoroughly until completely grit-free. Place in a large kettle with parsley, bay leaf, garlic, salt, pepper, wine and water. Cover tightly. Steam over low flame for 15–20 minutes or until shells open. Jerk pot upwards from time to time to turn mussels. Remove mussels. Strain liquid through cheesecloth. Remove top shells, cut beards from mussels and place on a large platter. Bring liquid to a full boil. Then pour over mussels. Serves 4.

VONGOLE IMBOTTITE
Stuffed Clams

2 dozen large clams
1 cup fine bread crumbs
2 tsp. dry parsley
1/4 tsp. thyme
2 cloves minced garlic
1 tsp. dry basil

salt to taste
1/2 tsp. crushed red pepper seeds
1 tbs. grated Romano cheese
6 tbs. olive oil
2/3 cup tomato sauce
1 large glass water

Scrub tightly closed clams well until completely grit-free. Place clams in a large kettle. Cover tightly. Steam over low flame for 20 minutes or until shells open. Discard the top shells.

In a bowl, combine bread crumbs, parsley, thyme, garlic, basil, salt, red pepper seeds, cheese and olive oil. Place 1 tsp. of mixture on each clam. Place clams in a large, shallow 12"x16" baking pan. Pour 1 tsp. of tomato sauce on each clam. Pour water on bottom of pan. Bake in a preheated oven at 425°F. for 5 minutes. Serves 6.

CODE D'ARAGOSTA AL FORNO
Baked Lobster Tails

3 medium frozen lobster tails, thawed
2 tsp. dry parsley *or* 1 sprig fresh minced parsley
salt to taste
pepper to taste (optional)

3 tbs. olive oil
juice of 1 medium lemon
1 cup water

Split lobster tails in half lengthwise. Remove swimmerettes and sharp edges. Sprinkle each with parsley and salt (and pepper if desired). Pour olive oil and lemon juice on each tail.

Pour water on bottom of a shallow 7"x11" baking pan. Place lobster tails in pan. Bake in a preheated oven at 375°F. for 25 minutes or until tender. Serves 3.

ARAGOSTA OREGANATA
Baked Lobster Oregano

2 live lobsters (1 1/2 lbs. each)
1 cup water
2 tbs. dry bread crumbs
1 tsp. oregano
2 tbs. grated pecorino *or* Romano cheese
2 cloves minced garlic

1 tbs. fresh minced parsley *or* 1/2 tsp. dry
    parsley
salt to taste
1/8 tsp. cayenne
1/2 cup olive oil

Plunge lobsters into boiling water, head first. Remove from water. When cool, place lobster on its back. With a knife, make a split in lobster from head to tail. Spread open with hands. Crack large claws. Remove black vein, the small sac on the back of the head and green spongy lungs. Do not remove green liver and coral.

Place lobsters, cut sides up, in a shallow 12"x16" baking pan with 1 cup of water. Combine bread crumbs, oregano, cheese, garlic, parsley, salt and cayenne. Sprinkle each lobster with an equal amount of the mixture. Pour 1/4 cup of olive oil over each. Bake in a preheated oven at 375° for 25 minutes or until tender. Serves 2–4.

ARAGOSTA CON SALSA DI FUNGHI
Baked Lobster with Mushroom Sauce

2 live lobsters (2 lbs. each)
1/4 lb. sliced mushrooms
3 tbs. butter
3 tbs. flour
1 1/2 cups hot milk

1/8 tsp. dry mustard
salt to taste
1 tbs. chopped fresh parsley
1/4 cup dry white wine
1/4 cup grated Parmesan cheese

In a large kettle, put enough water to cover lobsters and add 1 tbs. salt for each quart of water. Over high flame, bring to a full boil. Plunge lobsters into the boiling water head first. Cover. Lower flame. Simmer for 11–12 minutes. Shell should be bright red.

Remove cooked lobster from water. When cool, place lobster on its back. With a knife, make a split in lobster from head to tail. Spread open with hands. Crack large claws. Remove black vein, the small sac on the back of the head and green spongy lungs. Do not remove green liver and coral. Remove meat from body and claws. Keep tail shells to fill. Cut up lobster meat.

To make sauce, melt butter in a medium-size saucepan. Add mushrooms and sauté over low flame until tender. Remove mushrooms. Stir flour into butter until well blended. Add hot milk gradually and stir until thickened.

In a large bowl, mix lobster meat, mushrooms, mustard, salt and parsley. Stir into sauce. Slowly add white wine. Blend well and spoon into lobster tail shells. Sprinkle with grated Parmesan cheese. Place lobster tails in a shallow 7"x11" baking pan. Bake in a preheated oven at 400°F. until cheese begins to melt. Serves 4.

GRANCHIE FRITTI
Fried Soft-Shell Crabs

6 fresh or frozen soft-shell crabs*
1 large beaten egg
1/4 cup fine cracker crumbs

salt and pepper
olive oil
lemon wedges

Plunge fresh soft-shell crabs into boiling water. Clean, wash and dry crabs. Dip in egg. Roll in cracker crumbs combined with salt and pepper. In a large skillet, fry two at a time in enough olive oil to keep them afloat until crabs are light brown on both sides. Serve with lemon wedges. Serves 3.

*From April to December hard-shelled crabs shed their shells and are then called soft-shelled crabs.

GAMBE DI GRANCHIO AL FORNO
Baked King Crab Legs

2 12-oz. pkgs. pre-cooked frozen king crab legs
8 oz. can tomato sauce
1 tbs. olive oil

1/4 cup melted butter
1 cup flavored bread crumbs
lemon wedges

Thaw king crab legs. In a medium-size bowl, combine tomato sauce with olive oil. Arrange crab legs on a shallow 12"x16" baking pan. Brush each leg with melted butter. Sprinkle each leg generously with bread crumbs. Pour tomato sauce over each leg. Bake in a preheated oven at 400°F. for 15 minutes. Serve with lemon wedges. Serves 3–4.

SUCCULENT MEATS & GAME

When it comes to meats, the primary goal in the Italian mind is the cut which will most properly fit the method of preparation and therefore offer the most satisfaction.

Veal is highly prized in the Italian cuisine. From the following recipes one can see the magic that can be created with it. Beef steaks, leg of lamb, pork chops, sausage, liver, pheasant and rabbit are all deliciously transformed with these cherished formulas.

The following bits of information are intended to be useful to all meat and game lovers.

Beef—Fine-quality ground or chopped beef is obtained from tender round steak or top-grade chuck cut. A good-quality steak for individual servings is the club steak. Porterhouse is also a choice cut and should always be cut thick.

Veal—the meat from young calves that have been milk-fed and are under twelve weeks of age. Veal cutlets, veal scallopine and veal birds are all obtained from the leg of the calf. This type of cut should be thin and pounded still thinner to break connective tissues and muscle fibers for tenderness.

Veal chops cut from the loin are best.

Veal should be cooked until well done.

Pork—should be cooked slowly and until very well done. There are three types of pork chops: loin, rib and shoulder. Those cut from the loin are the best quality. Shoulder of pork and loin are two of the best choices for roasting.

Liver—should be freshly cut and cooked until nicely browned for about 6–7 minutes. Overcooking toughens it. Always serve immediately.

Lamb—The finer chops are from the loin. A good thickness is 1 1/2 inches. Spring lamb is available in spring (when it is about four months old).

Sausage—Italian sausage can be purchased in Italian butcher shops, Italian specialty stores and pork stores, or in supermarkets. The finest, of course, are obtained from the small shops. The varieties are: sweet, hot, cheese and fennel.

Prick sausages with fork to release fat before cooking.

For Roasting—a meat thermometer may be used.

Choose a thermometer with degrees of Fahrenheit, not just stages of doneness for the various meats. Be sure to insert the thermometer correctly: Place as near the center of the roast as possible and in the thickest part. The tip should not touch bone or fat.

Frozen lamb need not be thawed before cooking, but it requires extra cooking time. Unthawed roasts may take one and a half times as long to cook as fresh roasts of the same weight and shape. The amount of additional cooking time needed depends on the size and shape of the meat cut and on the cooking temperature.

Lamb and other meats should be thawed in the refrigerator. But if you don't have time to thaw frozen meats in the refrigerator, you can speed up thawing by placing the meat in a watertight wrapping and immersing it in cold water.

Broiling Tips—Put aluminum foil in the bottom of broiler pan to simplify cleaning.

Turn meat by sticking fork into the fat, not the lean—or use tongs.

Broil frozen meat at a low temperature to prevent surface from charring before interior thaws. Increase cooking time.

Check doneness by cutting a slit in the meat near the bone and noting interior color. Rare beef is reddish pink, medium is light pink and well-done is light brown.

Lamb is usually preferred medium or well-done. Medium lamb has a grayish-tan interior with a tinge of pink. Well-done lamb is grayish-tan with no trace of pink.

Storing Cooked Meats—Cooked meats should be covered or wrapped and stored in the refrigerator. Rapid cooling of meats and meat-combination dishes helps prevent bacterial growth. Because bacteria grow best between 45° and 120°F., the food should be taken through that temperature range as quickly as possible.

If you prepare enough of a meat dish for more than one meal, quickly cool and refrigerate or freeze the portion that you intend to serve later. Meat left on the serving platter (part of a roast, for example), should be refrigerated or frozen as soon as the meal is finished.

MEAT THERMOMETER TEMPERATURE CHART

CUT	WEIGHT RANGE	INTERNAL MEAT TEMPERATURE
Beef		
Standing Rib Roast	4-6 lbs.	140°F. rare 160°F. medium 170°F. well done
Veal		
Shoulder of Veal	3-5 lbs.	170°F. well done
Stuffed Breast of Veal	5 lbs.	165°F. well done
Lamb		
Roast Leg of Lamb	5 lbs.	160°F. rare 170°F. medium 180°F. well done
Roast Rolled Stuffed Lamb	5-6 lbs.	
Pork		
Pork Loin	3-5 lbs.	170°F. well done
Rolled Shoulder of Pork	3 lbs.	175°F. well done

BEEF

BISTECCA CALABRESE
Beefsteak Calabrian

1 porterhouse steak, 1-inch thick (2 lbs.)	2 tbs. olive oil
1 clove minced garlic	6 tbs. wine vinegar
2 sprigs chopped fresh parsley	3 tbs. water
1/2 tsp. oregano	salt and freshly ground pepper to taste

Slash the fat on steak in several places. Cut a piece of fat from steak and rub the inside of a large skillet. Place steak in skillet over moderate flame. Cook on both sides to desired doneness (rare, medium, well done). Remove steak to hot platter.

In a bowl, combine garlic, parsley, oregano, olive oil, vinegar and water. Place in same pan with drippings. Bring to a boil. Pour over steak. Sprinkle steak with salt and freshly ground pepper. Serve immediately. Serves 2–4.

Being a fish fancier, meat was not a favorite fare with Father. But this steak dish he introduced to Mother was a must, filling the kitchen with its piquant aroma.

BISTECCA ROSMARINO
Rosemary Steak

1 porterhouse steak, 1 inch thick (2 lbs.)
1/4 cup melted butter
1 tbs. olive oil

1 large clove minced garlic
1/2 tsp. crushed rosemary
salt and freshly ground pepper to taste

Slash the fat on steak in several places. Grease broiler rack with a piece of fat trimmed from steak. Preheat broiler to 350°. Broil steak about 3 inches from flame until brown on both sides. Combine butter, olive oil, garlic and rosemary. Spread over steak. Cook half a minute more. Remove to a hot platter. Sprinkle with salt and freshly ground pepper and serve immediately. Serves 2—4.

Serve with Fried Potatoes and Tomato and Onion Salad.

BISTECCA ALLA FIORENTINA
Beefsteak Florentine

1 porterhouse steak (2 lbs.), 1 inch thick
2 pats butter

salt to taste
freshly ground pepper to taste

Slash the fat on steak in several places. Grease broiler rack with a piece of fat trimmed from steak. Preheat broiler to 350°. Broil steak about three inches from flame, turning frequently, until well done on the outside but rare inside. When done, spread with butter. Remove to a hot platter. Season with salt and freshly ground pepper. Serve immediately. Serves 2—4.

BISTECCA ALLA CACCIATORA
Beefsteak, Hunter's Style

1 sirloin steak (2 lbs.), 1 inch thick
2 tbs. butter
salt and pepper to taste
1/2 cup dry Marsala

1/2 clove minced garlic
1/2 tsp. fennel seeds
1 tbs. tomato puree

Slash the fat on steak in several places. In a large skillet, cook steak in hot, melted butter over moderate flame until brown on both sides. Season with salt and pepper. Remove to a hot platter and keep warm. Add dry Marsala to skillet and simmer. Add garlic, fennel seeds, and tomato puree. Mix. Cook 1 minute longer and pour over steak. Serves 2—4.

MANZO LESSO CON SALSA
Boiled Beef with Italian Sauce

3 lbs. beef brisket (lean as possible)
water to cover
2 stalks celery, cut in half
1 large carrot
1 onion

1 large ripe tomato, cut up
2 sprigs fresh parsley
1 potato
salt and pepper to taste

In a large pot, place beef brisket, celery, carrot, onion, tomato, parsley, potato, salt, pepper and water to cover. Over high flame, bring to a boil. Skim off fat as it accumulates. Lower flame. Cover. Simmer about 3 hours or until brisket is tender. When done, remove remaining fat from top.

Remove brisket and place on platter. Cut fat away from meat. Strain vegetables from broth and serve the clear broth. May also be used as a base for other soups. Serve sliced boiled beef with Green Pepper Sauce or Green Sauce (pp. 73–74). Serves 4–5.

POLPETTONE
Meat Loaf

1 lb. ground beef	1 clove minced garlic
3 slices crumbled bread without crusts (soaked in about 1/3 cup milk)	1 tbs. fresh minced parsley *or* 1 tsp. dry parsley
2 eggs	3 heaping tbs. grated Romano cheese
1 small chopped onion	salt and pepper to taste
1 tsp. dry basil	olive oil

In a large bowl, combine beef, bread, eggs, onion, basil, garlic, parsley, cheese, salt and pepper. Mix well. Grease a shallow 7"x11" baking pan with olive oil. Place meat in pan and form into an oval shape. Make a slight dent lengthwise in middle of loaf. Brush top with olive oil. Cook in a preheated oven at 350°F. for 45 minutes or until done. Serves 4.

POLPETTONE IMBOTTITO
Stuffed Meat Loaf

1 lb. ground beef	dash of marjoram
1 egg	1 tbs. minced fresh parsley *or* 1 tsp. dry parsley
2 slices crumbled bread, without crusts (soaked in 1/4 cup milk)	1 small chopped onion
3 tbs. grated pecorino *or* Romano cheese	salt and pepper to taste

Stuffing:
2 strips proscuitto
5 thin strips provolone (3 inches long, 1/4 inch wide)
1 hard-boiled egg (sliced lengthwise)

Topping:
8 oz. can tomato sauce

In a large bowl, combine beef, egg, bread, cheese, marjoram, parsley, onion, salt and pepper. Mix thoroughly. Divide in half. In a shallow 7"x11" baking pan greased with olive oil, mold half of meat into oval shape. Flatten slightly. Arrange proscuitto, provolone and egg on meat. Place remaining meat on top and mold, pressing edges down. Bake in a preheated oven at 375°F. for 25 minutes or until brown. Then top with tomato sauce. Bake 5 minutes more or until well heated. Serves 4.

MANZO ARROSTO
Roast Beef

4–6 lbs. standing rib roast
onion salt, garlic salt *or* salt to taste
freshly ground pepper to taste

Have butcher cut off short ribs, feather bone and chine bone from roast. Do not have ribs cracked. Tie roast with white string. Stand roast on rib bones in a large shallow roasting pan (deep enough to hold drippings). Preheat oven to 325°F. Cook meat uncovered, without added liquid, to desired doneness. No basting is necessary.

Rare:	18–20 min. per lb.
Medium:	24–26 min. per lb.
Well Done:	30 min. per lb.

For 10-inch ribs, allow about 30 minutes less time.

For easier slicing, allow roast to stand a few minutes after removing from oven. Cut string. Slice and sprinkle with onion salt or garlic salt or salt and pepper. Serve with Baked Stuffed Potatoes, Buttered Carrots, Green Salad and Cherry Slices. Serves 4–6.

MANZO IN UMIDO CON VINO BIANCO
Beef Stew with White Wine

1 1/2 lbs. round steak *or* top-grade chuck	1 bay leaf
flour	1/2 cup dry white wine
7 tbs. olive oil	10-1/2-oz. can beef consommé
1 large chopped onion	10 1/2 oz. water
15 oz. can plum tomatoes, mashed	salt and pepper to taste
1 clove minced garlic	1 cup frozen peas
1 sliced carrot	5–6 sliced mushrooms
1 stalk chopped celery	

Remove fat from beef. Cut meat into 1-1/2-inch cubes. Dredge beef pieces in flour. In a Dutch oven or a heavy pot, brown meat in hot olive oil. Remove. Set aside. In same pot, cook onion over low flame until yellow. Add plum tomatoes, garlic, carrot, celery, bay leaf, white wine, consommé, water, salt and pepper. Bring to a boil over high flame. Add meat. Cover. Cook over low flame for 1 1/2 to 2 hours or until tender, stirring occasionally. Then add peas and mushrooms. Continue to simmer for 15 minutes. Serves 3–4. (**See color photo on p. 7.**)

STUFATO DI MANZO AL VINO ROSSO
Beef with Red Wine

3 lbs. top round (boneless)	salt and pepper to taste
flour	pinch of sage
2 tbs. butter *or* margarine	pinch of thyme
1/4 cup olive oil	pinch of oregano
2 thinly sliced medium onions	red wine
1 clove minced garlic	

Remove fat from beef. Cut beef into 1-1/2-inch cubes. Dredge in flour. In a large skillet with hot, melted butter and olive oil, cook beef until brown. Add onions, garlic, salt, pepper, sage, thyme and oregano. Add enough red wine to cover meat. Cover. Over low flame, simmer for 2 to 2 1/2 hours, according to tenderness of meat. Stir occasionally. If too much evaporation occurs, add a small amount of beef broth. Serves 6.

BRACIOLA CON SALSA
Beef Roll with Gravy

1 lb. top round steak
5 tbs. olive oil
Sauce with Meatballs (p. 76)

Stuffing:

2 thin slices salami
4 or 5 thin pieces provolone (3 in. long)
1/4 sliced medium onion
1 hard-boiled egg, sliced lengthwise

1/2 tsp. dry parsley *or* 1 tbs. fresh minced parsley
pepper to taste
butter

Have steak cut 1/4-inch thick. Going crosswise on steak, make rows of each stuffing ingredient (salami, provolone, onion, egg). Sprinkle with parsley and pepper. Dot with butter. Then roll steak carefully so that ingredients will not fall out. Tie well from one end to another with white cord.

Heat olive oil in a medium-size skillet. Add beef roll and brown on all sides over medium flame. Set aside. Meanwhile, follow directions for Sauce with Meatballs. When sauce is half done (after simmering 40 minutes), add beef roll. Simmer for 45 minutes more. Stir occasionally. Then remove meat and turn onto a platter. Cut cord from roll. Slice. Serve with meatballs as an accompaniment to pasta served with the sauce. Serves 6.

TRIPPA IN UMIDO
Honeycomb Tripe Stew

2 lbs. semi-cooked honeycomb tripe
4 qts. water
4 tbs. olive oil
1/2 chopped small onion
1 lb. 3 oz. can plum tomatoes, mashed
1 cup water

1 whole clove garlic
pinch of oregano
4 medium quartered potatoes
1 stalk chopped celery
salt and pepper to taste
1/3 cup grated Romano cheese

Cut semi-cooked tripe into strips 3 inches long and 1/2 inch wide. Wash well. In 4 quarts of water, cook tripe covered over low flame for 2 hours. Drain.

Heat olive oil in a large saucepan. Add onion and cook over low flame until yellow. Then add tomatoes, water, tripe, garlic, oregano, potatoes, celery, salt and pepper. Cover. Bring to a boil over high flame. Lower flame and simmer, stirring occasionally, until tripe and vegetables are tender and sauce is done (35 minutes or longer). Remove garlic. Serve hot with grated cheese. Serves 4–5.

BRACIOLE SAPORITE
Savory Thin Beefsteaks

1 lb. top round
flour
1/2 cup dry white wine
1/3 cup beef stock

pinch of pepper
pinch of salt
4 tbs. bacon fat

Marinade:

1 cup wine vinegar
1/2 cup water
1/2 small chopped onion
1/2 small chopped carrot

1/2 chopped stalk of celery
1 small bay leaf
2 cloves

Place marinade in a small enamel pot. Bring to a full boil over high flame. Lower flame and simmer for 10 minutes. Let cool.

Have butcher cut top round into four 1/4-inch-thick slices (for *braciole*). Place meat in a large bowl (not a metal one). Pour cooled marinade over meat. Cover with aluminum foil. Let stand in a cool place for 1 hour. Drain. Dry well with absorbent paper.

Dredge beef well in flour. Put 2 tbs. of bacon fat in a large skillet over a high flame. When fat starts to bubble, add two steaks and let brown quickly on both sides. Remove and place on a platter. Add remaining bacon fat and place remaining two steaks in pan to also brown quickly on both sides. Lower flame. Return the first two steaks to pan. Add wine, beef stock, salt and pepper. Cover pan. Cook for 35 minutes or until tender. If too much evaporation occurs, add a little beef stock. The fourth steak may be cut into thirds and served to each person. Serves 3.

Serve with Fried Potatoes, Beets in Sauce, and Paula's Pear Dessert.

CROCHE DI MANZO
Beef Croquettes

1 1/2 cups ground beef
1/2 cup boiled spinach, drained and chopped
1 strip proscuitto, chopped
salt and pepper to taste
pinch of nutmeg
2 tbs. grated Romano cheese

1 egg
3/4 cup fine dry bread crumbs
1 egg (beaten and diluted with 1 tsp. water)
1/4 cup olive oil
lemon slices

In a large bowl, place ground beef, spinach, proscuitto, salt, pepper, nutmeg, cheese and egg. Mix well. Form into oval balls about the size of an egg. Roll in bread crumbs. Then dip in slightly diluted egg with a pinch of salt added. Roll again in bread crumbs.

In a large skillet with hot olive oil, cook croquettes over medium flame until brown on all sides. Serve hot with lemon slices. Serves 3–4.

Beef and Celery Roll

Photo courtesy of Florida Celery Advisory Committee.

BRACIOLA DI MANZO E SEDANO
Beef and Celery Roll

2 lb. flank steak	1/2 tsp. ground oregano
1 1/4 tsp. onion salt	1/2 lb. sliced mozzarella
1/4 tsp. ground black pepper	1 tbs. olive oil
5 pascal celery ribs	8 oz. can tomato sauce
1/4 cup dry bread crumbs	1/4 cup water
1/4 cup grated Parmesan cheese	1/4 tsp. garlic powder

Score steak on one side with a sharp knife. Combine onion salt and pepper and rub into both sides of meat. Cut celery into lengths the width of the meat and arrange over scored side of meat. Sprinkle with bread crumbs, Parmesan cheese and oregano. Top with mozzarella, reserving two slices for later use. Roll jelly-roll fashion. Secure with white string from one end to the other. Heat olive oil in Dutch oven. Brown meat on all sides. Remove from heat. Add tomato sauce, water and garlic powder. Return to heat and simmer covered for 1 1/2 hours or until tender, turning meat occasionally. Ten minutes before cooking time is up, place two slices of cheese on top of meat. Cover and cook 10 minutes more. Remove to serving dish and slice.

If desired, serve with sauce made by blending 1 cup water mixed with 2 tbs. flour into gravy in Dutch oven. Cook until thickened, stirring with a wooden spoon. Serves 6–8. **(See photo above.)**

POLPETTE ITALIANI
Italian Meatballs

3/4 lb. ground beef
1/4 lb. ground pork
3/4 cup bread crumbs (moistened in milk)
2 eggs
1/4 cup grated Romano cheese

1 tbs. fresh minced parsley *or* 1/2 tsp. dry parsley
1 clove minced garlic
salt and pepper to taste
1/4 cup olive oil

In a large bowl, mix beef, pork, bread crumbs, eggs, cheese, parsley, garlic, salt and pepper. Form into balls. In a large skillet with hot olive oil, cook meatballs over medium flame until well-browned on all sides. Makes about 14. Serves 7.

MINIATURE MEATBALLS

If miniature meatballs are desired for antipasto, use same amount of ingredients but shape them smaller, about the size of a walnut. Before serving, spear each one with a toothpick.

VEAL

COTOLETTE DI VITELLA ALLA PARMIGIANA
Veal Cutlets, Parmesan

1 lb. veal cutlets
2 eggs
3/4 cup bread crumbs
2 tbs. grated Parmesan cheese
1 small clove minced garlic

1/2 tsp. dry parsley *or* 1 1/2 tbs. fresh minced parsley
salt and pepper to taste
1/3 cup olive oil
mozzarella slices (not too thin)

Sauce:
3 tbs. olive oil
1 tbs. chopped onion
8 oz. can tomato sauce

1/2 clove minced garlic
1/2 tsp. dry basil
pepper to taste

Have veal cutlets pounded thin. In a shallow bowl, beat eggs well. In a shallow dish, combine bread crumbs, cheese, garlic, parsley, salt and pepper. Dip cutlets in eggs. Then roll in bread crumb mixture. Heat 1/3 cup olive oil in a large skillet. Cook cutlets over moderate flame until golden brown on both sides.

Meanwhile, prepare the sauce: Heat 3 tbs. olive oil in a small saucepan. Over low flame, sauté onion until yellow. Add tomato sauce, garlic, basil and pepper. Cook until heated.

Coat the bottom of a shallow 12"x16" baking pan with some sauce. Arrange veal cutlets on top. Top each cutlet with a mozzarella slice. Pour remainder of sauce over them. In a preheated oven at 375°F., cook for 8–10 minutes or until cheese melts. Serves 4.

VITELLA CON SALSA DI VINO
Veal with Wine Sauce

1 lb. thin veal cutlets
4 tbs. butter
1/4 cup grated Parmesan cheese
1/4 cup flour

1/2 tsp. dry parsley
1/8 tsp. garlic powder
pepper to taste

Wine Sauce:
1 cup hot water
3 beef bouillon cubes

1/2 cup dry white wine
2 tbs. flour

Combine grated cheese, flour, parsley, garlic, and pepper in a shallow bowl. Dredge veal cutlets in this mixture. In a large skillet with hot, melted butter, cook meat over moderate flame until brown and tender on both sides. Remove to hot platter. Add water and bouillon cubes to skillet, scraping brownings from bottom of pan. Simmer for three minutes. Combine wine and flour. Add slowly to skillet. Stir until smooth and thick. Pour hot sauce over veal cutlets. Serves 4.

VITELLA TONNE
Veal with Tuna Sauce

2 lbs. boned leg of veal
3 fillets of anchovy
1/4 medium onion (stuck with 2 cloves)
1 bay leaf

1 sliced carrot
1 stalk chopped celery
1 tsp. chopped fresh parsley
salt and pepper to taste

Remove fat and tendons from meat. Cut anchovies in small pieces and distribute on meat. Roll meat and tie with white string (not too tight).

Into a Dutch oven or large, heavy pot, pour enough water to fully cover meat. Add onion, bay leaf, carrot, celery, parsley, salt and pepper. Bring to a boil over high flame. Then add meat. Lower flame. Cover pot. Simmer for 1 1/2 hours or until tender. Remove meat from pot.* Let cool completely. Untie it and slice very thinly. Fill a 2-1/2-quart casserole dish with veal slices.

Tuna Sauce:
4 oz. canned tuna fish in olive oil
2 fillets of anchovy
1/4 or 1/2 cup olive oil

juice of 1 lemon
2 tbs. capers (unsalted)

Make a paste of tuna (oil included) and the anchovies. Add olive oil gradually. Add lemon juice and then capers. This sauce should be very fluid.

Cover veal slices with tuna sauce. Refrigerate for 24 hours. Serves 4–6.

This makes a wonderful summer dish. Serve as antipasto also, if desired.

*Stock obtained from boiling the veal may be strained for preparing risotto or other uses.

COTOLETTE DI VITELLA IMPANATI
Breaded Veal Cutlets

1 lb. veal cutlets
3/4 cup bread crumbs
2 tbs. grated Romano cheese
1/2 tsp. dry parsley

1 small clove minced garlic
salt and pepper to taste
2 beaten eggs
1/3 cup olive oil

Have veal cutlets cut and pounded thin. In a shallow dish, combine bread crumbs, cheese, parsley, garlic, salt and pepper. Dip cutlets in beaten eggs. Then roll in bread crumb mixture. Heat olive oil in a large skillet. Cook cutlets over moderate flame until brown on both sides. Serves 4. **(See photo below.)**

Breaded Veal Cutlets   Photo courtesy of National Live Stock and Meat Board.

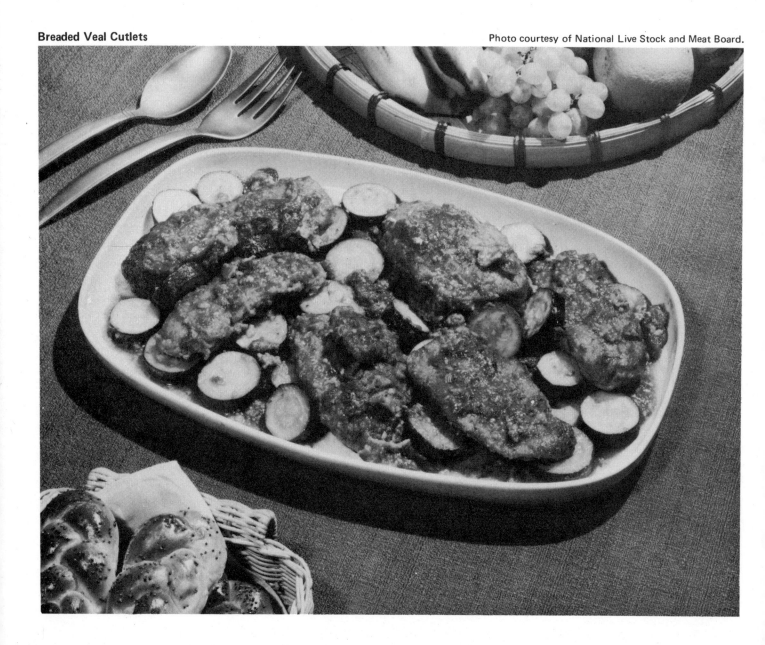

BRACIOLINE DI VITELLA ALL' UCCELLETTO
Veal Cutlets All' Uccelletto

1 lb. veal cutlets
1/4 cup olive oil
3 tbs. butter

1/2 tsp. dry sage leaves
salt and pepper to taste
juice of 1 large lemon

Have veal cutlets cut very fine and pounded. Heat olive oil and butter in a large skillet. Add sage leaves and simmer for 2 minutes. Then put in cutlets. Season with salt and pepper. Cook over moderate flame until brown and tender on both sides. Before removing from heat, add lemon juice. Serve with drippings left in pan. Serves 4.

SALTIMBOCCA
Veal Rolls, Roman Style

1 lb. thin veal cutlets, pounded
1 1/2 slices proscuitto (cut into 2-inch strips)
crumbled dry sage leaves

1/4 cup grated Romano cheese
salt and pepper to taste
6 tbs. butter

Cut veal cutlets into 2-inch squares. On each square, place a strip of proscuitto, a crumbled sage leaf and some grated cheese. Roll square carefully. Fasten with toothpick lengthwise. Sprinkle with salt and pepper. Heat butter in a large skillet. Cook veal rolls over moderate flame until golden brown on all sides. When done, remove toothpicks. Serve with drippings left in pan. Serves 4.

SCALLOPINE AL MARSALA
Veal with Marsala

1 1/2 lbs. veal cutlets
flour
salt and pepper to taste

1/4 cup butter
1/2 cup dry Marsala
lemon wedges

Have cutlets cut and pounded thin. Dredge cutlets in flour. Then sprinkle on both sides with salt and pepper. Heat butter in a large skillet. Cook cutlets over moderate flame until brown on both sides. Add Marsala and let veal cook 1 minute longer. Serve with lemon wedges. Serves 6.

ROLLINI DI VITELLA ALLA SICILIANA
Veal Rolls, Sicilian Style

2 lbs. veal cutlets
1/2 cup grated pecorino *or* Romano cheese
1 tsp. dry parsley
black pepper to taste
3 slices proscuitto (cut into 3-inch strips)
butter

1/2 cup olive oil
1 cup bread crumbs
1 medium onion (cut in eighths)
salt and pepper to taste
olive oil

(Continued on following page.)

Have cutlets cut and pounded thin. Cut into 4-inch squares. Place squares on board. In a small bowl, combine cheese, parsley and pepper. Put an equal amount of this mixture on each square. Place a proscuitto strip on top of each. Dot with butter. Roll tightly. Dip in olive oil. Dredge in bread crumbs. Fasten with toothpicks. Separate onion slices. Stick an onion slice on both ends of toothpick, pressing onion against veal roll.

Lightly grease a shallow 12"x16" baking pan. Put veal rolls in it, sprinkling both sides with salt and pepper. Drizzle with olive oil. Bake in a preheated oven at 375°F. for 40 minutes or until brown and tender on both sides. After 20 minutes, turn to cook other side. When done, remove toothpicks. Serves 8.

These are among Mother's specialties for important occasions, except we become too impatient for them and sometimes have these delicacies for Sunday dinner.

MINIATURE VEAL ROLLS, SICILIAN STYLE

If miniature veal rolls are desired for antipasto, use same amount of ingredients, but cut veal into 2-inch squares. Repeat same procedure. After cooking, remove sticky toothpicks and spear with clean ones.

COTOLETTE DI VITELLA IMBOTTITE
Stuffed Veal Cutlets

2 lbs. veal cutlets
1 tbs. butter
2 2-oz. cans fillets of anchovy
1/4 lb. proscuitto *or* Virginia ham (cut in medium-size pieces)

6 tbs. grated Romano cheese
2 beaten eggs
1 cup bread crumbs
1/2 cup olive oil

Have veal cutlets cut and pounded thin. If too large, cut each in half. In a small saucepan with hot butter, mash and cook anchovies over low flame until dissolved. Evenly distribute anchovies and proscuitto pieces on each cutlet. Sprinkle generously with grated cheese. Fold one edge over the other. Fasten with toothpicks. Dip cutlets in egg. Roll in bread crumbs. Heat olive oil in a large skillet. Cook meat over moderate flame until tender and brown on all sides. When done, remove toothpicks. Serves 8.

COSTATELLE DI VITELLA ALLA PIZZAIOLA
Veal Chops Alla Pizzaiola

6 large veal shoulder chops
6 tbs. olive oil
2 1/2 cups mashed canned plum tomatoes
2 1/2 cups hot water
6 medium quartered potatoes

1 clove minced garlic
1 large can peas, drained
1 tsp. oregano
salt to taste
pinch of crushed red pepper seeds

Heat olive oil in a large, deep skillet. Add veal chops, tomatoes, water, potatoes, garlic, oregano, salt, pepper and crushed red pepper seeds. Bring to a boil over high heat. Lower flame. Cover partially and simmer for 30 minutes. Stir sauce and turn chops occasionally. Add peas. Cover. Cook for 10 minutes or until chops are tender. Serves 6.

VITELLA RIPIENA AL FORNO
Rolled Stuffed Veal Roast

5 lbs. shoulder of veal

3 Italian sweet sausages (without casings)

salt and pepper

1 clove minced garlic

4 strips bacon

Have shoulder boned. Spread it open and sprinkle with salt. Break sausages in small pieces and distribute on shoulder. Sprinkle with pepper and garlic. Roll tightly. Rub outside with pepper. Tie with white string. Put in a 7"x11" baking pan or dish. Arrange bacon strips across top of shoulder. Roast in a preheated oven at 325°F. for 2 3/4 hours or until tender. Baste occasionally. Remove from oven and let stand 5 minutes. Cut string. Slice. Serves 6.

Serve with Potato Croquettes, Stuffed Mushrooms with Purée of Peas, Red Pepper Salad and Hot Coffee Spongecake.

PANZETTA DI VITELLA RIPIENA ALLA SICILIANA
Stuffed Breast of Veal, Sicilian

5 lb. breast of veal

1 tbs. olive oil

salt and pepper

2 tsp. rosemary

5 slices bacon

Stuffing:

1 lb. sweet Italian sausage (without casings)

1/2 medium onion, chopped

2 cups cooked rice (*al dente*)

2 hard-boiled eggs, cut in 1/4-inch cubes

3 tbs. grated Romano cheese

2 tsp. dry parsley *or* 3 tbs. fresh minced parsley

salt and pepper to taste

Have butcher cut a pocket in the large end of meat.

Crumble sausages and cook in a large skillet over low flame until meat loses its red color. Add onion. Cook until yellow. Place in a large bowl. Add remainder of stuffing ingredients. Mix. Fill breast of veal. Skewer ends together. Rub oil over veal. Sprinkle with salt, pepper and rosemary. Place in a 10"x14"x2" baking pan. Arrange bacon slices over meat. Roast in a preheated oven at 325°F. for 2 hours and 40 minutes or until tender. Baste occasionally with pan juices. Remove from oven and let stand for a few minutes for easier slicing. Serves 6.

FRICASSEA DI VITELLA CON FUNGHI
Fricassee of Veal with Mushrooms

1 1/2 lbs. boneless veal shoulder (in 2-inch cubes)

1/2 cup + 1 tbs. butter *or* margarine

1 large onion, finely chopped

1 large bay leaf

1 whole stalk celery

salt and pepper to taste

1 cup dry white wine

3 tbs. flour

2 1/2 cups hot beef broth *or* bouillon

1/2 cup milk

1/3 lb. fresh mushrooms

juice of 1/2 lemon

2 egg yolks

1/2 cup heavy cream

In a Dutch oven, place 1/2 cup butter, onion, bay leaf and veal. Wash celery, dry, remove leaves and add to mixture. Over low flame, allow to simmer, turning meat until all sides turn a

(Continued on following page.)

golden brown color. Season with salt and pepper. Add wine slowly. When wine evaporates, sprinkle meat with flour, stirring constantly. Add hot broth and milk gradually and mix well. Cover. Simmer for 1 hour or until meat is cooked through.

Meanwhile, wash and slice mushrooms. In a small skillet, melt remaining butter (1 tbs.), add lemon juice and cook mushrooms over low flame until they become limp. Set aside.

When veal is done, remove from pan with slotted spoon. Discard celery stalk and bay leaf from sauce. Beat egg yolks in a small bowl. Continue to beat while adding heavy cream and sauce from pan. Then put veal back in pan. Add mushrooms and this mixture. Mix. Heat through, but do not let boil because eggs will curdle. Serves 4.

Serve with rice seasoned with butter and grated Parmesan cheese.

LAMB

COSTATELLE D'AGNELLO ALLA PIZZAIOLA
Lamb Chops Alla Pizzaiola

4 large lamb shoulder chops (1 inch thick or less)	4 quartered potatoes
1/4 cup olive oil	1 clove minced garlic
1 sliced medium onion	1/4 tsp. oregano
1 1/4 cups canned plum tomatoes, mashed	salt and pepper to taste
2 1/2 cups hot water	

Heat olive oil in a Dutch oven or deep skillet. Cook onion over low flame until yellow. Add lamb chops, tomatoes, water, potatoes, garlic, oregano, salt and pepper. Over high flame, bring to a boil. Lower flame. Cover partially and simmer for 45 minutes or until tender. Stir sauce and turn chops occasionally. If too much evaporation occurs, add a small amount of hot water. Serves 4.

AGNELLO IN UMIDO
Lamb Stew

2 lbs. boneless lamb (shoulder), in 1-inch cubes	1 large carrot, cut in 2-inch strips
3 tbs. olive oil	1 cup frozen peas
1 medium chopped onion	1 tsp. dry parsley *or* 1 tbs. fresh chopped parsley
1 clove minced garlic	
1 lb. 3 oz. can plum tomatoes, mashed	1/2 tsp. marjoram
3 cups water	salt and pepper to taste
6 medium potatoes, quartered	

In a deep pot or Dutch oven, place olive oil, onion and garlic over low flame. Sauté until yellow. Remove with a slotted spoon. Set aside. Add lamb and brown over medium flame. Add tomatoes. Cook for 5 minutes. Add water, onion and garlic. Cover. Allow to come to a boil over high flame. Lower flame. Simmer for 30 minutes. Add potatoes, carrot, peas, parsley, marjoram, salt and pepper. Cover and cook for 30 minutes more or until meat and vegetables are tender. Stir occasionally. Serves 6.

COSTATELLE D'AGNELLO AI FERRI
Broiled Lamb Chops

4 large lamb shoulder chops (1 inch thick)
juice of 1 lemon
2 tbs. olive oil

1 clove minced garlic
1/2 tsp. dry parsley
salt and pepper to taste

Slash fat around edge of meat to prevent curling. In a small bowl, beat lemon juice, olive oil, garlic, parsley, salt and pepper. Brush lamb chops on both sides with this mixture. Preheat broiler. Place chops in broiler pan. Broil until brown (about 6–7 minutes for medium or well done). Turn chops and broil other side for same amount of time. Serves 4. **(See photo below.)**

Broiled Lamb Chops

Photo: Fred G. Korth. Courtesy of National Live Stock and Meat Board.

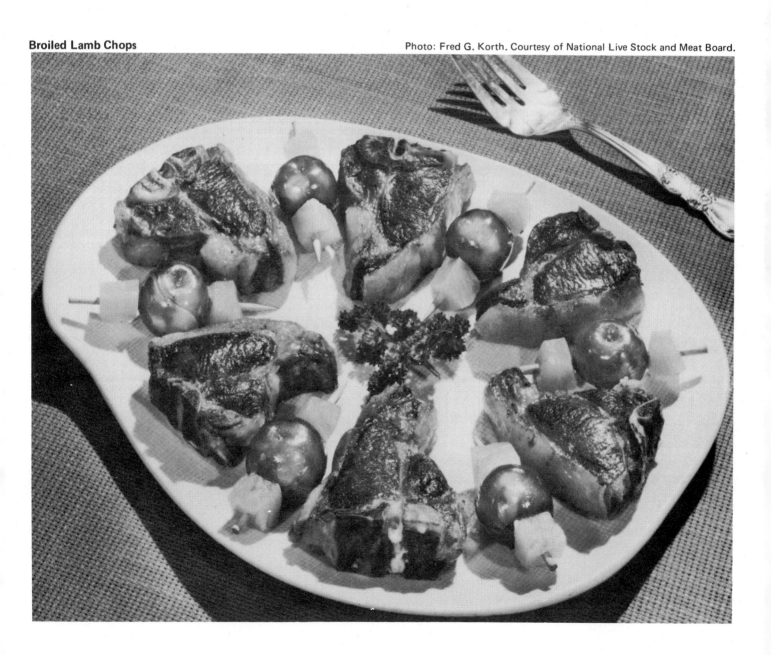

AGNELLINO AL FORNO
Roasted Whole Spring Lamb

7 lb. spring lamb	salt and pepper
garlic	1 cup olive oil
rosemary	1 cup water

Wipe meat with a damp cloth. Rub with garlic, rosemary, salt and pepper. Place lamb in a 10"x14"x2" baking pan. Combine olive oil and water. Pour on bottom of pan. Roast in a preheated oven at 325°F. for 10 minutes. Lower oven temperature to 250°. Continue roasting for 1 1/2 to 2 hours or until tender. Baste frequently. Remove from oven and let stand 5 minutes. Serve very hot. Serves 7–8. For suggested accompaniments, refer to Easter Menu.

The classic Italian Easter dish is roast spring lamb reflecting with its *contorno* (accompaniments) the freshness of spring and celebration of this solemn feast.

In Campania, a region around the Bay of Naples, Easter lamb is roasted in a round pan with lard, potatoes and onion. But throughout the regions, lamb is prepared in various ways at this time. Rome serves its lamb in a *brodetto*, a creamy soup containing lard, onion, chopped proscuitto, white wine and egg yolks beaten with lemon juice.

ABBACCHIO RIPIENO AL FORNO
Roast Rolled Stuffed Lamb

5–6 lb. leg of lamb

Stuffing:

1/2 lb. finely chopped veal	salt and pepper to taste
1/2 lb. finely chopped proscuitto	pinch of oregano
1/2 cup bread crumbs	1 clove minced garlic
1/4 lb. finely chopped salami	1 tbs. finely chopped fresh parsley
1 large egg	1 tbs. grated Parmesan *or* Romano cheese

Have bone removed from leg of lamb. Do not remove fell (skin) from lamb. Wipe meat with a damp cloth. Mix all stuffing ingredients together and spread over lamb, leaving about 1 1/2 inches clear around edges of meat. Roll and tie tightly with white string. Rub meat with oil and salt.

Place stuffed leg of lamb with fat side up on a rack in a 9"x13"x2" roasting pan. Roast in a preheated oven at 325°F. for 2 1/2 to 3 hours, according to weight. Baste occasionally. Remove from oven and let stand 5 minutes. Cut string. Serve very hot on a warm platter with drippings from pan. Serves 6–8.

ABBACCHIO AL FORNO CON ROSMARINO
Roast Leg of Lamb with Rosemary

5 lb. leg of lamb
1 large clove garlic
2 tbs. flour
salt and pepper

1 tsp. rosemary
1 medium sliced onion
2 cups hot water

Do not remove fell (skin) from lamb because this holds meat together and makes it juicier. Wipe meat with a damp cloth. Rub with garlic. Sliver garlic. Make 3 or 4 small slashes in surface of meat and insert garlic pieces. Dredge meat in flour. Sprinkle with salt, pepper and rosemary.

In a 9"x13"x2" roasting pan, place leg of lamb with fat side up. Roast in preheated oven at 325°F. for 30 minutes. Add onion to pan. Roast for 30 minutes longer, turning onion occasionally. Add hot water to pan. Continue cooking, basting occasionally, for 1 1/2 hours or until done. Remove from oven and let stand for 5 minutes before carving. Serve roast very hot on a warm platter. Serves 6—7. **(See photo below.)**

May be served with Hot Whipped Potatoes, Steamed Carrots, Eggplant and Pimiento Salad and Ice Cream with Strawberry Sauce.

Roast Leg of Lamb with Rosemary Photo courtesy of National Live Stock and Meat Board.

AGNELLO BRASATO CON VINO BIANCO
Braised Lamb with White Wine

3 lbs. boneless lamb shoulder (in 1-inch cubes)
2 tbs. olive oil
3 tbs. butter
2 medium chopped onions
1/2 tsp. thyme

1/2 cup dry white wine
1/4 cup hot water
2 heaping tbs. tomato sauce
1 large clove minced garlic
salt and pepper to taste

Heat olive oil and butter in a deep, heavy skillet or Dutch oven. Cook lamb slowly over moderate heat until brown. Add onion and cook until golden. Add thyme, white wine, hot water, tomato sauce, garlic, salt and pepper. Mix. Cover tightly. Cook over low flame for 1 hour or until lamb is tender. Stir occasionally. If too much evaporation occurs, add a small amount of boiling water. Serves 4–5.

Serve with Italian rice.

PORK

ARROSTO DI MAIALE
Roast Loin of Pork

5 lb. loin of pork
1 clove garlic, slightly crushed
salt and pepper to taste

rosemary
a few cloves

Have butcher cut through the chine bone to make the roast easy to carve. Wipe meat with a damp cloth. Rub garlic over pork loin. Rub with salt, pepper and rosemary. Insert cloves on top. Place in a 7"x11" roasting pan and cook in a preheated oven at 325°F. for 3 hours or until very well done. Let stand a few minutes before carving. Serves 6.

Serve with Fried Potatoes, Squash with Vinegar, Steamed Carrots, Mixed Salad and Baked Apples.

COSTATELLE DI MAIALE FRITTI
Fried Pork Chops

8 loin pork chops (1 inch thick or less)
olive oil
1 cup flour
1/4 tsp. thyme

1/8 tsp. garlic powder
salt and pepper to taste
6 tbs. butter *or* margarine
juice of 1 large lemon

Slash fat around edges of chops to prevent curling. Dip chops in olive oil. Then dredge in flour combined with thyme, garlic powder, salt and pepper. In a large skillet with hot melted butter, cook pork chops over low flame until well done and brown on both sides. Serve with lemon juice. Serves 4.

COSTATELLE DI MAIALE IMPANATI
Breaded Pork Chops

8 loin pork chops (1 inch thick or less)
1 large egg
2 tbs. water
1 cup bread crumbs
1 clove minced garlic

1/4 tsp. oregano
1 tsp. dry parsley *or* 1 tbs. chopped fresh parsley
2 tbs. grated Romano cheese
salt and pepper to taste
1/2 cup olive oil

Slash fat around edge of chops to prevent curling. In a shallow bowl, beat egg with water. In a shallow dish, combine bread crumbs, garlic, oregano, parsley, cheese, salt and pepper. Dip pork chops in egg. Roll in bread crumb mixture. Heat olive oil in a large skillet. Add pork chops to hot oil and cook over low flame until well done and brown on both sides. Serves 4.

COSTATELLE DI MAIALE ALLA CREMONA
Pork Chops Cremona

4 loin pork chops
2 tsp. rosemary
2 tsp. chopped fresh sage *or* 1/2 tsp. dry sage
1 tbs. butter *or* margarine

salt and pepper to taste
1/2 clove chopped garlic
1/2 cup dry Marsala
water

Slash fat around edges of chops to prevent curling. In a small bowl, combine rosemary, sage, salt, pepper and garlic. Sprinkle on pork chops. Melt butter in a large skillet. Brown chops in hot butter over low flame until brown on both sides. Pour enough water into pan to cover chops and cook about 45 minutes. When water has almost evaporated and chops are brown and well done, add dry Marsala and simmer 3 minutes. Serves 4.

PIEDE DI PORCO CON SALSA
Pig's Feet with Gravy

5 medium pig's feet
3 tbs. olive oil
1/2 small onion, chopped
7 oz. can tomato paste

4 1/2 cups hot water
salt and pepper to taste
1 tsp. dry basil *or* 3 or 4 fresh basil leaves
1 clove minced garlic

Have pig's feet split in half. Cover with water and boil for 30 minutes. Drain.

Heat olive oil in a large saucepan. Add onion and sauté over low flame until golden. Add tomato paste and water. Stir until dissolved. Add salt, pepper, basil and garlic. Over high flame, bring to a boil. Add pig's feet. Lower flame and cover partially. Simmer for about 1 1/2 hours or until pork is well done and tender. Stir occasionally. Serves 5.

SPALLA DI PORCO CON VEGETALI
Rolled Shoulder of Pork with Vegetables

3 lb. shoulder of pork
4 quartered potatoes
1/2 tsp. dry sage leaves
4 quartered onions

1/2 cup or more beef broth *or* bouillon
salt and pepper to taste
1 lb. frozen peas

Have the butcher bone and stuff shoulder with garlic and parsley, then roll and tie. Wipe meat with a damp cloth. Sprinkle with sage. Place in a 9"x13"x2" roasting pan. Roast in a preheated oven at 325°F. for 1 1/2 hours. Then add beef broth and potatoes and onions seasoned with salt and pepper to bottom of pan. Cook for 1 hour more or until meat and vegetables are thoroughly cooked. Baste vegetables frequently with pan juices. Fifteen minutes before meat is done, add peas. Sprinkle with salt and pepper to taste and mix with other vegetables and juices. Remove meat from oven and let stand a few minutes. Cut string and slice. Serves 4.

SALSICCIA CON CIPOLLE E PATATE
Sausage with Onions and Potatoes

2 lbs. Italian sweet sausage
6 medium potatoes, cut in eighths

3 medium sliced onions
salt and pepper to taste

Puncture sausages with fork. In a 10"x14"x2" baking pan, place sausages with potatoes and onions. Sprinkle salt and pepper on potatoes and onions only. Sprinkle sausages with pepper. Cook in a preheated oven at 375°F. for 45 minutes or until well done. Halfway through cooking time, turn sausages and vegetables. Serves 6.

SALSICCIA FRITTA
Fried Sausage

2 1/2 lbs. Italian sweet sausage
water
juice of 2 lemons

In a large skillet, put enough water to coat bottom. (This reduces shrinkage of sausage.) Puncture sausage with fork. Place in pan. Cook sausage over low flame until brown on both sides. Serve with lemon juice. If desired, eliminate lemon juice and serve sausages hot with fried Italian green peppers and onions. Serves 4–6.

Fried Sausage is a food reserved for celebration in Sicily. When Mother was a girl in Ciminna, the Feast of the Immaculate Conception would be observed on December 8 by processions of villagers trudging uphill to the Mother Church in the early evening. After services, villagers strolled by the light of sporadic bonfires to the nearby *cantini* (combination grocery stores-restaurants) to enjoy the traditional dish of fried sausage with bread accompanied by ruby red wine.

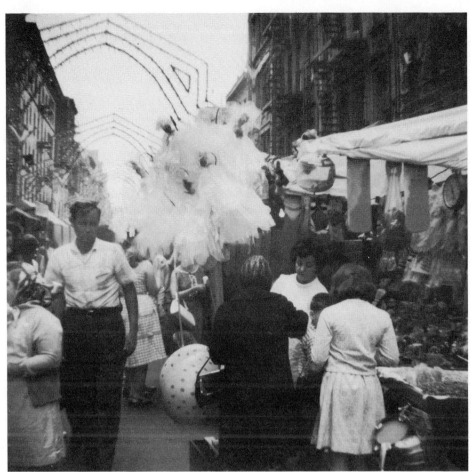

Photo: Pauline N. Barrese.
Courtesy of Encore Magazine.

Among other religious feasts held annually in New York, the St. Anthony Feast is celebrated by Italians June 1—13. As in their ancient *paesi* (villages) of Italy, the gaiety, music and spontaneity still exist long after the great immigration. So do the quaint stands with their traditionally bountiful display of *biscotti* (cookies), *torrone* (nougat), *ceci* (roasted chickpeas), *semenzi* (salted squash and sunflower seeds), and *noce* (pistachio nuts), among other good things.

But mostly, the marvelous wafting fragrance of sizzling grilled sausage rising above the merriment draws villagers and tourists to savor them, deliciously smothered with fried peppers and onions in small bread rolls called *panini*.

Meanwhile, inside the St. Anthony church foyer, the faithful give offerings for "holy bread" symbolizing "providence for the poor."

SALSICCIA AL GRIGLIA
Grilled Sweet Sausage

2 lbs. Italian sweet sausage

Preheat broiler. Place sausage in a loose circle on broiler rack about 6 inches from a medium flame. Puncture sausages with fork. Broil about 30 minutes or until thoroughly cooked, turning to brown both sides. Serve hot with roasted peppers or fried Italian peppers and onions.

Italian hot sausage may also be cooked in this manner. Serves 4.

CUORE DI PORCO CON SALSA
Heart of Pork with Tomato Sauce

2 hearts of pork (1 1/2 lbs.)
1/4 cup olive oil
1 small chopped onion
1 clove minced garlic
1 bay leaf

2 large fresh ripe tomatoes, skinned and
  chopped
salt to taste
pinch of crushed red pepper seeds

Wash hearts in warm water. Trim away gristle and the larger blood vessels. Cover hearts with boiling water and cook for 5—6 minutes. Drain. Cut into bite-size pieces.

Heat olive oil in a medium-size saucepan. Add onion and cook over low flame until yellow. Add heart, garlic and bay leaf. Cover. Simmer for 10—15 minutes, stirring occasionally. Add tomatoes, salt and crushed red pepper seeds. Cover. Simmer for 20 minutes more or until tender. Remove bay leaf. Serves 3.

LIVER

FEGATO ALLA VENEZIANA
Liver, Venetian Style

1 lb. calves' liver
4 tbs. butter
1 medium sliced onion
salt and pepper to taste
1/4 cup red wine

1 tbs. wine vinegar
1/2 tsp. dry parsley *or* 1 tbs. minced fresh
  parsley
1/4 tsp. thyme leaves

Cut liver into 1-1/2-inch cubes. Heat butter in a large skillet and sauté onion over low flame until yellow. Add liver. Over high flame, cook for 6—7 minutes or until nicely browned on all sides. Stir frequently. When done, season with salt and pepper. Mix. Remove onion and liver to hot platter.

To drippings in pan, add wine, vinegar, parsley and thyme. Bring to a boil. Pour over liver. Serve at once. Serves 3.

FEGATO CON CIPOLLA
Liver with Onion

1 lb. calves' liver (in 1-1/2-inch cubes)
4 tbs. olive oil
1 medium chopped onion

1 large bay leaf
salt and pepper to taste

Heat olive oil in a large skillet. Sauté onion until yellow. Add liver and bay leaf. Over high flame, cook for 6—7 minutes or until nicely browned on all sides. Stir frequently. When done, season with salt and pepper. Mix. Remove bay leaf. Serve immediately. Serves 3.

FEGATO IMPANATO IN FORNO
Baked Liver Cutlets

1 lb. calves' liver
1 beaten egg
3/4 cup bread crumbs
1 tbs. grated Romano cheese

2 tbs. minced fresh parsley *or* 1 tsp. dry parsley
salt and pepper to taste
4 tbs. olive oil
butter

Cut liver in 1/4-inch thick slices. In a shallow dish, combine bread crumbs, cheese, parsley, salt and pepper. Dip liver in egg. Dredge in bread crumb mixture. Coat a 14" round baking pan with olive oil. Place liver in pan. Dot with butter. Place pan in lowest point of oven. Bake in preheated oven at 400°F. for 5 minutes on each side or until brown. Place on a hot platter and serve immediately. Serves 3–4.

FEGATO ALLA CACCIATORA
Liver, Hunter's Style

1 1/3 lbs. calves' liver
6 medium onions
7 tbs. butter

6 tsp. flour
1/2 cup dry white wine
salt and pepper to taste

Peel onions. Slice and place in a large bowl with water to cover for 2 hours. Drain onions and dry well. Remove veins and membrane from liver. Cut into thin slices.

In a large skillet, melt butter over very low flame. Place onions in pan and sauté for 30 minutes covered. Onions should be tender but not brown. Stir occasionally.

Dredge liver slices in flour seasoned with salt and pepper. Add to onions. Over high flame, cook liver 1 minute on one side or until crispy brown. Turn. Brown other side for about the same amount of time. Add wine. Let cook for 1 minute more. Place on a hot platter and serve immediately. Serves 4.

FEGATINI DI PORCO TRIFOLATI
Sautéed Pork Livers

8 pork livers
2 tbs. olive oil

salt and pepper to taste

Have butcher place livers in pork net* with bay leaf. Heat olive oil in a large skillet and cook livers over high flame until nicely browned on both sides. Stir frequently. Sprinkle with salt and pepper. Place on a hot platter and serve immediately. Serves 4.

*Pork net is a membrane covering pork intestines.

FEGATO DI VITELLA ALLA MILITARE
Veal Liver, Military Style

1 lb. calves' liver
2 tbs. olive oil
2 tbs. butter
2 small chopped scallions

1 tsp. dry parsley *or* 1 tbs. minced fresh parsley
salt and pepper to taste
juice of 1 lemon

Remove veins and membrane from liver. Cut liver into thin slices. Heat olive oil and butter in a large skillet and sauté scallions until yellow. Add liver. Over high flame, cook on one side for 1 minute or until crispy brown. Turn. Add parsley. Cook until brown for about the same amount of time on other side. Add salt and pepper. Mix. Place on a hot platter. Serve immediately with drippings and lemon juice. Serves 3.

GAME

FAGIANO AL FORNO CON VEGETALI
Roast Pheasant with Vegetables

3 lb. pheasant
2 tbs. butter
salt and pepper to taste
1/2 tsp. dry sage leaves, crumbled

6 tbs. olive oil
4 quartered potatoes
1 large quartered onion
2 large sliced carrots

Cut pheasant into serving pieces. Wash. Dry with absorbent paper. Rub pieces with butter. Sprinkle with salt, pepper and sage. In a 9"x13"x2" roasting pan, place olive oil, pheasant, potatoes, onion and carrots. Sprinkle vegetables with salt and pepper. Roast in a preheated oven at 375°F. for 1 hour or until pheasant and vegetables are tender. Turn occasionally. Serves 4.

FAGIANO BRASATO CON VINO ROSSO
Braised Pheasant with Red Wine

4 lb. pheasant
1/4 cup olive oil
1/4 cup butter

salt and pepper to taste
1 tsp. oregano
1/2 cup dry red wine

Cut pheasant into serving pieces. Wash. Dry with absorbent paper. Heat olive oil and butter in a deep skillet or a Dutch oven. Add pheasant and sprinkle with salt, pepper and oregano. Cook over medium flame for about 15 minutes or until brown. Add red wine. Cover. Over low flame, simmer for 30 minutes or until tender. Serves 4—5.

FAGIANO IMBOTTITO
Stuffed Pheasant

3 lb. pheasant (whole)

2 tbs. butter

salt and pepper to taste

Stuffing:

1 tsp. olive oil

1/2 lb. chopped sausage (without casings)

1 small minced onion

1 pheasant liver, cut up

1 pheasant gizzard, cut up

1 egg

4 slices crumbled bread (without crusts)

2 tbs. grated Parmesan cheese

1/2 tsp. dry parsley *or* 1 tbs. chopped fresh
   parsley

pinch of poultry seasoning

salt and pepper to taste

Clean and wash pheasant, keeping the liver and gizzard. Dry.

To prepare stuffing: In a medium-size skillet with 1 tsp. of olive oil, cook sausage, onion, liver and gizzard until light brown. Place in a large bowl. Add egg, bread, cheese, parsley, poultry seasoning, salt and pepper. Mix well.

Fill pheasant with stuffing. Sew or skewer together. Rub outside with butter. Sprinkle with salt and pepper. Place pheasant in a 9"x 13"x 2" roasting pan. Roast in a preheated oven at 325°F. for 1 hour 15 minutes or until tender. Baste occasionally. Serves 4.

CONIGLIO ALL'AURORA
Rabbit all'Aurora

1 rabbit (3 lbs.)

1/2 stick butter

1/4 cup olive oil

3 cloves crushed garlic

1 small chopped onion

1 jigger brandy

1/2 cup white wine

salt and pepper to taste

1/8 tsp. paprika

4 tbs. tomato paste

1/2 cup hot water

2 cups light cream

1 sprig minced fresh parsley

Have rabbit cleaned and cut into serving portions. Soak in cool water to cover with 1 tbs. of salt for 3–4 hours. Run under cool, clear water. Dry.

In a deep skillet or Dutch oven with hot butter and olive oil, cook rabbit over medium flame for about 15 minutes or until brown. Add garlic, onion and brandy. Increase heat and let brandy evaporate for about 1 minute. Lower flame. Add white wine, salt, pepper, paprika, tomato paste and water. Stir until tomato paste dissolves. Cover and simmer for about 40 minutes or until rabbit is tender. Remove garlic. Five minutes before rabbit is done, add cream and parsley. Stir until sauce is somewhat thick. Serves 4.

CONIGLIO FRITTO
Fried Rabbit

1 rabbit (3—4 lbs.)
2 thin strips salt pork, cut in pieces
3 tbs. butter
3 tbs. olive oil

1/2 tsp. rosemary
salt and pepper to taste
1/8 tsp. garlic powder
juice of 1 large lemon

Have rabbit cleaned and cut into serving portions. Soak in cold water to cover with 1 tbs. of salt for about 3—4 hours. Run pieces under cool, clear water. Dry with absorbent paper.

Brown salt pork in a large skillet. Remove. Heat butter and olive oil in the same skillet. Add rabbit and sprinkle with rosemary, salt, pepper and garlic powder. Sauté over medium flame until rabbit is brown and tender on both sides. Serve with lemon juice. Serves 4.

CONIGLIO IN UMIDO CON VINO BIANCO
Stewed Rabbit with White Wine

1 rabbit (3—4 lbs.)
flour
1/4 cup olive oil
salt and pepper to taste
3/4 tsp. dry sage leaves

1 small chopped onion
2 cloves minced garlic
3/4 lb. or 1 3/4 cups diced fresh tomatoes
   (without skins)
1/2 cup dry white wine

Have rabbit cleaned and cut into serving portions. Soak in cold water to cover with 1 tbs. of salt for 3—4 hours. Run pieces under clear, cool water. Dry.

Dredge rabbit pieces in flour. Heat olive oil in a large, deep skillet or Dutch oven. Add rabbit and cook over medium flame for about 10 minutes. Sprinkle with salt, pepper and sage. Add onion and garlic. Lower flame. Cook slowly for 10 minutes or until onion and garlic are light brown. Add tomatoes and wine. Stir. Cover and simmer for 30 minutes or until rabbit is tender. Turn occasionally. Serves 4.

PERNICE AL GRIGLIA
Broiled Partridge

4 lb. partridge
melted butter

garlic powder
salt and pepper to taste

Clean partridge and cut into serving portions. Wash. Dry with absorbent paper. Brush pieces with melted butter. Sprinkle with salt, pepper and a little garlic powder.

Preheat broiler to 350°. Place partridge in the broiler pan about 5 inches from flame. Broil one side until brown and tender. Brush with more melted butter every 5—10 minutes. Broil other side until brown and tender, brushing with melted butter. Partridge should be done in about 45 minutes. Transfer to a warm serving platter. Pour pan drippings over partridge pieces. Serves 4—5.

Serve with Rice Milanese, Fried Artichokes, Tomato Slices with Basil and Ladyfinger Delight.

PERNICE IN TEGAME
Pan-Fried Partridge

3 lb. partridge
3 tbs. olive oil
3 tbs. butter

1/2 tsp. dry sage leaves, crumbled
salt and pepper to taste

Clean partridge and cut into serving pieces. Wash. Dry with absorbent paper.

Heat olive oil and butter in a large skillet. Add partridge and sprinkle with sage, salt and pepper. Fry until brown and tender on all sides. Serves 3–4.

DELECTABLE WAYS TO SERVE POULTRY

If poultry is highly preferable fare to you, then it is hoped that among the following recipes there will be some dishes you will come back to prepare many times over. There are so many and varied ways you can cook poultry with different herbs to give it that "just right" flavor. I felt I should also include here delicious stuffings fit for the bird and two ways to make Chicken, Hunter's Style–a favorite among many.

SOME HELPFUL HINTS

Removing the bone from a chicken breast is not difficult. It makes it easier to eat and cook and is therefore worth the doing. Simply cut filmy skin covering the bone. Then snap it to remove. Flatten, and prepare as desired.

If you want to serve stuffed chicken sometime and the guest list is large, a capon would be more convenient because of its size. It is actually a young rooster gelded to make the meat tender and is cooked in the same manner as chicken.

Squabs are the nestlings of pigeons, usually marketed at about four weeks of age when they weigh from 3/4 to 1 pound. They are a tender delicacy to be experienced. Allow one for each serving.

When roasting a duck, it is well to remember to puncture it with a fork because it has a heavy layer of fat under the skin. This releases much of the fat. Place the duck on a rack while roasting. This will help to make it crisp and keep it from being submerged in its own grease.

One way to tell when fowl is done is to use a meat thermometer. It should be inserted so that the bulb is in the center of the inside thigh muscle (preferred) or the thickest part of the breast muscle. Be sure that the bulb does not touch a bone.

Leftover stuffings should be removed from all fowl as soon as possible. Place in a bowl and allow to cool. Then cover tightly with either aluminum foil or plastic wrap and place in the refrigerator. Stuffing can be reheated by wrapping it in aluminum foil and placing in a hot oven.

Leftover poultry meat should also be allowed to cool before being refrigerated.

PETTI DI POLLO IMPANATI
Breaded Chicken Breasts

4 medium chicken breasts
1 beaten egg
salt
fine dry bread crumbs

butter *or* margarine
lemon wedges
fresh parsley sprigs

Remove bone from chicken breasts. Wash. Dry with absorbent paper. Place between two sheets of wax paper and pound until thin. In a shallow bowl, beat egg and season with salt. Dip chicken breasts in egg; then dredge in bread crumbs.

Heat butter or margarine in a large skillet and sauté breasts until brown on both sides. Place on a warm platter. Garnish with lemon wedges and sprigs of fresh parsley. Serves 4.

PETTI DI POLLO CON PREZZEMOLO
Chicken Breasts with Parsley

2 large chicken breasts
1 large clove minced garlic
1 tsp. oregano

3 tbs. fresh minced parsley *or* 3 tsp. dry parsley
salt and pepper to taste
3 tbs. olive oil

Remove bone from chicken breasts. Wash. Dry with absorbent paper. Flatten. Cut each in half. Then sprinkle both sides with garlic, oregano, parsley, salt and pepper. Grease bottom of a 2-quart baking dish with olive oil. Place chicken breasts in dish. Coat entirely with 3 tbs. olive oil. Cook in a preheated oven at 350°F. for 45 minutes or until tender and brown. Serves 3–4.

PETTI DI POLLO AL CURRY
Chicken Breasts with Curry

4 large chicken breasts
1/4 lb. butter
1/2 cup dry white wine
salt to taste

1/2 tsp. cayenne
1 tsp. curry powder (optional)
2 tbs. flour

Remove bone and skin from breasts. Wash. Dry with absorbent paper. Heat butter in a large skillet. Sprinkle chicken breasts with salt and cook until brown and tender. Add white wine. Over high flame, bring to a boil. Lower flame. Mix in cayenne and curry powder. Cover for 2 minutes. Remove chicken from pan and keep warm. Add flour to pan drippings, mixing until sauce thickens. Place chicken on a platter and pour sauce over it. Serves 7–8.

POLLO CON SALVIA
Chicken with Sage

1 roasting chicken (4 lbs.)

juice of 1 large lemon

1 large clove garlic

1 tsp. minced fresh parsley

1/4 cup butter

1/4 cup olive oil

salt and pepper to taste

1/2 tsp. dry sage leaves

In a small bowl, beat lemon juice, garlic and parsley. Set aside. Wash and cut chicken into serving pieces. Dry well. Rub chicken with butter and oil. Sprinkle with salt, pepper and sage. Place chicken in a 10"x14"x2" pan. Cook in a preheated oven at 350°F. for 1 hour or until tender. After 30 minutes, turn pieces. When done, pour lemon mixture over chicken. Cook 1 minute longer. Serve very hot. Serves 4–6.

POLLO ALLA CACCIATORA #1
Chicken, Hunter's Style #1

1 frying chicken (3 lbs.)

1/4 cup olive oil

2 tbs. butter

1/2 tsp. dry sage leaves

1 medium onion, chopped

1 clove minced garlic

1 cup canned plum tomatoes, mashed

salt and pepper to taste

1/2 lb. frozen peas

1 cup hot water

Wash chicken and cut into serving pieces. Dry. In a large skillet, heat olive oil, butter and sage. Cook chicken over medium flame on both sides for 10 minutes. Add onion and garlic. Cook until golden. Then add tomatoes. Over low flame, simmer for 10 minutes, stirring frequently. Add salt, pepper, peas and water. Cover. Cook until chicken and peas are tender. Serves 3–4.

POLLO ALLA CACCIATORA #2
Chicken, Hunter's Style #2

1 frying chicken (3 lbs.)

flour

1/3 cup olive oil

1 large chopped onion

salt and pepper to taste

1/2 cup red wine

1 cup tomato sauce

1/4 lb. sliced fresh mushrooms

Cut chicken into serving pieces. Wash well. Dry with absorbent paper. Then roll in flour.

Heat olive oil in a large skillet and sauté onion over low flame until light brown. Remove onion and set aside. Place chicken pieces in same pan. Sprinkle with salt and pepper. When chicken is brown on both sides, return onion to pan with wine and tomato sauce. Cover. Simmer 15 minutes. Add mushrooms. Simmer 15 minutes more or until chicken is tender. Stir sauce and turn chicken occasionally. Serves 4. (See color photo on page 6.)

POLLO ALLA PARMIGIANA
Chicken Parmesan

2 lbs. roasting chicken (cut into serving pieces)
1 egg
2 tbs. water
1/2 cup flour

3/4 cup grated Parmesan cheese
salt and pepper to taste
1 tsp. oregano
3 1/2 tbs. melted butter

Wash chicken pieces. Beat egg and water in a shallow bowl. In another bowl, combine flour, 1/2 cup grated cheese, salt, pepper and oregano. Dip chicken in egg, then in flour and cheese mixture. Put chicken in a 2-1/2-quart casserole and pour melted butter over it. Bake in a preheated oven at 400°F. for 45 minutes, brushing occasionally with butter. Before serving, sprinkle with remaining grated Parmesan cheese. Serves 3–4.

POLLO CON FUNGHI
Chicken with Mushrooms

3 lbs. frying chicken
3 tbs. olive oil
3 tbs. butter
1 lb. fresh sliced mushrooms
1 strip chopped proscuitto
1 sprig chopped parsley

1 clove minced garlic
4 chopped scallions
salt and pepper to taste
5 tbs. canned plum tomatoes, mashed
1/2 tsp. oregano
1/2 cup dry white wine

Cut chicken into serving pieces. Wash. Dry with absorbent paper. Heat olive oil and butter in a large skillet. Add chicken and cook over medium flame for 25 minutes or until almost done. Add mushrooms, proscuitto, parsley, garlic, scallions, salt and pepper. Sauté for 5 minutes. Add tomatoes and oregano. Continue cooking for 10 minutes or until chicken is done. Turn occasionally. Add white wine. Cover. Cook for 1 minute. Serve hot. Serves 3–4.

POLLO ALLA DIAVOLO
Deviled Chicken

2 lbs. frying chicken
1/2 cup olive oil

salt to taste
cayenne to taste

Wash chicken. Then split chicken in half. Flatten halves as much as possible. Dry.
Heat olive oil in a large skillet. Add chicken and cook over medium flame until tender and golden brown. While cooking, sprinkle with salt and cayenne to taste. Brush pieces frequently with oil from pan until done. Serve very hot with drippings left in pan. Serves 2–3.

POLLO BRASATO CON SHERRY
Braised Chicken with Sherry

3 lbs. frying chicken
1 stick butter
1 finely chopped medium onion

salt and pepper to taste
1/4 cup water
1/4 cup dry sherry

Cut chicken into serving pieces. Wash. Dry with absorbent paper. Heat butter in a large skillet. Add chicken and cook over medium flame for 10 minutes. Then add onion and allow to become golden. Sprinkle with salt and pepper. Add water. Cover. Lower flame. Simmer for about 25 minutes or until tender. Turn pieces while simmering to cook other side. Add dry sherry and continue to cook for 10 minutes. Serves 3—4.

POLLO FANTASIA CON VEGETALI
Fancy Chicken with Vegetables

3 lbs. frying chicken, cut in serving pieces
2 tbs. butter
2 tbs. olive oil
salt and black pepper
pinch of rosemary
1/4 lb. fresh mushrooms

juice of 1/2 lemon
2/3 cup dry white wine
2 tbs. dry sherry
2 tbs. chicken broth *or* consommé
9 oz. pkg. frozen artichoke hearts
chopped fresh parsley

Wash chicken pieces and dry with absorbent paper. In a large skillet, over low flame, melt butter and heat olive oil. Raise heat to medium. Place chicken in pan. Sprinkle with salt and pepper. Cook until golden brown. Lower flame. Add rosemary. Cover. Let cook for 30 minutes or until tender, turning pieces now and then. Remove chicken from skillet and place on a serving platter. Keep warm.

Wash mushrooms, but do not soak. Slice and place in same skillet. Add lemon juice, white wine, dry sherry and broth.

Meanwhile, cook artichoke hearts according to package directions. Add to ingredients in skillet and mix. Heat thoroughly over medium flame. Then pour hot mixture over chicken pieces. Sprinkle with chopped fresh parsley and serve immediately. Serves 4.

POLLO ALLA CONTADINA
Chicken, Farmer's Style

1 frying chicken (3 lbs.)
1/2 cup olive oil
1/2 tsp. rosemary
1/8 tsp. garlic powder
salt and pepper to taste

4 strips chopped bacon
2 cups canned plum tomatoes, mashed
2 cups chicken broth
1/4 cup olive oil
4 quartered potatoes

Cut chicken in half. Wash. Dry with absorbent paper. Heat 1/2 cup olive oil in a large skillet or Dutch oven. Place chicken pieces in hot oil and sprinkle them with rosemary, garlic powder, salt and pepper. Cook over medium flame until chicken is golden brown. Then add bacon, tomatoes, and chicken broth. Over high flame, bring to a full boil. Lower flame. Cover partially and simmer until chicken is tender.

Meanwhile, in a medium-size skillet, heat 1/4 cup olive oil and fry potatoes until tender and golden. Add potatoes to chicken gravy. Simmer for 5 minutes. Serves 4.

POLLO IMBOTTITO
Stuffed Chicken

1 roasting chicken (4 lbs.)
2 tbs. butter
salt and pepper to taste

1/2 tsp. oregano
2 tbs. olive oil

Stuffing:

1/2 lb. ground beef, cooked
4 slices milk-soaked bread (without crusts)
1 egg
2 tbs. grated Romano cheese

1 tbs. fresh minced parsley *or* 1 tsp. dry parsley
1 small minced onion
salt and pepper to taste
pinch of poultry seasoning

Wash chicken and dry. Rub inside with 1 tbs. of butter. Combine stuffing ingredients. Stuff chicken. Sew or skewer together to prevent stuffing from falling out. Rub outside of chicken with 1 tbs. butter. Sprinkle with salt, pepper and oregano. Grease bottom of a 9"x13"x2" roasting pan with olive oil. Place chicken in pan. Roast in a preheated oven at 350°F. for 1 hour 15 minutes or until tender. Baste occasionally. Serves 6.

POLLO SICILIANA SAUTE
Sicilian Sautéed Chicken

1/2 lb. small onions
3 lb. chicken, cut in serving pieces
3 tbs. butter
1/4 cup olive oil
salt and pepper to taste

1/2 cup dry Marsala
2 peeled, seeded diced tomatoes
2 sprigs parsley
1/2 cup chicken stock

Peel onions. In a medium-size pot, place onions in enough salted water to cover. Boil 5 minutes. Drain. Heat butter and olive oil in a large skillet. Add chicken and onions and brown slightly on all sides. Season with salt and pepper and add dry Marsala. Over low flame, simmer until Marsala is reduced by half. Add tomatoes, parsley and chicken stock. Cover pan and continue to cook for 30 to 40 minutes or until tender, adding more stock if necessary. Arrange chicken on a hot platter and pour the sauce over it. Serves 4.

FEGATINI DI POLLO CON CIPOLLA
Chicken Livers with Onion

9 chicken livers
1/4 cup olive oil
2 tbs. butter

1 large sliced onion
1 tsp. dry parsley
salt and pepper to taste

Heat olive oil and butter in a medium-size skillet. Add chicken livers, onion and parsley. Cook over high flame for 7 minutes, stirring frequently. When done, sprinkle with salt and pepper. Serve immediately with pan drippings. Serves 3.

POLLO IMPANATO IN TEGAME
Pan-Fried Breaded Chicken

1 frying chicken (3 lbs.)
2 beaten eggs
1 cup fine bread crumbs
1 sprig fresh parsley, chopped

1 clove minced garlic
1/2 tsp. marjoram
salt and pepper to taste
1/2 cup olive oil

Have chicken cut into serving pieces. Wash. Dry with absorbent paper. In a shallow dish, combine bread crumbs, parsley, garlic, marjoram, salt and pepper. Dip chicken pieces in eggs. Roll in bread crumb mixture. Heat olive oil in a large skillet and fry chicken over medium flame until golden brown and tender. Serves 4.

CAPONE IMBOTTITO
Stuffed Capon

7 lb. capon
2 tbs. butter

salt and pepper to taste

Stuffing:

1 lb. Italian sweet sausage (skinned and crumbled)
6 finely chopped scallions
6 slices bread (without crusts), crumbled and
  moistened with milk
10 roasted chopped chestnuts

8 large green olives, pitted and chopped
8 chopped mushrooms
4 tbs. grated Parmesan cheese
2 eggs
salt and pepper to taste

Wash and dry capon with absorbent paper. In a large skillet, cook sausage and scallions for 10 minutes. Place in a bowl. Add crumbled bread, chestnuts, olives, mushrooms, cheese, eggs, salt and pepper. Mix. Stuff capon with mixture. Sew or skewer together. Rub butter over capon. Place in a 9"x 13"x 2" roasting pan. Sprinkle with salt and pepper. Cook in a preheated oven at 325°F. for 2 1/2 hours or until tender. Baste occasionally. Serves 7–8.

It has been recorded that capon stuffed with pine nuts, chicken liver, rice, grated lemon peel and fresh mint was a delicacy of the ancient Roman table and a specialty in the Brutus household. Well, this is our favorite recipe for stuffing a capon.

PICCIONE ALLA PERUGINA
Squab Perugian Style

3 squabs
3 tbs. olive oil
1 cup dry Marsala
2 tbs. olive oil

8 ripe green olives
4 fresh sage leaves *or* 3/4 tsp. dry sage leaves
salt and pepper to taste

Clean squabs. Wash thoroughly in water to which baking soda has been added. Rinse under clear water and then dry.

Heat 3 tbs. olive oil in a heavy 2-1/2-quart casserole. Brown squabs on all sides over medium flame. Remove from flame. Add Marsala, olive oil, olives, sage leaves, salt and pepper. Roast in a preheated oven at 300°F. for 50 minutes to 1 hour or until well done. Baste frequently. If more liquid is needed, add more Marsala. Serves 3.

PICCIONI CON VINO BIANCO
Squabs with White Wine

6 squabs
garlic powder
1/2 tsp. dry sage leaves
salt and pepper to taste
6 strips proscuitto, cut in halves

1/4 cup olive oil
1/2 stick butter
1/2 cup dry white wine
juice of 1 lemon

Clean squabs. Wash thoroughly in water to which baking soda has been added. Rinse under clear water and then dry. Sprinkle each cavity with garlic powder, sage, salt and pepper. Fill with 1/2 tsp. butter and 2 halves of proscuitto. Season outside of squabs with salt and pepper.

Heat olive oil and remaining butter in a large skillet and cook squabs over low flame until brown and tender on all sides. Add white wine. Remove from heat. Cover and let stand for 10 minutes. Skim excess fat from top. Add lemon juice and stir. Heat. Place squabs on a platter and pour liquid from pan over them. Serves 6.

ANITRA ALL' ARANCIO
Duck with Orange Sauce

4 lb. duck
salt and pepper
1 orange (peeled and quartered)

1 clove minced garlic
4 tbs. butter

Orange Sauce:
1 3/4 cups chicken stock
2 tbs. brandy
juice of 1 orange

1 duck liver, mashed
2 tsp. flour
2 tbs. butter

Have duck cleaned. Cut off tips of wings. Wash thoroughly, inside and out. Dry. Sprinkle inside of duck with salt. Sprinkle outside with salt and pepper. Place orange and garlic in cavity of duck. Heat 4 tbs. butter in a Dutch oven or deep skillet and cook duck on all sides, over low flame, until tender. When done, pour off fat and remove duck to a warm platter. Remove orange and garlic from cavity. To same pan, add chicken stock, brandy, orange juice, and duck liver. When it starts to boil, add flour and butter. Stir for 2—3 minutes or until somewhat thick. Pour hot orange sauce over individual servings of duck. Serves 4.

ANITRA BRASATO CON VINO ROSSO
Braised Duck with Red Wine

4 lb. duck
1 1/2 cups dry red wine
1 thinly sliced onion
1 bay leaf
1/2 tsp. oregano

1 sprig minced fresh parsley
1 clove crushed garlic
2 1/2 tbs. butter
salt and pepper to taste

Have duck cleaned and cut into serving pieces. Wash thoroughly. Dry. In a large, deep bowl, combine red wine, onion, bay leaf, oregano, parsley and garlic. Place duck in liquid. Cover. Marinate for 3 1/2 hours in refrigerator. Reserve marinade. Remove duck and place on a rack. Allow to dry.

Heat butter in a Dutch oven. Over medium flame, cook duck pieces seasoned with salt and pepper until golden. Pour off fat. Add marinade. Cover. Over low flame, simmer for 1 hour and 15 minutes or until tender. Turn pieces occasionally. Serves 4.

ANITRA ARROSTITO
Roast Duck

4 lb. duck
1 clove crushed garlic
1 medium onion, whole

1/2 stalk celery, cut in half
salt and pepper
rosemary

Have duck cleaned. Wash well inside and out. Dry. Rub inside of duck with garlic. Place onion and celery in cavity. Skewer or sew together. Rub outside with garlic, salt and pepper. Sprinkle with rosemary. Stand duck on a rack in a 9"x13"x2" roasting pan. Roast in a preheated oven at 325°F. for about 1 1/2 hours to 1 hour 45 minutes or until tender. Prick skin often while roasting to release fat. Discard onion and celery from cavity. Serves 4.

TACCHINO AL FORNO
Roast Turkey

4 lb. turkey
1 large clove crushed garlic
butter

salt and pepper
1/2 tsp. thyme
4 strips fat bacon

Clean and wash turkey. Dry with absorbent paper. Rub outside with garlic, butter and thyme. Rub inside with butter and then season inside with salt and pepper. Insert garlic. Sew or skewer opening together. Place in a 9"x13"x2" roasting pan. Arrange bacon strips over breast. Roast in a preheated oven at 350°F. for 1 hour 45 minutes or until tender. Baste frequently. Remove from oven. Let stand 20 minutes for easier carving. Serves 4.

TACCHINO ALLA FIORENTINA
Florentine Turkey

4–6 lb. turkey   salt
butter

Stuffing*:

1/4 lb. sweet Italian sausage (1/2 cup)   3 slices bacon
3 prunes   turkey liver and gizzard, chopped
1 pear, cut in half   1/4 cup dry white wine
3 tbs. chestnut purée

For Pan:

1 whole carrot   1/4 tsp. rosemary
1 whole turnip   1/2 slice chopped bacon
1 clove garlic, peeled and cut in half   1 onion stuck with 3 cloves

Clean, wash and dry turkey. Cook pear in boiling water to cover until tender. On a wooden board, chop and mix sausage, prunes, pear, chestnut puree and bacon. Place in a small saucepan and cook over medium flame for 2 minutes. Remove from heat. Add chopped liver, gizzard and wine.

Stuff turkey with mixture. Sew or skewer together. Rub turkey with butter and salt. Place in a 5-quart roaster. In bottom of pan, put 2 inches of water, carrot, turnip, garlic, rosemary, onion and bacon. Cover pan and braise turkey on top of stove for 1 hour over low flame. Remove garlic after first 10 minutes. Uncover and place roaster in a preheated oven at 325°F. Roast 10 to 15 minutes per pound, basting every half hour. When turkey is tender, remove from oven and let stand for 20 minutes before carving. Serves 4–6.

*This mixture serves more as a flavoring rather than a stuffing.

TACCHINO IMBOTTITO
Stuffed Turkey

10 lb. turkey
butter
3 tbs. olive oil

Stuffing:

3/4 lb. ground beef   1 cup cooked rice
1/2 lb. ground pork   8 chopped mushrooms
1 small minced onion   8 chopped roasted chestnuts
2 slices chopped proscuitto *or* ham   meat from 4 walnuts, chopped
1 sprig chopped fresh parsley   2 eggs
4 tbs. grated Parmesan cheese   salt and pepper to taste
1/2 tsp. basil   5 strips salt pork

Clean, wash and dry turkey. Rub inside with butter. Heat olive oil in a large skillet over medium flame and cook beef, pork and onion until light brown. Place in a large bowl. Add proscuitto, parsley, cheese, basil, rice, mushrooms, chestnuts, walnuts, eggs, salt and pepper. Mix well. Stuff turkey with mixture. Sew or skewer together. Rub outside with butter. Arrange salt pork strips over turkey. Place turkey in a 10"x14"x2" roasting pan. Cook in a preheated oven at 325°F. for 4 1/2 hours or until tender. Baste frequently. Remove from oven and let stand for 20 minutes for easier carving. Serves 10—12.

It is traditional, in Italy, for a large golden brown turkey to be triumphantly brought to the table to gladden the Christmas meal. Without a turkey or at least a large chicken, the holiday is not complete. Some prefer capon or duck, but turkey always lends more festivity to the day.

In the homes, the rejoicing centers around the *presepio*, a small representation of the birthplace of Christ, instead of around a Christmas tree. No evergreens are used, but flowers adorn the tables, and in many shops, small olive trees are hung with oranges.

VEGETABLES & SALADS 7

Ancient Roman agriculture has received special recognition because it was a favorite subject with Roman writers such as Varro, Columella and Pliny. Earlier than these and more celebrated was Cato the Censor who offers information from the plowing to the reaping of the crop.

To the list of vegetables produced in ancient Egypt and Greece, the Romans added celery to a soil primitively but thoroughly cultivated with the plow and harrow or the hoe and the rake.

The Romans were so mad for mushrooms that they became a symbol of luxury in Rome and were cooked in a set of utensils designed especially for them. The utensils were called *boletaria* and were never used for any "lesser food."

Regardless of preparation, vegetables are frequently refused by people today. But those who have tasted them with the Italian home touch agree that there is little room for improvement because of their distinct and delicious taste. Whether steamed, baked, fried or boiled, the blandest of vegetables is enhanced by the Italian cook with a few herbs and by cooking or preparing it with olive oil. In this manner, a simple salad of boiled string beans can become something surprisingly interesting and appetizing.

If she happens to live in the country, the Italian cook will most likely have her own vegetable garden to satisfy the needs of her cuisine. A garden answers her concern for the utter freshness of the product.

But gathering wild dandelions in fields or roadsides is another favorite introduction of hers to a delightful salad! If you like, try it some spring morning. After you've picked a nice bunch, rinse, dry and chill them. Then lightly toss with any desired Italian dressing. You're sure to be pleased with this *insalata franca* (free salad).

If, on the other hand, the Italian cook happens to be an urbanite, she's equally aware of the need for quality vegetables, knowing that they contribute an important vitality, unimpaired goodness and pleasure to everyone who experiences them.

Italians have such a high regard for the fresh vegetable that there is much hostility to frozen foods which have just recently taken over in Italy.

Surgelato is the name for frozen food and one is only now starting to hear the word spoken in Italian villages. Few Italian housewives would ever admit to their husbands that they are eating a *surgelato*.

But freezing does mean a wider variety of available foods in and out of season for Italians though it may run against the grain of vegetable purists who insist that there is "no substitute for the fresh vegetable."

You will also find in this chapter some favorite fish, meat and chicken salads.

A FEW VALUABLE TIPS

To Keep Parsley Fresh—Rinse parsley under cold water, then shake off excess water. Place bunch of parsley with stems in a glass container or pitcher. Pour water up to level of stems only. Keep on lowest shelf of refrigerator. Will keep crisp for several weeks or more.

Before Cooking Broccoli—Cut off the lower tough portion of the broccoli. Then peel the bottom inch of the remaining stalk. Remove any wilted leaves. Separate stalks. Split larger ones lengthwise until all are about the same thickness. Soak in cold water with 1 teaspoon of salt for 15—20 minutes to rid it of any tiny insects. Then run under clear, cool water.

MELENZANA FRITTA
Fried Eggplant

1 medium eggplant
salt
2 medium-size eggs
1/2 cup flour
3/4 cup bread crumbs

1 tsp. dry parsley *or* 1 tbs. fresh minced parsley
salt to taste
pepper to taste
3/4 cup olive oil

Peel eggplant. Cut crosswise into 1/4-inch-thick slices. In a colander, place a layer of eggplant slices. Sprinkle lightly with salt. Continue process until all of eggplant is used. Place a dish on eggplant. Place a pot filled with water on dish to force bitter fluid out of eggplant. Let stand for about three hours. (It is advisable to put colander in sink.) Dry slices.

In a shallow bowl, beat eggs well. In another shallow dish, combine flour, bread crumbs, parsley, and a small amount of salt and pepper. Dip eggplant in eggs. Dredge in bread crumb mixture. Heat olive oil in a large skillet and fry eggplant until golden brown on both sides. Drain on absorbent paper. Serves 5–6.

MELENZANA ALLA PARMIGIANA
Eggplant Parmesan

1 large eggplant
salt
2 large eggs
1 1/2 cups dry bread crumbs

1 tbs. chopped fresh parsley
small amount of salt
pepper to taste
3/4 cup olive oil

Sauce:

2 lbs. fresh plum tomatoes, cut in pieces
1 clove minced garlic
1/4 cup olive oil

1 tbs. chopped onion
4 basil leaves, chopped
salt and pepper to taste

Topping:

3 tbs. grated Parmesan cheese
1/2 lb. thinly sliced mozzarella

Wash and cut eggplant crosswise into 1/4-inch-thick slices. Place in layers in a colander, sprinkling each layer lightly with salt. Place a dish on eggplant. Place a pot filled with water on dish to force bitter fluid out of eggplant. (It is advisable to place colander in sink.) Let stand for about 3 hours. Dry slices with absorbent paper.

In a shallow bowl, beat eggs. Dip eggplant slices in eggs. Then dredge in bread crumbs combined with parsley, a small amount of salt and pepper. Heat olive oil in a large skillet and sauté eggplant slices until golden brown on both sides. Drain on absorbent paper.

Meanwhile, in a large saucepan, simmer tomatoes and garlic for 10 minutes. Then sieve tomatoes. In another saucepan, heat olive oil and cook onion until yellow. Add tomatoes, basil, salt and pepper. Cook for 15 minutes, partially covered.

Coat the bottom of a 2-quart casserole with a little sauce. Place some eggplant slices in a layer. Pour some sauce on them and distribute a few slices of mozzarella. Continue process until all ingredients are used, ending with mozzarella. Sprinkle top with Parmesan cheese. Bake in a pre-heated oven at 375° until sauce is well heated and mozzarella melts. Serves 6.

MELANZANE RIPIENI
Stuffed Eggplants

8 small eggplants (about 5 inches long)
8 small cloves garlic, quartered
32 slices provolone (1 inch long, 1/4 inch wide)

3 1/2 tsp. dry basil
salt and pepper to taste
1/2 cup olive oil

Sauce:

2 tbs. olive oil
1 tbs. chopped onion
1 tbs. tomato paste
8 oz. can tomato sauce
8 oz. water

1 clove minced garlic
1 tsp. dry basil *or* 3 large fresh basil leaves,
    chopped
salt and pepper to taste

Remove stems from eggplants. Wash. Dry with absorbent paper. Remove four 1/2-inch-wide strips of peel lengthwise from eggplants (leaving peel in between strips). Where peel is removed, make 1-inch slash. In each slash, insert 1 quartered clove of garlic, 1 provolone slice, and some basil. Sprinkle eggplants with salt and pepper.

Heat 1/2 cup olive oil in a large skillet and cook eggplants until golden brown. Meanwhile, heat 2 tbs. olive oil in a Dutch oven and, over low flame, sauté onion until yellow. Add tomato paste and water. Stir until dissolved. Add tomato sauce, garlic, basil, salt and pepper. Over high flame, bring to a boil. Lower flame. Add eggplants. Simmer for 20 minutes, partially covered, turning eggplants after 10 minutes. Stir sauce occasionally. Serve with sauce. Serves 4.

PATATE IMBOTTITE AL FORNO
Stuffed Baked Potatoes

6 medium baking potatoes
1 beaten egg
pinch of nutmeg
2 tbs. grated Parmesan cheese
1 tbs. minced scallions
2 tbs. butter *or* margarine

1 tbs. minced fresh parsley
salt and pepper to taste
1/4 cup milk
very fine bread crumbs
butter *or* margarine

Scrub potatoes well. In boiling water to cover, cook potatoes until almost tender. Cut each potato in half lengthwise. Scoop out potato pulp, being careful to leave shells intact. Put potato pulp through ricer or mash until very smooth. Add egg, nutmeg, cheese, scallions, butter, parsley, salt, pepper and milk. Beat until well blended and very smooth. Fill potato shells with mixture. Sprinkle tops with bread crumbs. Dot each with butter or margarine.

Place potatoes in a shallow 12"x16" baking pan. In a preheated oven, bake at 375°F. for 20 minutes or until a golden crust forms on top of potatoes. Serves 6.

PATATE ARROSTITI
Roast Potatoes

12 small potatoes
1 tbs. olive oil

1/2 cup pork fat, cut in pieces
salt and pepper to taste

Pare potatoes. Wash. Dry with absorbent paper. Grease bottom of a 2-1/2-quart casserole with olive oil. Place potatoes in dish. Put pork fat on potatoes. Sprinkle with salt and pepper. Bake in a preheated oven at 375°F. for 30–45 minutes or until tender. Turn occasionally. Serves 3–4.

PATATE CON CREMA
Potatoes with Cream

4 medium potatoes

4 pats butter *or* margarine

2 tsp. flour

light cream *or* milk (warm)

1 or 2 tbs. grated Parmesan cheese

salt and pepper

Wash potatoes. Boil in skins until tender. Peel. Cut in slices. Place in a medium-size bowl. Flavor hot potatoes with butter. Sprinkle with flour and mix. Add a small amount of warm (not boiling) light cream or milk to moisten flour. Mix. Right before serving, add grated Parmesan cheese, salt and pepper to taste. Serve hot. Serves 4.

TORTA DI PATATE ALLA NAPOLETANA
Neapolitan Potato Pie

2 lbs. potatoes

8 oz. grated mozzarella

2 slices minced proscuitto *or* ham

6 large eggs

4 tbs. grated Romano cheese

2 tsp. chopped fresh parsley

salt and pepper to taste

bread crumbs

Scrub potatoes thoroughly. Boil potatoes with skins in salted, boiling water for 20 minutes or until tender. Peel. Put potatoes through a ricer or mash until smooth. Place in a large bowl. Add mozzarella, proscuitto, eggs, cheese, parsley, salt and pepper. Mix well.

Grease an 8"x8"x2" baking dish. Sprinkle the bottom lightly with bread crumbs. Place potato mixture in dish. Bake in a preheated oven at 375° until golden brown. Serves 8.

CROCHE DI PATATE
Potato Croquettes

1 lb. potatoes

2 tbs. grated pecorino *or* Romano cheese

1 egg

1 clove minced garlic

1/2 tsp. dry parsley *or* 1 tbs. fresh minced parsley

1/4 cup bread crumbs

salt and pepper to taste

1/2 cup flour

1/2 cup olive oil

Scrub potatoes well. Boil potatoes with skins in salted, boiling water for 20 minutes or until tender. Drain. Peel. Put through a ricer or mash until smooth. Allow potatoes to cool. In a bowl, mix potatoes, cheese, egg, garlic, parsley, bread crumbs, salt and pepper. Form into oval-shaped croquettes about 3 inches long and 1 1/2 inch wide. Roll in flour. Heat olive oil in a large skillet and sauté croquettes over moderate flame until golden brown on both sides. Serves 4.

TORTA DI PATATE
Potato Pie

2 lbs. potatoes
3 eggs
1/2 cup grated Parmesan cheese
1 tbs. fresh chopped parsley *or* 1/2 tsp. dry
    parsley
1 tbs. butter

2 slices diced ham
salt and pepper to taste
bread crumbs
1/2 lb. ricotta
pinch of salt

Scrub potatoes well. Boil potatoes with skins in salted, boiling water for about 20 minutes or until tender. Drain. Peel. Put potatoes through a ricer, or mash until smooth. Place in a large bowl. Add 2 eggs, Parmesan cheese, parsley, ham, butter, salt and pepper.

Coat the bottom of a greased 2-quart casserole with bread crumbs. Place half the potato mixture in the casserole. Spread ricotta, seasoned with a pinch of salt, over it. Top with remaining potato mixture. Beat remaining egg well and brush it on top of potatoes. Bake in a preheated oven at 375°F. for about 35 minutes or until golden brown. Serves 6.

PATATE FRITTE
Fried Potatoes

4 medium potatoes
flour

olive oil for deep frying
salt to taste

Peel and wash potatoes. Slice 1/4 inch thick. Let potato slices stand for 2 hours in cold water, changing water to keep cold. Dry with absorbent paper. Dredge potatoes in flour. Fry in deep, hot olive oil until golden. Drain on absorbent paper. Sprinkle with salt. Serves 4.

PATATE CALDE SBATTUTE
Hot Whipped Potatoes

4 potatoes
1 tbs. butter
1 sprig minced fresh parsley
1 slice finely chopped Virginia ham

onion powder to taste
salt and white pepper to taste
1/3 cup warm milk

Scrub potatoes well with a stiff brush. In boiling, salted water to cover, cook potatoes in skins for about 20 minutes or until tender. Drain. Then peel. Put potatoes through a ricer or mash until smooth. Add butter, parsley, ham, onion powder, salt and pepper. Add milk gradually while whipping well with wire whisk until potatoes are very smooth. Serves 4.

Because Father had more than a slight aversion to butter, he insisted that Mother add olive oil to his whipped potatoes. After many years of this practice, Mother decided to test his perception one day by serving them with butter instead. Amazingly, he raved over them, even having a second helping, at which she smiled secretly.

PATATE CON SALVIA
Potatoes with Sage

4 potatoes
1/2 cup olive oil

1/4 tsp. crushed sage leaves
salt and pepper to taste

Peel and wash potatoes. Dry. Cut into eighths. In a large skillet, heat olive oil with sage. Add potatoes. Fry until golden. When almost done, sprinkle with salt and pepper. Serves 4.

CAVOLO E PATATE AFFOGATI
Steamed Cabbage and Potatoes

1 medium head cabbage
1/4 cup olive oil
1 medium sliced onion

2 peeled sliced potatoes
salt and pepper to taste

Wash cabbage. Remove core. Then chop. Heat olive oil in a large saucepan. Add onion and cook over low flame until slightly yellow. Add cabbage, potatoes, salt and pepper. Cover. Over low flame, steam for 45 minutes or until tender, stirring frequently. If too much evaporation occurs before vegetables are done, add a small amount of hot water. Serves 4.

PEPERONI VERDE E PATATE FRITTE
Fried Green Peppers and Potatoes

4 medium Italian green peppers (frying peppers)
  or bell peppers
3 medium potatoes
1/2 cup olive oil

salt to taste
1/2 tsp. crushed red pepper seeds
1 medium sliced onion
2 beaten eggs

Remove stems and seeds from peppers. Wash. Dry with absorbent paper. Cut into 1/2-inch-wide strips. Peel potatoes and cut into slices 1/8 inch thick.

Heat olive oil in a large skillet. Add potatoes and peppers; sprinkle with salt and crushed red pepper seeds and cook over low flame for 15 minutes or until almost tender. Turn occasionally. Then add onion. When golden brown, add eggs. Stir until eggs are done. Serves 4—5.

May be served as a delicious accompaniment to chicken or as a sandwich (especially good with crusty Italian bread).

Coming home for lunch as school children, we were frequently met by the drifting aroma of this dish two flights below our apartment. We entered the kitchen gratified to find Mother making delicious, nourishing sandwiches of it for us.

FAGIOLINI E PATATE
String Beans and Potatoes

1 lb. string beans
3 medium potatoes, quartered
6 tbs. olive oil
1 medium onion, chopped
3 tbs. finely chopped fresh tomato

1 clove minced garlic
6 1/2 cups water
salt and pepper to taste
1/4 cup grated Romano cheese

Wash string beans and remove tips. Heat olive oil in a large pot. Add onion and sauté over low flame until yellow. Add tomato. Simmer for 3 minutes. Add garlic and water and bring to a boil over high flame. Lower flame to medium. Add string beans. Cover the pot partially. After 20 minutes, add potatoes, salt and pepper. Cook for another 30 minutes or until tender. Serve with grated Romano cheese. Serves 3. May be served as a main dish.

ZUCCHINI AL ACETO
Squash with Vinegar

2 lbs. zucchini (Italian squash)
1/2 cup olive oil
2 whole cloves garlic
4 or 5 tbs. wine vinegar

salt to taste
pinch of crushed red pepper seeds *or* black
    pepper to taste
2 finely chopped mint leaves

Scrub zucchini well. Remove stem and blossom ends. Slice zucchini crosswise into 1/4-inch-thick slices. In a large skillet, cook zucchini in hot olive oil over medium-low flame until tender and golden brown on both sides. Remove zucchini to a medium-size bowl. In the same oil, cook garlic over low flame until golden. Stir in vinegar, salt and crushed red pepper seeds or pepper and heat well. Remove garlic. Pour liquid over zucchini. Toss lightly. Sprinkle with fresh mint. Serve hot or cold. Serves 4.

ZUCCHINI CON SALSA DI POMODORO
Squash with Tomato Sauce

6 medium-size zucchini (Italian squash)
1/2 cup olive oil
1 medium chopped onion
1 cup canned plum tomatoes, mashed
2 tbs. fresh chopped basil *or* 1 tsp. dry basil

salt to taste
black pepper to taste *or* pinch of crushed red
    pepper seeds
1/4 cup grated Romano cheese

Scrub zucchini well. Remove stem and blossom ends. Cut crosswise in 1/4-inch-thick slices. In a large skillet, cook zucchini in hot olive oil over medium-low flame until light brown on both sides. Remove from pan. In same oil, sauté onion over low flame until golden. Add tomatoes, basil, salt and pepper. Cook for 10 minutes. Add zucchini. Mix. Cook for 5 minutes more. Place in a bowl and sprinkle with grated Romano cheese. Serves 6.

During World War II, many Americans raised "victory gardens" as part of the national defense effort. Employed as a railroad mechanic, Father managed to grow, among other things, squash and tomatoes in a cleared plot in the railroad yard. It was not unusual for him to come home proudly displaying an array of colorful vegetables accompanied by a bunch of marigolds, his favorite flowers, for Mother. We anticipated this fresh summer delight of squash augmented by tomato sauce.

Zucchini Casserole

CASSERUOLA DI ZUCCHINI
Zucchini Casserole

3 tbs. olive oil	pinch of rosemary
1 medium onion, thinly sliced	pinch of sage
1 lb. ground beef *or* 2 cups ground leftover cooked beef	pinch of thyme
	dash of garlic powder *or* garlic salt
three 8 oz. cans tomato sauce	1 tbs. sugar
1 cup Burgundy, Claret or other red dinner wine	salt and pepper to taste
1/4 tsp. oregano	6–7 medium zucchini (2 lbs.)
1/4 tsp. basil	grated Parmesan cheese

Heat olive oil in a Dutch oven or large, heavy skillet. Add onion and beef and cook, stirring frequently, until meat is nicely browned. Add tomato sauce, wine, oregano, basil, rosemary, sage, thyme, garlic powder, sugar, salt and pepper. Cover and simmer very gently for 1 hour, stirring occasionally.

While sauce is cooking, wash zucchini and trim off ends. Cook whole in boiling salted water for about 15 minutes or just until tender. Drain. When cool enough to handle, cut lengthwise in halves and arrange, cut side up, in a single layer in a greased shallow baking dish. Pour sauce over zucchini. Bake in a preheated oven at 350°F. for 45 minutes. Serve with grated Parmesan cheese. Serves 5–6.

Makes an ideal entree for a spring buffet. Serve with a tossed green salad, crusty Italian bread and Strawberries with Meringue for dessert. **(See photo above.)**

ZUCCHINI RIPIENI
Stuffed Squash

4 medium-size zucchini (Italian squash)
1/4 cup olive oil
1/2 lb. ground beef
1/2 medium onion, chopped

2 tbs. grated Romano cheese
1 egg
salt and pepper to taste

Scrub zucchini thoroughly. Remove stem and blossom ends. Cut into halves lengthwise. In a medium-size pot, cook in boiling, salted water for 12 minutes, covered. Drain. Remove pulp and chop well.

Meanwhile, heat olive oil in a large skillet. Add beef and onion and cook over medium flame for 10 minutes. Remove from heat. Combine with zucchini pulp, cheese, egg, salt and pepper. Fill squash with mixture and place in a greased baking dish. Bake in a preheated oven at 375°F. for 15 minutes or until tender. Serves 4.

PEPERONI IMBOTTITI #1
Stuffed Peppers #1

8 Italian green peppers *or* medium-size bell
   peppers*
1 lb. spinach
1/4 cup olive oil
1/2 lb. ground beef
1/2 minced medium onion

1/2 cup fine dry bread crumbs
1/4 cup grated Romano cheese
1 egg
salt and pepper to taste
olive oil

Wash peppers and remove seeds and stems. Dry with absorbent paper. Wash spinach thoroughly, until grit-free. Put spinach in a large pot with water still clinging to the leaves. Cover and cook for 5 minutes (without adding extra water). Drain well and chop finely.

Heat olive oil in a medium-size skillet. Add beef and onion. Cook over medium flame until beef loses its red color. Remove to a large bowl. Add spinach, bread crumbs, cheese, egg, salt and pepper. Mix well. Fill peppers. Arrange peppers in a greased 2-1/2-quart casserole. Pour some olive oil over them. Sprinkle with salt. Bake in a preheated oven at 375°F. for 30 minutes or until tender. Serves 8.

*If using bell peppers, parboil 5 minutes and drain before stuffing.

PEPERONI IMBOTTITI #2
Stuffed Peppers #2

8 Italian green peppers *or* medium bell peppers*
1/2 lb. chopped Italian sweet sausage (without
   casings)
1 small chopped onion
4 sliced mushrooms
1 cup cooked rice

1 tsp. dry parsley
2 tbs. grated Romano cheese
1 egg
salt and pepper to taste
olive oil

Wash peppers well. Remove seeds and stems. Dry. In a medium-size skillet, cook sausage over low flame. When nearly done, add onion. Cook until onion is yellow. Place in a large bowl. In same pan, cook mushrooms for 5 minutes. Remove and chop. Combine sausage mixture with mushrooms, rice, parsley, cheese, egg, salt and pepper. Fill peppers with stuffing. Place peppers in a greased 2-1/2-quart casserole. Coat peppers with olive oil. Sprinkle with salt and pepper. Bake in a preheated oven at 375°F. for 30 minutes or until tender. Serves 8.

*If using bell peppers, parboil 5 minutes and drain before stuffing.

PEPERONI ARROSTITI
Roasted Peppers

2 lbs. red bell peppers*
1 clove minced garlic
3 tbs. olive oil

1/2 tsp. oregano
salt to taste
pinch of crushed red pepper seeds

Wash and dry peppers. Place on broiler rack 6 inches below medium flame. Roast about 10 minutes or until skins blacken and blister on all sides. Turn frequently to prevent burning. Remove and place peppers in a paper bag. Close tightly. Let stand for 10 minutes. (This process makes removing skins easier.) Remove skins, stems and seeds. Cut lengthwise into 1/2-inch-thick strips.

Place peppers in a medium-size bowl. Add garlic, olive oil, oregano, salt and pepper. Mix well. May be served warm or cold with fish, fowl or meat; or, if desired, as a delicious sandwich. Serves 6.

*If red bell peppers are not available, buy green bell peppers. Place them in a paper bag and close tightly. Let stand until they turn red. Maturing time depends on size.

PEPERONI VERDI E CIPOLLE FRITTE
Fried Green Peppers and Onions

6 Italian green peppers *or* 4 large bell peppers
2 large onions, cut into 1/2-inch cubes

6 tbs. olive oil
salt and pepper to taste

Cut peppers into 1/2-inch cubes. Heat olive oil in a large skillet over low flame. Add peppers. Raise flame to medium. Fry until peppers are half-tender. Lower flame. Add onions. Season with salt and pepper. Cook until peppers and onions are tender. Stir frequently. Serves 6.

Delicious with Fried or Grilled Italian Sausage.

POMODORI VERDI FRITTE
Fried Green Tomatoes

4 medium green-wrap tomatoes*
1 egg
2 tbs. flour
2 tbs. fine dry bread crumbs

2 or 3 fresh minced basil leaves *or* 1/8 tsp. dry basil leaves
salt and pepper to taste
1/2 cup olive oil

Wash tomatoes. Remove tops and slice tomatoes horizontally 1/4 inch thick. Remove seeds.

(Continued on following page.)

In a small bowl, beat egg well. Dip slices in egg. Then dredge in combined flour and bread crumbs, basil, salt and pepper.

Heat olive oil in a large skillet. Fry tomato slices over low flame until golden brown on both sides. Drain on absorbent paper. Serve immediately. Serves 4.

Serve with steak, sausage, meatballs, fish or omelets.

*Green-wrap tomatoes are those that have been picked before they are ripe and stored for winter consumption.

PISELLI FRESCHI CON UOVA
Fresh Peas with Eggs

2 lbs. very young fresh peas *or* frozen peas
6 eggs
4 strips diced bacon

1 chopped medium onion
1 cup beef bouillon
salt and pepper to taste

If fresh peas are used, shell them. In a large skillet, cook bacon over low flame until crisp. Remove and set aside. Cook onion in bacon fat for 2 minutes. Add beef bouillon, peas and pepper. Cover. Simmer over low flame for about 10 minutes or until tender. If bouillon evaporates before peas are tender, add small amount of boiling water. Add bacon and mix. Test for salt; if needed, add a little.

In three rows (2 eggs to a row), break eggs carefully on top of peas. Sprinkle lightly with salt and pepper. Cook for 5 minutes more or until eggs are set. Serves 6.

PISELLI CON SALSA
Peas with Sauce

1 lb. frozen peas
3 tbs. butter *or* margarine
2 finely sliced small onions
2 tbs. flour
2 cups hot beef broth *or* bouillon

salt and pepper to taste
1 tsp. sugar
a few lettuce leaves, shredded
1/2 tbs. butter *or* margarine

In a medium-size saucepan, heat 3 tbs. butter or margarine. Add onion and cook over low flame until tender and golden. With a wooden spoon, mix in flour well. Add hot broth gradually and stir constantly until smooth and somewhat thick. Add peas. Season with salt and pepper. Simmer until peas are half-cooked (about 5 minutes), stirring frequently. Add sugar, wet lettuce leaves and 1/2 tbs. butter. Continue cooking until peas are tender (about 5 minutes). Serves 4.

Serve with fowl, lamb, beef or pork.

PISELLI CON SPARAGI
Peas with Asparagus

1 lb. frozen peas
1 lb. fresh asparagus
1/4 cup olive oil
4 strips diced bacon

1/2 medium minced onion
salt and pepper to taste
1 cup boiling water

Wash asparagus. Cut into 1-inch pieces. Discard tough ends. Heat olive oil in a large saucepan. Over low flame cook bacon and onion until yellow. Add peas, asparagus, salt and pepper. Cover. Steam over low flame for 8 minutes. Then add water. Cook covered for 10 minutes more or until tender. Stir occasionally. If too much evaporation occurs, add some hot water. Serves 4.

CAROTE AL BURRO
Buttered Carrots

1 bunch tender carrots (1 1/4 lbs.)
1/2 tsp. sugar
butter *or* margarine

1 tbs. dry white wine
salt and pepper to taste

Scrape carrots. Leave whole. Wash. In a large pot, boil carrots in salted water with sugar until tender (but not overcooked). Drain. Cut into thin slices. Season with butter, white wine, salt and pepper. Serves 4.

CAROTE AFFOGATI
Steamed Carrots

4 medium carrots
3 tbs. butter

salt to taste
1/2 tsp. sugar

Scrape carrots. Wash. Then cut into 1/8-inch-thick slices. Heat butter in a small saucepan. Add carrots, sprinkle with salt, cover and cook until tender, stirring occasionally. A few minutes before carrots are done, add sugar. Stir. Serves 2–3.

CARCIOFI CON VINO BIANCO
Artichoke Hearts with White Wine

6 frozen artichoke hearts
3 tbs. olive oil
1 small finely chopped onion
1 tbs. fresh minced parsley *or* 1 tsp. dry parsley
1 clove minced garlic

salt and pepper to taste
pinch of mint
2 1/2 tbs. white wine
1/2 cup chicken stock

Heat olive oil in a medium-size saucepan and sauté onion over low flame until yellow. Add artichoke hearts, parsley, garlic, salt, pepper and mint. Over low flame, cook for 5 minutes. Add white wine and chicken stock. Cover. Continue cooking until tender. Serves 3.

CARCIOFI IMBOTTITI NAPOLETANI
Stuffed Artichokes Neapolitan

8 fresh young globe artichokes
24 chopped Gaeta olives *or* black olives
2 large cloves minced garlic
2 sprigs finely chopped fresh parsley
2 tbs. unsalted minced capers

salt and pepper to taste
1 1/2 cups water
1/2 tsp. salt
olive oil
fine bread crumbs

Lay artichokes on sides. Cut about 1/2 inch from tips of artichoke leaves. Cut off all spine tips. Pull off loose leaves around bottom. Wash. Remove any excess water from between leaves by holding artichokes upside down and tapping.

In a medium-size bowl, combine olives, garlic, parsley and capers. With this mixture, stuff between leaves. Sprinkle between with salt and pepper to taste.

Pour 1 1/2 cups of water with 1/2 tsp. salt on bottom of an 8"x8"x2" baking dish. Place artichokes upright and snug in dish. Pour olive oil generously over each artichoke. Sprinkle tops with bread crumbs. Bake in a preheated oven at 350°F. for 45 minutes or until outer leaves come off easily. Serves 8.

CARCIOFI ARROSTITI
Roasted Artichokes

6 medium-size fresh globe artichokes
4 cloves minced garlic
6 sprigs fresh parsley, finely chopped

salt and pepper to taste
1/2 cup olive oil
12 tbs. olive oil

Lay artichokes on sides. Cut about 1/2 inch from tips of artichoke leaves. Cut off all spine tips. Pull off loose leaves around bottom. Wash. Remove any excess water from between leaves by holding artichokes upside down and tapping. Stuff with garlic and parsley between leaves and sprinkle between with salt and pepper.

In a large saucepan with 1/2 cup of olive oil, place artichokes upright and snug. Pour 2 tbs. of olive oil over each artichoke. Cover. Cook over low flame until artichokes are tender or outer leaves come off easily. Serves 6.

CARCIOFI FRITTI
Fried Artichokes

15 oz. can artichoke hearts in brine
flour
2 lightly beaten eggs

flavored bread crumbs
deep olive oil
lemon wedges

Drain artichokes. Rinse in cold water and drain well. Cut into quarters. Dredge in flour lightly. Dip in eggs and dip in bread crumbs, coating well.

In a large skillet with hot olive oil (deep enough to make them float), fry artichoke slices until a golden brown. Serve hot with wedges of lemon. Serves 6.

If desired, may also be served as an appetizer.

CARCIOFI IMBOTTITI ALLA SICILIANA
Stuffed Artichokes, Sicilian Style

4 medium-size fresh globe artichokes
3/4 cup bread crumbs
2 tbs. grated Romano cheese
1 tsp. dry parsley *or* 1 1/2 tbs. finely chopped
    fresh parsley

1 clove minced garlic
salt and pepper to taste
4 tbs. olive oil
3 cups water
1/3 tsp. salt

Lay artichokes on sides. Cut about 1/2 inch from tips of artichoke leaves. Cut off all spine tips. Pull off loose leaves around bottom. Wash artichokes. Remove excess water from between leaves by holding upside down and tapping.

In a small bowl, combine bread crumbs, cheese, garlic, parsley, salt and pepper. Divide mixture into four parts. Stuff between artichoke leaves.

In a medium-size saucepan with 3 cups of water and 1/3 tsp. of salt, place artichokes to stand upright and snug. Pour 1 tbs. of olive oil over top of each artichoke. Cover pan partially. Over low flame, cook for 25–30 minutes or until outer leaves can be easily removed. Serves 4.

We wait for spring globe artichokes every year to experience their tender, fresh flavor. Mother's stuffing enhances them and perhaps will tempt those who find the artichoke a vegetable holding impenetrable mysteries. But it really has no secrets, except to deeply please those who will give a few moments to learn how to prepare and eat it.

To eat: Pull off petals one by one and eat only the tender base part of the leaf and stuffing by drawing between teeth. Discard remaining part of leaf on a dish. Continue until you come to a fuzzy center or "choke" which you remove with a spoon by scooping it out. Cut artichoke base or heart into bite-size pieces.

SPARAGI AFFOGATI
Steamed Asparagus

2 lbs. fresh asparagus
1/4 cup olive oil
1 small chopped onion
2 large ripe tomatoes, finely chopped

1 clove minced garlic
salt and pepper to taste
1 cup hot water
1/4 cup grated Romano cheese (optional)

Wash asparagus. Cut into 2-inch pieces. Discard tough ends. Heat olive oil in a medium-size saucepan and sauté onion over low flame until slightly tender. Add tomatoes. Cook for 3 minutes. Add asparagus, garlic, salt and pepper. Stir. Cover and steam for 4–5 minutes. Add 1 cup hot water. Cover. Continue cooking for 8–20 minutes or until tender. The length of cooking time depends on the thickness and tenderness of the stalks. In case too much evaporation occurs, add some hot water.

If desired, sprinkle with grated Romano cheese. Serves 6.

SPARAGI IN PASTELLA
Asparagus in Batter

1/2 lb. fresh asparagus
corn oil for deep frying

Batter:

1 egg, separated
1/2 cup sifted flour
salt and pepper to taste

1/2 tbs. olive oil
about 1/2 cup cold water

Wash asparagus. Cut into 2-inch pieces. Discard tough ends. In a medium-size bowl, beat egg yolk. Add flour, salt, pepper, olive oil and enough water to make a consistency of pancake batter (about 1/2 cup). Beat well. Cover and let stand for 1 hour. When ready to use, beat egg white until stiff. Fold into mixture. Dip asparagus pieces in batter. Fry in deep, hot corn oil until tender and golden brown. Drain on absorbent paper. Serves 6.

BARBABIETOLE IN SALSA
Beets in Sauce

1 lb. can whole beets *or* 5 fresh cooked beets
3 tbs. butter
1 medium sliced onion
1 tbs. flour
1 cup hot chicken broth *or* bouillon

1 tbs. wine vinegar
pinch of cumin seeds
salt and pepper to taste
1 tbs. grated Parmesan cheese

Cut beets into strips. Set aside. In a medium-size skillet, sauté sliced onions in hot butter over low flame until yellow. Add flour and stir into onions until well blended. Then gradually add hot broth and stir until smooth. Add beets, vinegar, cumin seeds, salt and pepper. Mix well and let heat through, stirring occasionally until sauce thickens slightly. Place in a serving bowl and sprinkle with grated Parmesan cheese. Serve immediately. Serves 4.

SCAROLA SAPORITA
Savory Escarole

2 lbs. escarole
2 qts. salted water
1/4 cup olive oil
1 large clove minced garlic

2 tbs. canned plum tomatoes, mashed
salt and pepper to taste
grated Parmesan *or* Romano cheese (optional)

Remove undesirable leaves from escarole. Wash escarole and cut leaves in half crosswise. In a large pot, bring salted water to a boil. Add escarole. Cook, partially covered, over high flame for 15 minutes (water must boil vigorously).

Meanwhile, in a medium-size saucepan over low flame, heat olive oil with garlic until oil starts to bubble. Then add tomatoes. Cook for 1 minute and set aside. Lift out escarole with a fork and place in saucepan with oil, tomatoes, salt and pepper. Mix well. Let cook over medium flame, covered, for 5 minutes. If desired, sprinkle individual servings with grated Parmesan or Romano cheese. Serves 6. Serve with boiled fish or any type of meat.

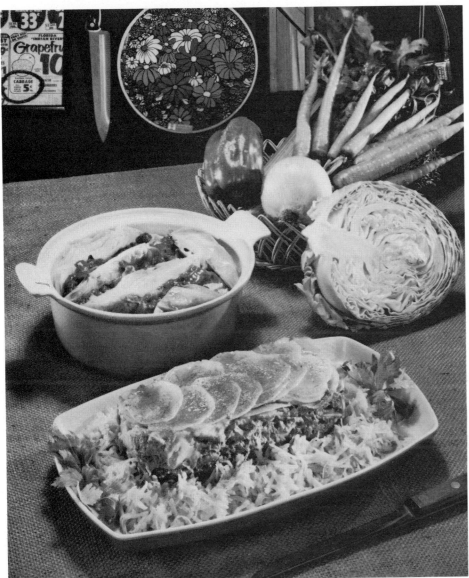

Cabbage Casserole

Photo courtesy of Western Growers Association.

CASSERUOLA DI CAVOLO
Cabbage Casserole

1 lb. fresh cabbage
three 8 oz. cans tomato sauce
1 lb. ground beef
2 tbs. olive oil
1/4 cup cooked rice
1 cup thinly sliced onion

1 clove minced garlic
1 medium carrot, sliced paper-thin
1/2 tsp. basil
1/2 tsp. sugar
salt and pepper to taste

In a greased 1-1/2-quart casserole, place 2-inch wedges of cabbage with core removed. Combine tomato sauce, beef, olive oil, rice, onion, garlic, carrot, basil, sugar, salt and pepper. Pour sauce over cabbage. Cover. Bake in a preheated oven at 350°F. for 1 hour. Serves 6. **(See photo above.)**

DI POMODORO
String Beans with Tomato Sauce

1 lb. string bea...
1 1/2 qts. ...ed boiling water
8 oz. ca... tomato sauce
1/4 cup olive oil

... tsp. oregano
...ove minced garlic
...epper to taste
1/4 cup grated Romano cheese

Wash string beans and remove tips. In 1 1/2 quarts salted, boiling water, cook string beans for 15 minutes. Drain.

In a small bowl, combine tomato sauce, olive oil, oregano, garlic and pepper. Pour a little of this mixture on the bottom of a 1-1/2-quart casserole. Place a layer of string beans topped with some sauce and grated cheese. Repeat process in this order until all ingredients are used. Cover tightly with aluminum foil. Bake in a preheated oven at 375°F. for 15 minutes or until tender. Serves 4.

CAVOLFIORE IN TEGAME
Pan-Fried Cauliflower

1 medium head cauliflower
1 large egg, beaten
3/4 cup bread crumbs
1 tbs. flour
1 tbs. grated Parmesan cheese
1 sprig finely chopped parsley

1 clove minced garlic
pinch of nutmeg
salt and pepper to taste
1/4 cup butter
1/4 cup olive oil

Remove stalk and outer leaves from cauliflower. Soak head in 2 quarts of cold water with 1 teaspoon salt for 30 minutes to rid it of any tiny insects it may have. Rinse in clear, cool water. Separate into flowerets. In a large pot, cook, covered, in a small amount of boiling, salted water until tender but firm. Drain well and dry with absorbent paper.

In a small bowl, beat egg until frothy. In a shallow dish, combine bread crumbs, flour, cheese, parsley, garlic, nutmeg, salt and pepper. Dip flowerets in egg and then in bread crumb mixture.

In a large skillet, heat butter and olive oil. Cook cauliflower until golden brown on both sides. Remove with spatula. Drain on absorbent paper. Serves 4–6.

May also be served as antipasto.

CAVOLFIORE CON SALSA DI POMODORO E PEPERONE
Cauliflower with Tomato and Pepper Sauce

1 medium head cauliflower
1/2 small chopped green pepper
1 tbs. butter *or* margarine
1 tbs. flour

1/2 tsp. salt
1 clove minced garlic
1 tbs. vinegar
1 cup canned tomatoes

Remove stalk and outer leaves from cauliflower. Soak head in 2 quarts of cold water with 1 teaspoon salt for 30 minutes to rid it of any tiny insects it may have. Rinse in clear, cool water. Separate into flowerets. In a large pot, cook, covered, in a small amount of boiling, salted water just until tender.

In a small saucepan, sauté green pepper in hot butter. Add flour, salt and garlic, mixing well. Add vinegar and tomatoes and cook until thickened. Drain cauliflower and place in a platter. Pour tomato sauce over it and serve very hot. Serves 4.

SPINACI AFFOGATI
Steamed Spinach

2 lbs. spinach
2 tbs. olive oil

1 clove minced garlic
salt and pepper to taste

Remove undesirable leaves from spinach. Wash thoroughly until all grit is removed. Place spinach with water clinging to leaves and salt in a large pot. Cover. Steam over low flame for 7–8 minutes. Drain well. Add olive oil, garlic and pepper. Continue to steam for 3–4 minutes. Serves 4.

SPINACI CON SALSA DI FORMAGGIO
Spinach with Cheese Sauce

2 lbs. spinach
pinch of salt
2 tbs. butter *or* margarine
2 tbs. flour

1 cup milk
salt and pepper to taste
1 beaten egg yolk
4 tbs. grated Romano cheese

Remove undesirable leaves from spinach. Wash well until grit-free. Place spinach dripping with water in a large pot. Sprinkle with a pinch of salt. Cover. Steam over low flame for 5 minutes. Drain very well. Press out excess liquid with a wooden spoon. Chop spinach coarsely.

In a medium-size saucepan, melt butter over low flame. Add flour. Stir with wooden spoon until smooth. Gradually add milk. Season with salt and pepper. Stir constantly until slightly thick. Remove from flame. Add egg yolk gradually and stir. Add grated Romano cheese. Mix. Fold spinach into cheese sauce. Serves 6.

TORTA DI SPINACI E RISO
Spinach and Rice Pie

1/3 cup raw rice
10 oz. fresh spinach
2 tbs. butter (divided)
pinch of nutmeg
1 1/2 tbs. finely chopped onion
1/3 cup grated Parmesan cheese

2 slices ham, finely chopped
1 egg
salt and pepper to taste
fine bread crumbs
1 oz. grated processed Gruyere cheese

Boil rice in salted water until tender. Drain well. Place in a bowl.

Remove undesirable leaves from spinach. Wash well until grit-free. Fill a 6-quart pot three-fourths full of water. Bring to a full boil. Place spinach in pot. (This will cause water to stop boiling.) Bring to a full boil and remove from stove immediately. Drain well. Press out excess liquid

(Continued on following page.)

with a wooden spoon. On a wooden board, chop spinach coarsely. Place hot spinach in a large bowl. Add 1 tablespoon of butter. Mix until butter melts. Add nutmeg and mix.

In a small skillet, sauté onion and ham in 1 tablespoon of hot butter until onion is yellow and ham is light brown. Add to rice. Mix well. Add rice and cheese to spinach. Mix. Taste for salt. If desired, add salt with pepper. Beat egg until frothy. Add and blend well.

Grease a 9" pie pan. Sprinkle lightly with bread crumbs. Spoon in spinach mixture and spread evenly in pan. Bake in a preheated oven at 375°F. for 20 minutes. Sprinkle top with grated Gruyere cheese. Cook for 10 minutes more or until cheese melts. Serves 4.

BROCCOLI SAUTE
Sautéed Broccoli

1 head broccoli (1 3/4 lbs.)
1/2 cup olive oil

1 small minced onion
1 cup grated Parmesan cheese

Clean and wash broccoli. Split into small spears. Soak in cool water with 1 tsp. of salt for 15 minutes. Run under clear water. In a medium-size pot, place spears in 1 inch of boiling, salted water. Cover. Steam until broccoli is almost tender (about 10 minutes). Drain well.

Heat olive oil in a medium-size skillet and sauté onion for 5 minutes over low flame. Then add broccoli and sauté until lightly browned and tender. Sprinkle with grated cheese before serving or pass cheese separately. Serves 6.

BROCCOLI CON LIMONE
Broccoli with Lemon

1 medium head broccoli
1 clove crushed garlic (optional)
1/4 cup olive oil

salt and freshly ground black pepper to taste
juice of 1 small lemon

Clean and wash broccoli. Split into spears. Soak in cool water with 1 tsp. of salt for 15 minutes. Run under clear water. In a medium-size pot, place broccoli spears in 1 inch of boiling, salted water. Cover. Steam until broccoli is tender (about 15 minutes). Add crushed garlic, if desired. Stir a few times. Drain and discard garlic. Place broccoli in a medium-size bowl. Combine olive oil, salt, pepper and lemon juice. Pour over broccoli. Toss. Serves 4.

BROCCOLI CON SALSICCIA
Broccoli with Sausage

1 medium bunch broccoli
2 tbs. olive oil
1/2 lb. Italian sweet sausage (without casings and broken up)

1 clove minced garlic
salt and pepper to taste
1 cup hot water

Clean and wash broccoli. Split into spears. Soak in cool water with 1 tsp. of salt for 15 minutes. Run under clear water. Cut into 3-inch pieces.

Heat olive oil in a deep saucepan and cook sausage and garlic for 10 minutes. Add cut stems to pan and stand broccoli with flower sides up. Add salt and pepper. Cook over low flame for 5 minutes. Mix broccoli with sausage mixture. Add water. Over high flame, bring to a boil. Lower flame. Cover. Continue simmering for 15—20 minutes or until broccoli and sausage are well done. Turn occasionally. Serves 4.

FUNGHI AFFOGATI
Steamed Mushrooms

1 lb. mushrooms
1/4 cup olive oil
1 clove minced garlic
1/2 tsp. dry parsley *or* 1 tbs. fresh minced
    parsley

1/3 tsp. oregano
salt to taste
pinch of crushed red pepper seeds *or* black
    pepper

Wash mushrooms quickly, but do not soak. Cut into thick slices. In a medium-size saucepan, place mushrooms, olive oil, garlic, parsley, oregano, salt and pepper. Cover. Simmer over low flame for 8—10 minutes or until tender, stirring occasionally. Serves 4.

FUNGHI IMPANATI SAUTE
Sautéed Breaded Mushrooms

1 lb. mushrooms
1 cup salted, boiling water
1 egg
1/2 cup fine bread crumbs
2 tbs. grated Romano cheese

1 tsp. dry parsley *or* 1 tbs. finely minced
    parsley
salt and pepper to taste
1/2 cup olive oil

Wash mushrooms quickly, but do not soak. Remove stems. In a medium-size pot, cook mushrooms and stems for 1 minute in 1 cup of salted, boiling water. Drain.

In a shallow bowl, beat egg well. In a shallow dish, combine bread crumbs, cheese, parsley, salt and pepper. Dip mushrooms and stems in egg. Roll in dry mixture. Heat olive oil in a large skillet. Add mushrooms and cook until golden brown. Serves 4.

FUNGHI ALLA SICILIANA
Mushrooms, Sicilian Style

1 lb. mushrooms
1/4 cup olive oil
1 small chopped onion
2 tbs. canned plum tomatoes, mashed

1 clove minced garlic
1/4 tsp. oregano
salt and pepper to taste

Wash mushrooms quickly, but do not soak. Slice. Heat olive oil in a medium-size pot. Add onion and cook over low flame until yellow. Add tomatoes. Cook for 2 minutes. Add mushrooms, garlic, oregano, salt and pepper. Simmer for 8—10 minutes or until tender, stirring occasionally. Serves 4.

FUNGHI IMBOTTITI SAPORITI
Savory Stuffed Mushrooms

1 lb. large mushrooms
2 tbs. olive oil

Stuffing:

1 cup bread crumbs
2 tbs. grated Romano cheese
1 clove minced garlic
1 sprig minced fresh parsley

1/4 tsp. oregano
salt to taste
pinch of crushed red pepper seeds
1/4 cup olive oil

Wash mushrooms quickly, but do not soak. Remove stems.* In 1 cup of boiling, salted water, cook mushrooms for 1 minute. Drain.

In a small bowl, combine stuffing ingredients. Stuff mushrooms. Place in a shallow 12"x16" baking pan with 1 cup of water plus 2 tbs. of olive oil. Bake in a preheated oven at 375°F. for 15—20 minutes or until tender. Serves 6.

*Use stems in omelets, soups or stuffings.

FUNGHI IMBOTTITI CON PURE DI PISELLI
Stuffed Mushrooms with Purée of Peas

1 lb. large mushrooms
chicken broth
butter

Stuffing:

2 10-1/2-oz. pkgs. frozen peas
1 3/4 cups water
2 tsp. sugar
1/2 tsp. basil leaves (dry)

1/4 cup chopped onion
1 tbs. butter *or* margarine
salt and pepper to taste
grated Gruyere *or* Swiss cheese

In a medium saucepan, bring salted water to a boil over high flame. Add sugar, basil and peas and stir. Cover. When water boils again, uncover. Lower flame to medium-low and let cook for 10 minutes or until tender. Stir peas occasionally.

Meanwhile, in a small skillet, melt butter over low flame. When butter starts to bubble, add onions and sauté for 5 minutes or until soft (do not brown). Add pepper and mix. Remove from flame and place onions with butter in a bowl. When peas are done, drain. Purée peas through a sieve in same bowl with onions. (You should have approximately 1 1/4 cups of purée.) Mix well. Set aside.

Wash mushrooms quickly, but do not soak. Remove stems (save for omelets, soups, stews, or sauces). In a medium-size saucepan over medium flame, bring to a simmer enough broth (measured) to cover mushrooms. Add mushrooms and lower flame. Then melt butter in a small saucepan. (The amount of butter is determined by the amount of broth needed to cover. If you need 2 cups of broth, use 2 tbs. of butter. If more cups of broth are needed, match in tablespoons of butter.) Add melted butter to mushrooms and mix. Let poach for 8—10 minutes. Drain and turn mushrooms upside down on absorbent paper.

Fill hollows of mushrooms with pea purée. Top each one with some grated Gruyere or Swiss cheese. Place on a greased shallow baking pan and broil in preheated broiler 4 inches from flame until browned. Serves 6.

SALADS

INSALATA DI CARCIOFI
Artichoke Salad

6 medium-size artichoke hearts (canned
    in brine)
1 tbs. finely chopped pimiento
1/4 cup olive oil

3 tbs. white vinegar
1/4 tsp. oregano
salt and pepper to taste

Rinse artichoke hearts. Drain. In a bowl, place artichoke hearts and pimiento. Chill. Mix olive oil, vinegar, oregano, salt and pepper. Pour over vegetables. Toss lightly. May be served chilled or at room temperature. Serves 2.

INSALATA DI FAGIOLINI
String Bean Salad

1 lb. string beans
1 medium sliced onion
1 clove minced garlic
5 tbs. olive oil

1/4 cup or more white vinegar
1 tsp. oregano
salt and pepper to taste

Wash string beans and cut off tips. Cook string beans in 1 1/2 quarts of rapidly boiling, salted water about 30 minutes or until tender. Drain. Cut into 1-1/2-inch pieces. Place string beans in a salad bowl. Add onion and garlic. Mix olive oil, vinegar, oregano, salt and pepper. Pour over salad. Toss well. May be served warm or cold. Serves 6.

INSALATA DI MELENZANA E PIMENTO
Eggplant and Pimiento Salad

1 medium eggplant
2 tbs. pimiento, cut into 1/4-inch cubes
3 tbs. olive oil
2 tbs. wine vinegar

1/2 tsp. oregano
1 tbs. chopped parsley
salt to taste
pinch of crushed red pepper seeds

Peel eggplant. Cut in half lengthwise. Then cut into 1/2-inch thick slices lengthwise. Boil in water to cover with 1 tsp. of salt for 7—10 minutes or until tender. Drain. Cut into 1-inch cubes. Place eggplant and pimiento in a salad bowl. Mix olive oil, vinegar, oregano, parsley, salt and pepper. Pour over eggplant. Toss well. Serve warm or chilled. Serves 4.

INSALATA DEL GIARDINO
Garden Fresh Potato Salad

2 lbs. new potatoes
1 stalk chopped celery
1/2 chopped red bell pepper
1 medium chopped cucumber
1/4 cup chopped onion
8 chopped olives

1/4 cup mayonnaise
1/4 cup white vinegar
salt and pepper to taste
1 tsp. sugar
2 tbs. fresh chopped parsley
paprika

Scrub potatoes. Cook in skins in boiling, salted water until tender. Drain. Peel. Slice potatoes. Place in a bowl. Add celery, red pepper, cucumber, onion and olives. In another bowl, blend mayonnaise, vinegar, salt, pepper and sugar until smooth. Add to potato mixture. Mix. Sprinkle with paprika and parsley. Chill. Serves 6.

INSALATA DI PATATE
Potato Salad

8 medium new potatoes
1 medium chopped onion
2 tbs. finely chopped pickled sweet red pepper
1/2 medium cucumber, chopped

1/2 cup olive oil
1/4 cup wine vinegar
1 tbs. chopped parsley
salt and freshly ground pepper to taste

Scrub potatoes well. Boil with skins in salted, boiling water to cover until tender. Drain. Peel. Slice potatoes. Place in a salad bowl. Add onion, pickled red pepper and cucumber. Mix olive oil, vinegar, parsley, salt and pepper. Pour over potatoes. Toss lightly. Serve warm or chilled. Serves 8.

INSALATA DI PATATE E ACCIUGHE
Potato and Anchovy Salad

4 medium new potatoes
4 fillets of anchovy, minced
1 tsp. minced capers (unsalted)
1/2 cup chopped celery

1 finely chopped small onion
1/4 cup olive oil
3 tbs. wine vinegar
pepper to taste

Scrub potatoes well. Boil with skins in slightly salted water to cover until tender. Drain. Peel. Cut into 3/4-inch cubes. Place in a salad bowl. Add fillets of anchovy, capers, celery and onion. Mix olive oil, vinegar and pepper. Pour over potatoes. Toss well. Taste for salt. If desired, add some. Serve warm or at room temperature. Serves 4.

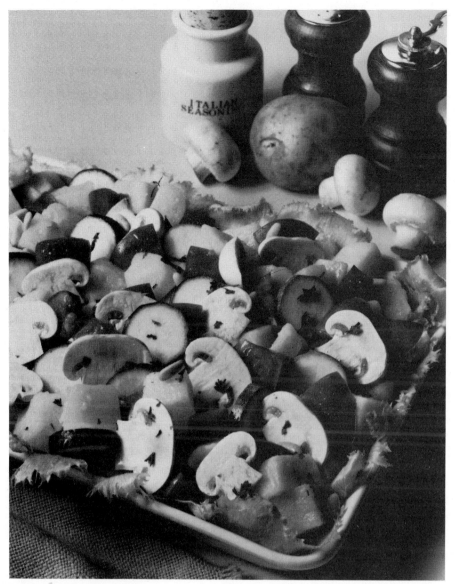

Potato and Zucchini Salad   Photo courtesy of American Mushroom Institute.

INSALATA DI PATATE E ZUCCHINI
Potato and Zucchini Salad

1/2 lb. fresh mushrooms
4 cups cooked, peeled and diced new potatoes
1 lb. (3 medium) sliced zucchini
1 diced tomato
1/4 cup finely chopped onion
salt and coarse ground black pepper to taste
1/3 cup olive oil

2 tbs. lemon juice
1 tsp. dry parsley *or* 2 tsp. chopped fresh
  parsley
1/8 tsp. oregano
1/2 tsp. dry basil *or* 1 tsp. chopped fresh basil
1/4 cup pine nuts (optional)

Wash mushrooms quickly, but do not soak. Pat dry and slice mushrooms (makes about 2 1/2 cups). In a large bowl, combine mushrooms, potatoes, zucchini, tomato and onion. Set aside. Combine remaining ingredients, except nuts. Mix well and pour over vegetable mixture. Toss well. Chill thoroughly. Serve sprinkled with pine nuts. Serves 6. **(See photo above.)**

INSALATA DI SPARAGI
Asparagus Salad

2 lbs. fresh asparagus
1/4 cup olive oil

3 tbs. wine vinegar
salt and pepper to taste

Wash asparagus well. Cut it into 2-inch pieces. Discard tough ends. Cook in boiling, salted water for 10–12 minutes or until tender. Drain. Place in a salad bowl. Mix olive oil, vinegar, salt and pepper. Pour over asparagus. Toss. Serve warm or chilled. Serves 6.

INSALATA AGRUMARIO
Citrus Fruit Salad

3 large navel oranges
3 large thick-skinned lemons
salt and freshly ground pepper to taste

1/4 cup olive oil
lettuce

Peel oranges and lemons. Slice thin. Place in a bowl. Sprinkle with salt and pepper. Pour olive oil on fruit. Mix. Arrange on a bed of lettuce on a platter. Allow to stand at least 20 minutes before serving. Serve at room temperature. Serves 6.

Serve with duck, roast beef, lamb or pork.

INSALATA DI RISO
Rice Salad

3/4 cup raw rice
2 tbs. tuna in olive oil, flaked
2 stalks chopped celery
2 fresh roasted peppers (red and yellow)

2 tbs. olive oil
salt and pepper to taste
juice of 1 lemon
2 finely chopped hard-boiled eggs

Boil rice until firm but not hard (*al dente*). Drain. Place in a bowl. Add tuna and celery. Cut peppers in julienne strips. Add peppers, olive oil, salt, pepper and lemon juice. Toss well. Garnish with finely chopped hard-boiled eggs. Chill in refrigerator before serving. Serves 4.

Serve with roast chicken, baked potatoes and mixed salad.

INSALATA MISCHIATA
Mixed Salad

1 medium head escarole *or* romaine
1 pickled sweet red pepper, chopped
3 chopped scallions
3 tbs. wine vinegar

5 tbs. olive oil
12 Sicilian black olives (pitted)
salt and pepper to taste

Remove undesirable leaves from escarole. Rinse thoroughly in cool water. Dry. Tear into bite-size pieces. In a bowl, place escarole, red pepper, scallions and olives. Chill. Add olive oil, vinegar, salt and pepper. Toss. Serves 4.

INSALATA VERDE ALLA PARMIGIANA
Green Salad Parmesan

4 cups bite-size pieces chicory
4 cups bite-size pieces Bibb lettuce
4 cups bite-size pieces escarole
1/4 cup olive oil

1 small clove garlic
1 cup croutons
1/2 cup grated Parmesan cheese

Dressing:
3/4 cup corn oil
1/3 cup tarragon-flavored vinegar

In a large salad bowl, place chicory, lettuce and escarole. Chill. Heat olive oil in a small saucepan. Add garlic and cook over low flame until brown. Discard garlic and add croutons. Cook until golden. Drain and cool. Add croutons to greens. Toss. Arrange grated Parmesan cheese around edges of bowl. Then toss all ingredients with corn oil and vinegar. Serves 6.

INSALATA DI PEPERONI ROSSI
Red Pepper Salad

4 medium red bell peppers
1/4 cup olive oil
3 tbs. white vinegar

1/4 tsp. oregano
1 clove minced garlic
salt and pepper to taste

Wash peppers. Remove stems, seeds and membranes. In boiling water to cover with 1/2 tsp. salt, cook peppers for 1 minute. Drain. Let cool. Slice lengthwise into 1/2-inch strips. Place peppers in a bowl. Mix oil, vinegar, oregano, garlic, salt and pepper. Pour over peppers. Toss well. Serve at room temperature. Serves 4.

INSALATA DI CETRIOLO E POMODORO
Cucumber and Tomato Salad

1 large cucumber, thinly sliced
2 medium sliced tomatoes
1 stalk chopped celery
1 small sliced onion
1/4 tsp. oregano

1/2 tsp. dry basil *or* 3 fresh chopped basil
 leaves
salt and pepper to taste
1/4 cup olive oil

Combine chilled vegetables in a bowl. Then add remaining ingredients. Toss well. Serves 4.

INSALATA DI PEPERONI VERDI
Green Pepper Salad

4 medium green bell peppers
1 sliced medium onion
1/4 cup olive oil
3 tbs. white vinegar

1/4 tsp. oregano
salt to taste
pinch of crushed red pepper seeds

Wash peppers. Remove stems, seeds and membranes. Cut into julienne strips. In a bowl, place chilled peppers and onion. Combine olive oil, vinegar, oregano, salt and crushed red pepper seeds. Pour over peppers. Toss. Serves 4.

INSALATA DI POMODORO E CIPOLLA
Tomato and Onion Salad

4 medium sliced tomatoes
1 small sliced onion
1/2 tsp. oregano

4 large fresh basil leaves, chopped
1/4 cup olive oil
salt and pepper to taste

Place all ingredients in a salad bowl. Toss. Serve at room temperature. Serves 4.

INSALATA DIMENATA
Tossed Salad

1 clove garlic
1 head romaine lettuce
4 tomatoes, cut in wedges
1/2 cup chopped stuffed olives
1 sliced endive

1/2 bunch sliced scallions
1/2 cup narrow provolone strips
1/4 lb. proscuitto, cut in narrow strips,
    or Virginia ham
onion rings

Italian Dressing #1
1/4 tsp. dry mustard
1/2 tsp. salt
1/4 tsp. freshly ground pepper

1/4 tsp. minced garlic
1 tbs. wine vinegar
1/4 cup olive oil

Rub salad bowl with garlic. Tear chilled romaine into bite-size pieces. Add tomatoes, olives, endive and scallions. Arrange strips of provolone and proscuitto on salad. Add Italian dressing. Toss. Arrange onion rings on top. Serves 4–6.

INSALATA CON MAIONESE
Salad with Mayonnaise

1/2 head romaine lettuce
2 sliced boiled beets
2 sliced boiled potatoes
4 chopped fillets of anchovy
8 pitted, mashed Italian green olives

1 tsp. prepared mustard
1/4 cup olive oil
2 tbs. wine vinegar
salt to taste
mayonnaise

Wash lettuce. Dry. Tear chilled lettuce into small pieces in bowl. Add chilled beets and potatoes, anchovies, olives, mustard, olive oil, vinegar and salt. Toss. Then cover top of salad with mayonnaise. Serves 4.

INSALATA DI MANZO
Beef Salad

2 lbs. boiled beef brisket, cut in 1/2-inch cubes
2 oz. can fillets of anchovy
1/4 cup olive oil
2 sprigs minced fresh parsley

4 tbs. beef stock
pepper to taste
3 tbs. wine vinegar

In a small saucepan, place anchovies, olive oil, parsley, beef stock and pepper. Over low flame, stir until anchovies dissolve and liquid is heated. Place beef in a salad bowl. Pour sauce and vinegar over it. Toss well. Serve warm or chilled. Serves 6.

INSALATA DI GAMBERI
Shrimp Salad

1 lb. small fresh or frozen shrimp, thawed
1 clove minced garlic
1 sprig minced fresh parsley

3 tbs. olive oil
salt and pepper to taste
juice of 1 lemon

Shell and de-vein fresh shrimp. Wash well. In boiling, salted water to cover, cook shrimp over low flame for 6 minutes. Drain well. Place in a bowl. Chill. Add garlic, parsley, olive oil, salt, pepper and lemon juice. Toss. Serve on chilled lettuce leaves. Serves 3.

INSALATA DI MERLUZZO
Whiting Salad

2 lbs. fresh whiting
2 tsp. chopped fresh parsley
1 clove minced garlic
salt and pepper to taste

3 tbs. cold fish stock
1/3 cup olive oil
juice of 2 lemons

Clean and wash fish. In a pot with simmering, salted water to cover, cook fish over low flame, covered, for 15 minutes or until tender. Drain; reserve 3 tbs. of fish stock. Cool. Remove skin and bones from fish and cut into bite-size pieces. Place in a bowl. Chill. Add parsley, garlic, salt, pepper, fish stock, olive oil and lemon juice. Toss. Serve warm or chilled. If chilled, serve on lettuce leaves. Serves 4.

INSALATA DI POLLO E TONNO
Chicken and Tuna Salad

2 cups cooked chicken (boiled or roasted)
1 cup canned tuna with olive oil, flaked
2 celery stalks, cut in julienne strips 2 in. long
2 tbs. capers (unsalted)

2 tbs. sliced stuffed olives
2 sliced hard-boiled eggs
lettuce leaves
mayonnaise

Remove skin from chicken. Cut chicken in narrow 3-inch-long strips. Place chicken, tuna, celery and capers in a deep plate. Moisten ingredients with mayonnaise. Garnish around plate with crisp lettuce leaves. Distribute olive and egg slices over salad. Place in refrigerator until serving time. Serves 4.

Makes a delicious luncheon or buffet salad.

INSALATA DI SCAROLA E TONNO
Escarole and Tuna Salad

1/2 medium head escarole
7 oz. can tuna fish in olive oil, flaked
1 small sliced onion
1/2 sliced cucumber
10 pitted green olives, sliced

3 tbs. pickled sweet red pepper, sliced
3 tbs. olive oil
salt and pepper to taste
juice of 1 lemon

Remove undesirable leaves from escarole. Rinse in cool water. Drain. Dry. Tear into bite-size pieces. Chill. In a salad bowl, place escarole, tuna fish, onion, cucumber, olives, red pepper, olive oil, salt, pepper and lemon juice. Toss. Serves 4.

INSALATA DI TONNO FRESCO
Fresh Tuna Salad

2 lbs. fresh tuna
3 qts. boiling water
1 clove minced garlic
1 sprig minced fresh parsley
1/4 tsp. oregano

8 chopped pitted green olives
salt and pepper to taste
1/4 cup olive oil
juice of 1 large lemon

Place tuna on a heat-proof dish. Wrap in cheesecloth and tie. Put into 3 qts. of simmering, salted water and cook, covered, for 15–20 minutes or until tender. Drain. Remove cheesecloth and cool fish. Then chill in refrigerator.

In a bowl, break tuna into chunks. Add garlic, parsley, oregano, olives, salt, pepper, olive oil and lemon juice. Toss well. Serve on lettuce. Serves 6.

INSALATA DI SCUNGILLI
Conch Salad

8 large boiled conches
1 clove minced garlic
1 sprig chopped fresh parsley
1 tbs. chopped pickled sweet red pepper

salt and pepper to taste
1/4 cup olive oil
juice of 1 large lemon

Purchase already-boiled conches. Cut off hard outer cover. Clean. In salted, boiling water to cover, cook over low flame, covered, for 30 minutes or until tender. Drain and cool. Cut meat into 3/4-inch chunks. Place in a bowl. Add garlic, parsley, red pepper, salt, pepper, olive oil and lemon juice. Toss. Serve at room temperature. Serves 4.

INSALATA DI POLPO
Octupus Salad

2 lbs. octopus
3 qts. boiling water
1 clove minced garlic
2 sprigs chopped fresh parsley
salt to taste

black pepper *or* crushed red pepper seeds to
    taste
1/4 cup olive oil
juice of 1 large lemon

In 3 qts. of simmering, salted water, cook octopus, covered, until tender. Drain. Allow to cool. Cut into bite-size pieces. Place in a bowl. Add garlic, parsley, salt, pepper, olive oil and lemon juice. Toss. Serve at room temperature. Serves 6.

INSALATA DI STOCCO
Stockfish Salad

2 lbs. soaked stockfish *or* fresh or frozen cod
    fillets
2 cloves minced garlic
2 sprigs chopped fresh parsley

salt and pepper to taste
4 tbs. olive oil
juice of 1 large lemon

Wash stockfish well in cool water. Bring 3 qts. of salted water to a boil. Add fish and simmer, covered, over low flame for 25 minutes or until tender. Drain. Cool. Cut into bite-size pieces. In a bowl, place stockfish, garlic, parsley, salt, pepper, olive oil and lemon juice. Toss well. Serves 6.

If desired, garnish with sliced stuffed olives. Serve at room temperature.

If using cod fillets, place fresh or thawed fillets on a heat-proof dish, wrap in cheesecloth and tie. Place in 3 quarts of boiling, salted water and simmer, covered, for 10–20 minutes or until tender. Drain. Remove cheesecloth. Cool fish. Prepare as above.

INSALATA DI ARAGOSTA
Lobster Salad

2 cups cooked lobster meat
1/4 cup olive oil
1 large clove minced garlic
2 sprigs chopped fresh parsley

juice of 1 large lemon
salt and pepper to taste
paprika

Flake lobster meat. Chill. Add olive oil, garlic, parsley, lemon juice, salt and pepper. Toss well. Place on beds of chilled lettuce leaves. Sprinkle lobster mounds with paprika. Serves 4.

If desired, garnish with any one of the following: sliced stuffed olives, quartered hard-boiled eggs, anchovy fillets or strips of pimiento.

SALAD DRESSINGS

CONDIMENTO ITALIANO #1
Italian Dressing #1

1/4 tsp. dry mustard
1/2 tsp. salt
1/4 tsp. freshly ground pepper

1/4 tsp. minced garlic
1 tbs. wine vinegar
1/4 cup olive oil

In a jar, place mustard, salt, pepper, garlic and vinegar. Shake until mustard dissolves. Add olive oil. Shake vigorously until smooth. Use on any green salad.

CONDIMENTO ITALIANO #2
Italian Dressing #2

3/4 tsp. dry mustard
2 tsp. oregano
1 tsp. tiny capers (unsalted)
1 clove garlic, split

6 tbs. wine vinegar
1/2 tsp. salt
1/4 tsp. pepper
3/4 cup olive oil

In a jar, place mustard, oregano, capers, garlic, vinegar, salt and pepper. Shake until mustard dissolves. Add olive oil. Shake vigorously until smooth. Remove garlic. Shake well before using. Use 4 tbs. of dressing in salad for 4. Use on any green salad.

CONDIMENTO D'ACCIUGHE
Anchovy Dressing

1 large clove garlic
3 fillets of anchovy
1/2 cup olive oil

1/4 cup wine vinegar
1/2 tsp. paprika
1/4 tsp. salt

Work garlic and anchovies into a paste. Place in a jar. Add olive oil, vinegar, paprika, and salt. Shake vigorously until well blended. Refrigerate. Shake before using. Use on any green salad.

CONDIMENTO DI BASILICO
Basil Dressing

1 cup olive oil
8 3/4 tbs. wine vinegar
3/4 tsp. salt

1/3 tsp. pepper
1 1/2 tsp. dry basil
2 crushed cloves garlic

Combine all ingredients in a jar. Shake well. Remove garlic. Shake before using. Makes 1 1/2 cups. Use on any green salad.

CONDIMENTO DI GORGONZOLA
Gorgonzola Dressing

Add 1/3 cup plus 1 tablespoon of creamed Gorgonzola cheese to ingredients for Basil Dressing above. Shake well before using. Use on any green salad.

FINGER FOODS

8

Tourists in Rome have to a great extent changed the eating habits of Romans. Until a few decades ago, citizens of the Eternal City were still clinging to their two-thousand-year-old custom of eating the *caena*, the main meal, only in the evening. Halfway through the day, they depended on the *merenda,* a light noon meal, a word now connoting "snack," to sustain them between meals until sunset and the start of the real repast.

This chapter holds recipes for this type of food (also called *spuntini*) which does not require spoons or forks to enjoy. Besides being snacks, these foods are allowed the added distinction of being luncheon or supper dishes while a few are breads and rolls that can be served at meals.

Finger foods, Italian-style are tempting, choice foods to have over and over again. Many will come as a complete surprise to your guests while even those who have tasted Broccoli Calzone may have never experienced it quite like this.

Most of these finger foods can be served in paper dishes.

FOR BEST RESULTS

All-purpose, presifted, unbleached flour is recommended for recipes in this section. Flour, baking powder, sugar, butter, milk and eggs should be at normal room temperature. Cold ingredients retard rising of dough and proper baking.

Any type of yeast may be used in recipes that require it. But yeast must never be dissolved in cold or hot water. The temperature should be lukewarm for moist yeast and warm for dry yeast.

A good-size wooden board (about 24"x26") is important. It must be washed, dried and air-dried after each use. Cover when storing. A formica-surfaced area will also do nicely.

A long rolling pin (about 26" long and 1 1/4" round) may be cut to order at your local lumber yard. Wash, dry and air-dry thoroughly. Store by wrapping in a plastic wrap.

A pizza cutter makes cutting hot pizza wedges a simple task.

A HINT

To freshen stale bread rolls, place in a paper bag. Twist top of bag closed. Sprinkle outside of bag lightly with water. Place in a 375° oven for 15 minutes or until soft. Test by squeezing rolls from outside bag.

Salami Pizza

PIZZA DI ROSA
Rose's Pizza

Dough:

4 cups flour

1 tsp. salt

1 1/2 cups warm water

1 cake moist yeast (dissolved in 1/4 cup luke-warm water) *or* 1 pkg. dry yeast (dissolved in 1/4 cup warm water)

Combine flour and salt on a board. Make a well. Add dissolved yeast. Blend by rubbing mixture between palms of hands until mealy. Make a well again. Add water gradually. Blend and gather up.

On a lightly floured board, knead until extremely smooth. Place in a large bowl. Cover. Let rise in a warm place for 1 1/2 hours or until double in bulk, avoiding drafts.

Sauce:

1/4 cup olive oil

1 1/2 medium sliced onions

3 1/2 cups canned plum tomatoes, mashed

salt to taste

Topping:

8 oz. sliced mozzarella

light sprinkling of oregano

pepper to taste

4 tbs. olive oil

1/4 cup grated Romano cheese (for sprinkling on top)

(Continued on following page.)

To make sauce: Heat olive oil in a saucepan and sauté onion over low flame until yellow. Add tomatoes and salt. Cover. Simmer for 10 minutes, stirring occasionally.

When dough has risen, punch down and divide into two sections. Roll out dough to fit two lightly oiled 14" round baking sheets. Press dough out from center with fingers to the edges of baking pans. Press with fingers to puff up dough 1/2" away from edges (this will form a nice crust when baked).

Divide amount of sauce and topping into two even portions. Top each section of dough with mozzarella slices. Spoon tomato sauce on each (leaving 1/2" margin clear on edges where crust will form). Sprinkle with oregano, pepper and drizzle with olive oil (except edges). Let stand uncovered for 30 minutes.

Place sheets on grating as high as possible in oven. Bake in preheated oven at 400°F. for 20 minutes or until crust is golden brown. Before removing from oven, sprinkle with grated Romano cheese. Bake for 1 minute longer. Cut into wedges. Serve very hot. Makes 2 pizzas.

Anchovy Pizzas—Add only a pinch of salt to sauce as anchovies are salty. Drain a 2 oz. can of fillets of anchovy for topping each pizza. Cut anchovies into pieces and arrange on pizza. Omit mozzarella. Omit grated Romano cheese. Bake as Rose's Pizza.

Salami Pizzas—Cut or roll about 8 slices of salami for each pizza. Add before topping with mozzarella slices and cover with sauce. Omit grated Romano cheese. Bake as Rose's Pizza.

If desired, serve pizza with a tossed green salad with Italian dressing and have ice cream for dessert.

Being the favorite of rich and poor alike, the pizza originated in Naples and enjoys as much popularity as her songs.

Even when the tomato was still unknown, Italians made pizza one of their favorite foods. They were used as breads to carry in the hand and eat quickly.

In Mother's village, tomatoes were also not used on pizza. But a deep kinship was manifested between villagers on winter days whenever pizza or bread was made. For after a villager completed baking, on a particular day, it was customary to share the still-burning embers of her oven with a neighbor. The latter would arrive with a large copper brazier into which some embers were shoveled. Quickly returned home, the fuming bowl was then inserted into a three-legged wooden pedestal in the center of a room, upon which family members placed their feet to keep warm. The older folk would frequently place some of the embers in small copper hand-warmers, as well, which were carried as they moved about the house.

FOCACCIA
Onion Pizza

3 cups flour
1 tsp. salt
1 pkg. dry yeast (dissolved in 1/4 cup warm
    water)
1 cup warm water

1 tsp. olive oil
2 finely sliced onions
salt
1/2 cup olive oil

Place flour and 1 tsp. of salt on board. Mix. Make a well. Add dissolved yeast. Blend by rubbing mixture between palms of hands. Make a well. Add water gradually. Blend and gather up. Place 1 tsp. of olive oil on board. Knead dough on it until very smooth. Place in a large bowl. Cover. Let rise in a warm place until double in bulk or about 1 1/2 hours. Punch down. Roll out 1/4-inch thick.

Place in a greased, shallow baking pan (12"x16"). Press onion slices in dough, making dents with fingers. Spoon olive oil over all and press, making dents in dough to distribute oil. Sprinkle lightly with salt. Let stand uncovered. Allow to rise in a warm place (about 30 minutes).

Bake in middle section of a preheated 400° oven for 25 minutes or until golden. Serves 4–6.

For Northern Italians here, this is a Sunday morning breakfast treat after Mass. It is preferred, perhaps, even to cake.

PIZZILLE
Little Sweet Pizzas

2 cups flour
1/2 tbs. sugar
1/2 tsp. salt
1/2 tbs. olive oil
1 pkg. dry yeast (dissolved in 1/4 cup warm water)

3/4 cup warm water
1 tsp. olive oil
about 6 tbs. olive oil
sifted confectioners' sugar

On a board, combine flour, sugar and salt. Make a well. Pour in oil. Blend by rubbing between palms of hands until mealy. Then make a well again and add dissolved yeast. Work in same manner until well incorporated. Make another well and add water gradually. Blend and gather up. Lightly flour board and knead until very smooth. Place in a large bowl. Cover and let rise in a warm place for 1 1/2 hours or until double in bulk.

When dough rises, punch down and divide dough into 12 equal pieces. On board, pour 1 tsp. of olive oil and in a circular motion, spread out oil to an approximate diameter of 6 inches. This will serve as a working area for all the pizzas.

Take one piece of dough and roll under palm of hand into a ball. Then place ball of dough on oiled area and flatten out with fingers into a 5-inch disk. With a 1-inch round cutter (taken from inside a doughnut cutter), cut out a hole in the center of disk. Repeat this process until all dough has been used. (Shape only two at a time as you are ready for them so they will not shrink while they are waiting to be cooked.)

In a 6-1/4-inch cast-iron skillet, heat 1 1/2 tbs. of olive oil over medium flame. Fry pizzas until golden brown on both sides, using spatula to turn them. Drain on absorbent paper. Add 1 1/2 tbs. of olive oil to skillet for every three pizzas. The small cut-out pieces may also be fried. Sprinkle pizzas with confectioners' sugar and serve immediately. Serves 6 or more.

Serve with black coffee or any preferred beverage.

These sweet surprises have their origin in Naples. Mother claims that during the Great Depression, this was a common treat for some impecunious immigrant Neapolitan neighbors whose guests also enjoyed them.

PANE ABBRUSTOLITO ITALIANO
Italian Toast

14-inch loaf day-old Italian bread
3 large eggs
1/3 cup milk

salt to taste
1/4 cup olive oil
grated pecorino *or* Romano cheese

Cut bread into 1/2-inch-thick slices. In a shallow bowl, beat eggs well. Add milk and salt. Beat. Dip both sides of bread slices in mixture.

Heat olive oil in a large skillet. Fry slices until golden brown on both sides. Sprinkle each generously with grated pecorino or Romano cheese. Serve hot. Serves 4.

One day, leftover bread inspired Mother to create this delightful snack which tempts everyone into having more!

PANINI SOFFIATI ALLA MARMELLATA
Puffed Sweet Rolls with Marmalade

Batter:
1/4 cup butter
1/4 cup sugar
2 eggs
2 1/4 cups flour

2 tsp. baking powder
1/2 tsp. baking soda
1/2 tsp. salt
1 cup buttermilk *or* sour milk

Filling:
1/4 cup orange marmalade
1 tsp. grated orange rind

1/4 tsp. cinnamon
1/8 tsp. nutmeg

In a small bowl, mix marmalade, orange rind, cinnamon and nutmeg. Set aside.

In a medium-size bowl, cream butter with sugar until light and creamy. Add eggs one at a time, beating well after each addition. Sift flour with baking powder, baking soda and salt. Add gradually to egg and butter mixture. Add buttermilk gradually, mixing well each time. (Sour milk may be obtained by adding 1 tbs. of vinegar or lemon juice to 1 cup sweet milk.) Grease a 12-cup muffin pan (with 2 1/2" muffin molds). Place 2 tbs. of batter in each mold. Then place 1 level tsp. of filling in center of each. Continue to fill with remainder of batter until molds are 2/3 full.

Bake in a preheated oven at 400°F. for 20–25 minutes or until golden. Makes 12 rolls. Serve with hot tea or black coffee.

GUASTELLE
Sicilian Rolls

4 cups flour
1 tsp. salt
1 tbs. sugar
1 tbs. olive oil
1 pkg. dry yeast (dissolved in 1/4 cup warm water)

1 cup warm water
1 egg
1 tsp. water
sesame seeds
cornmeal

Combine flour, salt, and sugar and mix on a board. Make a well. Add olive oil and, by rubbing between palms of hands, incorporate oil with flour until slightly mealy. Make a well. Add and work in dissolved yeast in same manner. Make another well. Add water gradually. Blend and gather up. Knead on a lightly floured board until smooth. Place dough in a large bowl. Cover. Let stand in a warm place for 1 1/2 hours or until double in bulk, avoiding drafts.

Then punch down dough and divide into two sections. On a lightly floured board, knead slightly. Divide each section into 6 pieces. Shape into 12 smooth, round balls.

Sprinkle two 14" round baking sheets lightly with cornmeal to avoid sticking. Place 6 rolls on each baking sheet. Place one in the center and the other 5 around the pan, spacing each evenly. This space allows rolls to rise and expand. Flatten rolls slightly.

For sheen, beat egg with 1 tsp. water and brush tops of rolls. Sprinkle with sesame seeds and tap them down lightly. Cover. Let rise in a warm place for 1 hour or until double in bulk. Take rolls still covered to oven. Uncover and bake in a preheated oven at 425°F. for 20 minutes or until golden brown. If rolls do stick slightly, loosen them by using spatula with a scraping motion. Makes 12 rolls.

Often, right after taking the rolls out of the oven, Mother splits one or two in half, places them cut side up on a dish, drizzles them with olive oil and sprinkles them lightly with black pepper. The combination of hot, steaming bread with these ingredients is wonderfully fragrant and delicious.

Besides rolls, Sicilians mold their bread in several shapes—round, long, braided. There is also a long whole-wheat bread with a slash down the center.

Bread, prominent in the rituals of every religion since pagan days, represents the body, as wine represents the soul.

In Ciminna, breads were only baked round and heavily topped with sesame seeds. There is a surviving practice among some of making the sign of the cross with a knife in back of the bread before slicing it as a blessing and acknowledgement of divine providence.

CASTAGNE ARROSTITI
Roasted Chestnuts

1 lb. chestnuts

In a large bowl, soak chestnuts in water to cover for 2 hours. Slash through the shells on the flat side. Place chestnuts, cut sides up, on a 12"x16" baking sheet. Roast in a preheated oven at 400°F. about 20 minutes or until tender. Insert fork through cut in shell to test tenderness. Turn occasionally. Serves 6.

BISCOTTI DI GRANO CALABRESE
Whole Wheat Biscuits Calabrese Style

4 whole wheat biscuits*
1/4 cup olive oil

1/2 cup wine vinegar
salt and pepper to taste

In a jar, combine olive oil, vinegar, salt and pepper. Place biscuits in a dish. Pour dressing on both sides of biscuits. To eat, break into chunks. Serves 4.

*Whole wheat biscuits may be purchased at almost any Italian bakery.

This was one of my Calabrian father's favorite foods. It is a custom to bake whole-wheat bread in Reggio di Calabria and preserve it by placing thick slices of it back in the oven after being baked so it becomes dry and crusty.

When father was a boy, large batches of this bread were baked in this manner once a month, to eliminate daily baking. It was popular with men working long hours in the fields who, at lunchtime, ate these biscuits with a dressing of spiced olive oil and vinegar poured from a small bottle.

Sometimes the bread was baked in a round shape, sliced in half and returned to the oven. Father's mother would ingeniously utilize half of the loaf as a dish for a *frittata* (omelet) or other foods.

CALZONE DI BROCCOLI
Broccoli Calzone

Dough:

4 cups flour
1 tsp. salt
1 tsp. sugar
1 tbs. olive oil

1 pkg. dry yeast (dissolved in 1/4 cup warm
   water)
1 1/4 cups warm water
1 tsp. olive oil

Combine flour, salt and sugar. Add 1 tbs. of olive oil, blending by rubbing mixture between palms of hands. Make a well. Add dissolved yeast. Work in the same manner. Add water gradually. Blend and gather up.

Place 1 tsp. of olive oil on wooden board. Knead dough on it until smooth. Place dough in a deep bowl. Cover with a piece of plastic wrap and a towel. Let rise in a warm place for 1 1/2 hours or until double in bulk. Punch down dough. Then knead once more for 1 minute. Divide into six equal parts. On a floured board roll out each section into an 8"x10" rectangle. About 30 minutes before dough has risen, prepare filling:

Filling:

1 1/2 medium heads broccoli
2/3 cup chopped provolone
2/3 cup chopped dry pork sausage

1 clove minced garlic
1/4 cup olive oil
salt and pepper to taste

Glaze:

1 egg
1 tsp. water

corn meal

Clean and wash broccoli. Separate stalks. Soak in cool water with 1 tsp. of salt for 15 minutes. Run under clear, cool water. Drain. Cook in a large pot of boiling, salted water for 5 minutes. Drain well. Chop. Place in a large bowl. Add provolone, sausage, garlic, olive oil, salt and pepper. Mix well. Divide into six equal portions.

On the long side of dough, place a portion of filling (about 2/3 cup, packed) in a strip 1 inch away from three edges of dough (nearest you). Flatten and smooth out filling with a spoon. Brush 1/2 inch of edges of complete dough with beaten egg diluted with 1 tsp. of water. Fold the empty side of dough over filling to evenly meet edge of other side. Tamp down all edges to seal very well. Flour fingers and turn edges under 1/4 inch. Continue process on other pieces of dough.

Sprinkle two 12"x16" baking tins with corn meal. Place three calzones on each tin (not touching each other). Tamp down edges well once again to make a perfect seal.

To glaze: Brush tops of calzones with remainder of beaten egg. Prick the top dough with a round toothpick, making holes about 1/2 inch apart all over the top. Use a rotating motion in order to assure piercing dough well (for necessary air vents). Be careful not to pierce bottom dough. Bake in a preheated oven at 375°F. for 30 minutes or until golden brown. Serve hot or cold. Makes 6.

Calzone may be reheated by wrapping in foil and placing in a preheated oven at 375°F. for 10–15 minutes.

CALZONE DI RICOTTA
Ricotta Calzone

Follow directions for dough in Broccoli Calzone. About 30 minutes before dough has risen, prepare the filling:

Filling:

1 1/2 lbs. ricotta	2 eggs
3 slices chopped proscuitto *or* Virginia ham	salt* and black pepper to taste
3 tbs. grated pecorino *or* Romano cheese	2 tbs. minced fresh parsley

Glaze:

1 egg
1 tsp. water

corn meal

Combine filling ingredients. Divide into six equal portions. Divide dough into six equal portions. Roll out each section to a 8"x10" rectangle.

On the long side of dough, place a portion of filling (about 2/3 cup) in a strip 1 inch away from the three edges of dough (nearest you). Flatten and smooth out filling with a spoon. Brush 1/2 inch of edges of complete dough with beaten egg diluted with 1 tsp. of water. Fold the empty side of dough over filling to evenly meet edge of other side. Tamp down all edges to seal very well. Flour fingers and turn edges under 1/4 inch. Continue process on other pieces of dough.

Sprinkle two 12"x16" baking tins with cornmeal. Place three calzones on each pan (not touching each other). Tamp down edges well once again to make a perfect seal.

To glaze: Brush tops of calzones with remainder of beaten egg. Prick the top dough with a round toothpick, making holes about 1/2 inch apart all over the top. Use a rotating motion in order to assure piercing dough well (for necessary air vents). Be careful not to pierce bottom dough. Bake in a preheated oven at 375°F. for 30 minutes or until golden brown. Serve hot or cold. Makes 6.

Calzone may be reheated by wrapping in foil and placing in a preheated oven at 375°F. for 10–15 minutes.   *If using proscuitto, add salt if desired. Add salt if Virginia ham is used.

CALZONE DI CARNE E VEGETALI
Meat and Vegetable Calzone

Follow directions for dough in Broccoli Calzone. About 30 minutes before dough has risen, prepare this filling:

Filling:

1 1/4 lbs. escarole
1/4 cup olive oil
1 clove minced garlic
1 tsp. salt
dash of pepper
2 heaping tbs. grated Romano cheese

8 oz. can sliced mushrooms, chopped *or*
    fresh mushrooms, chopped
1/2 lb. ground beef
1/2 lb. ground pork *or* sausages
1 medium chopped onion

Glaze:

1 egg
1 tsp. water

corn meal

Wash escarole. In a large pot, place escarole, olive oil, garlic, salt and pepper. Cover. Over low flame, steam for 8—10 minutes. Turn once while cooking. Place in a colander and press with a wooden spoon until well drained. Then chop. Place in a large bowl. If using fresh mushrooms, sauté for 3 minutes. Add cheese and mushrooms. Mix. In a large skillet cook beef and pork for 5 minutes. Add onion. Cook until meat is brown. Combine with escarole.

On the long side of dough, place a portion of filling (about 2/3 cup, packed) in a strip 1 inch away from three edges of dough nearest you. Flatten and smooth out filling with a spoon. Brush 1/2 inch of edges of complete dough with beaten egg diluted with 1 tsp. of water. Fold the empty side of dough over filling to evenly meet edge of other side. Tamp down all edges to seal very well. Flour fingers and turn edges under 1/4 inch. Continue process on other pieces of dough.

Sprinkle two 12"x16" baking tins with cornmeal. Place three calzones on each pan (not touching each other). Tamp edges down well once again to make a perfect seal. To glaze: Brush tops of calzones with remainder of beaten egg. Prick the top dough with a round toothpick, making holes about 1/2 inch apart all over the top. Use a rotating motion to assure piercing dough well (for necessary air vents). Be careful not to pierce bottom dough. Bake in a preheated oven at 375°F. for 30 minutes or until golden brown. Serve hot or cold. Makes 6.

Calzone may be reheated by wrapping in foil and placing in a preheated oven at 375°F. for 10—15 minutes.

Generally, calzone is deep-fried, but we like to bake ours.

In various regions of Italy, calzone takes on different shapes and fillings. When the dough is rolled around the filling, they look like trouser legs, therefore the name *calzone*.

HERO SANDWICH #1

1 loaf Italian bread
Caponatina (p. 29)
Swiss cheese, thinly sliced
1 finely sliced onion

1 finely sliced tomato
a few lettuce leaves
olive oil
salt and pepper to taste

Slice bread in half lengthwise. Cover one half with caponatina. Top with cheese, onion, tomato and lettuce. Brush other half with olive oil. Sprinkle with salt and pepper. Put slices together. Cut into serving portions.

HERO SANDWICH #2

1 loaf Italian bread
Roasted Peppers (p. 139)
Sicilian salami
thin slices of provolone

a few lettuce leaves
olive oil
pepper to taste

Slice bread in half lengthwise. Cover one half with roasted peppers. Top with salami, provolone and lettuce. Coat inside of other half with olive oil. Then sprinkle with pepper. Put slices together. Cut into serving portions.

HERO SANDWICH #3

1 loaf Sicilian Bread
piccalilli peppers
tuna fish
1 finely sliced onion

Sicilian green olives
olive oil
pepper to taste

Slice bread in half lengthwise. Cover one side with piccalilli peppers, tuna fish, onion and olives. Brush inside of other half with olive oil. Sprinkle with pepper. Put slices together. Cut into portions for individual servings.

All amounts used in hero sandwiches are according to taste. For a hot sandwich, omit lettuce, wrap sandwich in foil and bake in a hot oven for 15—20 minutes.

SOME FAVORITE EGG & CHEESE DISHES

9

Una Frittata (an omelet) is a popular Italian luncheon. It is frequently served as a meat substitute for supper, too. Italian-style omelets can be prepared with a large variety of vegetables, cheese and, surprisingly enough, with pasta, as well. Eggs are indispensable in the Italian diet. In our particular household, a week doesn't go by without our having at least three different *frittati*.

A few hints for good results when cooking eggs: They will beat up faster and to larger volume when brought to room temperature before using. Take from refrigerator only the amount of eggs needed. Occasionally blood spots appear in eggs. But they may be lifted out before cooking and do not alter the nutritive value or taste.

Frittati seem to be more successful in a heavy skillet. Be sure to remember to keep the flame low to assure tender and attractive eggs. Tools for turning are a spatula and, if you desire, a flat, round dish to help flap them over carefully in the skillet in one piece.

Also included in this collection are two sunny-side-up types and some sweet omelets you may serve as desserts.

FRITTATA DI MACCHERONI
Macaroni Omelet

3 cups cooked spaghetti
4 eggs
3 tbs. grated pecorino *or* Romano cheese

1 slice chopped proscuitto *or* Virginia ham
salt and pepper to taste
3 tbs. butter

Let spaghetti stand to cool and dry out. In a bowl, beat eggs, cheese, proscuitto, salt and pepper. In a large skillet, fry spaghetti in hot butter until light brown. Pour egg mixture over spaghetti. Cook over low flame. When set and golden brown on one side, turn and brown other side. Serves 3.

UOVA CON MOZZARELLA
Eggs with Mozzarella

4 eggs

4 oz. diced mozzarella

1 tsp. dried parsley *or* 1 tbs. chopped fresh
    parsley

1/8 tsp. garlic powder

salt and pepper to taste

4 tbs. olive oil

In a bowl, beat eggs thoroughly. Add mozzarella, parsley, garlic powder, salt and pepper. Mix well. Heat olive oil in a large skillet. Pour in egg mixture and cook over low flame. When set and golden brown on one side, turn and brown other side. Serves 3.

UOVA CON SALSICCIA
Eggs with Sausage

3 eggs

1/2 lb. Italian sweet sausage (casings removed)

2 tbs. olive oil

salt and pepper

Crumble sausages. Heat olive oil in a medium-size skillet. Add sausage and cook over low flame until well done. Beat eggs well with salt and pepper. Pour over sausages. When set and golden brown on one side, turn and brown other side. Serves 3.

FRITTATA DI SPARAGI
Asparagus Omelet

4 eggs

10 oz. pkg. frozen asparagus spears

1/4 cup olive oil

1/4 cup grated Romano cheese

salt and pepper

Cut asparagus spears into 2-inch pieces. Heat olive oil in a large skillet. Cook asparagus, covered, over low flame for 10 minutes or until tender. Season lightly with salt and pepper. Stir occasionally. Beat eggs thoroughly. Add cheese, salt and pepper. Beat until well-blended. Pour over asparagus. When set and brown on one side, turn carefully and brown other side. Serves 4.

Omelets have found their place in the hardy life of Sicilian peasantry. As in many parts of Sicily, much of a Ciminna peasant's time was spent reaching his work in the morning and returning at night, clip-clopping on his mule down the shadeless streets to and from the distant fields. To avoid tiresome commuting between field and home, he would often camp overnight in a *pagliaio*, a straw barn occasionally utilized as a shelter from bad weather as well. There he rested and slept with a Spartan discipline on a bed of straw. But before that, he ate his expedient though nutritious supper of an hours-old omelet accompanied by bread, olives, dried figs and nuts and downed by red wine from a *fiasco*, a terra-cotta flask with an enamel interior.

FRITTATA DI POMODORO FRESCO
Fresh Tomato Omelet

3 eggs
1 medium tomato, ripe
1/4 cup grated Romano cheese
1/2 tsp. dry parsley *or* 1 tbs. chopped fresh parsley

1 clove minced garlic
salt and pepper to taste
4 tbs. olive oil

In a bowl, beat eggs well. Remove seeds and skin from tomato. Chop. To eggs, add tomato, cheese, parsley, garlic, salt and pepper. Blend well. Heat olive oil in a medium-size skillet. Cook omelet over low flame until golden brown on one side. Turn and brown other side. Serves 3.

FRITTATA DI ZUCCHINI
Squash Omelet

4 eggs
1 lb. zucchini (Italian squash)
2 heaping tbs. flour

4 tbs. olive oil
salt and pepper

Scrub zucchini well. Remove stem and blossom ends. Dry. Cut into 1/4-inch slices. Then dip in flour. Heat olive oil in a large skillet. Cook zucchini slices over low flame until golden. Season lightly with salt and pepper. Beat eggs well with salt and pepper. Pour over squash. When firm and golden on one side, turn and brown on other side. Serves 4.

FRITTATA DI FORMAGGIO
Cheese Omelet

6 eggs
onion salt to taste
pepper to taste

1/2 tsp. rosemary, crushed
4 tbs. grated pecorino *or* Romano cheese
4 tbs. olive oil

In a bowl, beat eggs well. Then beat in onion salt, pepper, rosemary and cheese. Heat olive oil in a large skillet. Pour eggs in and cook over low flame. When set and golden brown on one side, turn and cook other side. Serves 4.

FRITTATA DI CARCIOFI
Artichoke Omelet

6 eggs
8 oz. pkg. frozen artichoke hearts
1/3 cup olive oil

salt and pepper
1 sprig chopped fresh parsley
2 tbs. grated Romano cheese

Heat olive oil in a large skillet. Cook artichoke hearts over low flame until tender and golden. Season lightly with salt and pepper. Meanwhile, beat eggs. Then beat in salt, pepper, parsley and cheese. Pour eggs over artichokes. Cook omelet until set and golden brown on one side; then turn and cook other side. Serves 4–5.

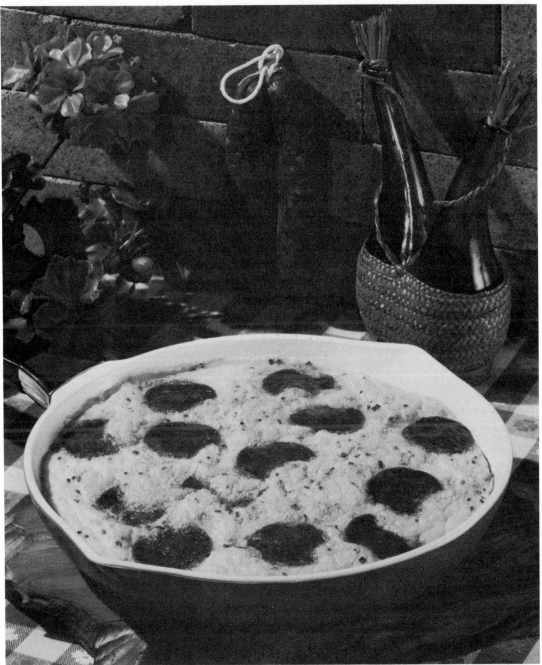

Eggs with Pepperoni   Photo courtesy of Poultry and Egg National Board.

UOVA CON PEPERONI
Eggs with Pepperoni

4 eggs

6 whole slices of pepperoni *or* 10 thin, diced
    slices of Sicilian salami

1 sprig minced fresh parsley *or* 1 tsp. dry
    parsley

pinch of salt

3 tbs. grated pecorino *or* Romano cheese

pepper (optional)

3 tbs. olive oil

    Beat eggs well. Add pepperoni, parsley, salt, cheese, and pepper if desired. Beat until well
blended. Heat olive oil in a large skillet. Cook omelet over low flame. When set and golden brown
on one side, turn and cook other side. Serves 3. **(See photo above.)**

UOVA CON PEPERONI VERDI
Eggs with Green Peppers

4 eggs
4 medium Italian green peppers
4 tbs. olive oil
1/2 medium chopped onion

4 strips chopped bacon
2 tbs. grated pecorino *or* Romano cheese
salt and black pepper *or* pinch of crushed
    red pepper seeds

Wash and dry peppers. Remove seeds. Slice and cut into 1-inch pieces. Heat olive oil in a large skillet. Add peppers and cook over low flame until almost done. Then add onion and bacon. Cook until vegetables are tender. Beat eggs. Add cheese, salt and pepper. Beat until well blended. Pour eggs over pepper mixture. When set and golden brown on one side, turn and cook other side. Serves 3.

FRITTATA NAPOLETANA
Neapolitan Omelet

3 cups cooked spaghettini with tomato sauce
4 eggs
1 tbs. dry parsley

2 tbs. grated Parmesan cheese
salt and pepper to taste
2 tbs. olive oil

In a bowl, beat eggs well. Beat in parsley, cheese, salt and pepper. Add spaghettini and mix. Heat olive oil in a large skillet. Cook mixture over low flame. When firm and golden brown on one side, turn and cook other side. Serves 3.

FRITTATA DI FUNGHI
Mushroom Omelet

4 eggs
1/2 lb. mushrooms
1 small chopped onion
3 tbs. olive oil

1 tsp. dry parsley *or* 1 tbs. chopped fresh
    parsley
1/4 cup grated Romano cheese
salt and pepper

Wash, dry and slice mushrooms. Heat olive oil in a large skillet. Add mushrooms and onion and season lightly with salt and pepper. Cover partially and cook over low flame until tender, stirring occasionally. In a bowl, beat eggs. Combine with parsley, cheese, salt and pepper. Pour over mushrooms and onion. When firm and golden, turn and cook on other side. Serves 3.

UOVA CON FEGATINI DI POLLO
Eggs with Chicken Livers

8 chicken livers
4 eggs
1 medium onion, sliced
6 tbs. olive oil

salt and pepper
1/2 tsp. dry parsley *or* 1 tbs. fresh chopped
    parsley

Chop chicken livers into bite-size pieces. Heat olive oil in a skillet. Add chicken livers and onion. Cook over high flame until nicely browned, stirring frequently. Season lightly with salt and pepper. Beat eggs with salt and pepper and then beat in parsley. Add to chicken livers in pan. Cook over low flame until set and golden brown on one side, then turn and cook other side. Serves 3.

FRITTATA DI RICOTTA
Italian Cheese Omelet

2 eggs
salt and pepper to taste
1/4 lb. ricotta
1/2 tbs. grated Parmesan cheese

1/2 tsp. dry parsley *or* 1 tbs. fresh chopped
    parsley
1 tbs. olive oil
1 tbs. butter

Beat eggs with salt and pepper. In a small bowl, combine ricotta, grated cheese, parsley, salt and pepper. Heat olive oil and butter in a medium-size skillet. Pour in eggs and cook over low flame until golden brown on one side. Turn. Spread ricotta mixture over omelet. Cook omelet until set. Then fold over. Continue cooking until golden brown on both sides. Serves 2.

UOVA CON SPINACI
Eggs with Spinach

1 lb. spinach
4 eggs
salt and pepper

2 tbs. grated Romano cheese
4 tbs. olive oil
1 clove minced garlic

Discard undesirable leaves from spinach. Wash spinach thoroughly until grit-free. Place in a pot. Season lightly with salt and pepper. Cover. Steam for 7 minutes or until tender. Drain well by squeezing liquid out with a wooden spoon.

Meanwhile, beat eggs. Combine with salt, pepper and cheese. Heat olive oil in a large skillet. Add spinach and garlic. Mix. Cook over low flame for 1 minute. Pour egg mixture over spinach. Cook until set and golden brown on one side, then turn and cook other side. Serves 4.

UOVA CON PROVOLONE
Eggs with Provolone

4 eggs
3 tbs. olive oil

4 tsp. grated provolone
pepper to taste

Into a large skillet with hot olive oil, break eggs carefully. Sprinkle 1 tsp. of grated provolone and pepper on each. Cook over very low flame until cheese melts. Serves 4.

UOVA IN SALSA DI POMODORO
Eggs in Tomato Sauce

6 eggs
1 cup homemade leftover tomato sauce

salt to taste
crushed red pepper seeds *or* black pepper

In a large skillet, heat sauce over medium flame. Lower flame. Break eggs carefully in pan.
Cook sunny-side up until egg whites are set. Season eggs with salt and a light sprinkling of either crushed red pepper seeds or black pepper. Serves 6. Delicious!

PESCI D'UOVA
Egg Fish

4 eggs
1 sprig finely chopped parsley *or* 1 tsp. dry
    parsley
1 clove minced garlic

6 tbs. grated Romano cheese
salt and pepper to taste
3 tbs. olive oil

In a bowl, beat eggs well. Add parsley, garlic, grated cheese, salt and pepper. Beat until well blended. In a large skillet, heat olive oil over low flame. Pour egg mixture in pan and cook until underside is set. Then, with spatula fold 1/4 of the omelet, pushing the omelet back in space left in pan so that folded end touches edge of skillet.

With spatula, force raw egg on top of omelet to other end of pan. (Tipping pan will help.) When set, carefully fold omelet twice over. Let cook on one side until golden brown. Turn with spatula to cook other side, enabling the omelet to cook within. Place omelet on platter. Cut crosswise in half or in thirds, according to amount of servings. Serves 2–3.

When bad weather would deter fish deliveries to Ciminna's marketplace on Fridays, villagers had this delicious omelet for supper instead, giving it the clever, metaphorical name of "egg fish" because of its long shape. They also cut it like a fish.

FRITTATA DOLCE
Sweet Omelet

4 eggs
salt to taste
2 tbs. butter

any preferred jam, jelly or marmalade
sifted confectioners' sugar

In a bowl, beat the eggs with salt until fluffy. Heat butter in a large skillet. Add the eggs and cook over low flame. When set and golden brown on one side, turn and cook other side. Remove from pan. Spread with favorite jam, jelly or marmalade and then fold. Sprinkle with confectioners' sugar. Serve as a dessert. Serves 2—3.

FRITTATA MONTATA
Omelet Soufflé

6 egg whites
3 egg yolks
grated peel of 1 lemon

a few drops lemon juice
1/2 cup sugar
sifted confectioners' sugar

Beat egg yolks, lemon peel, lemon juice with sugar. Then beat egg whites stiff and fold into egg yolk mixture. Transfer to an 8"x2" round buttered baking pan. Bake in a preheated oven at 400°F. After five minutes, make a few cuts in omelet and sprinkle with confectioners' sugar. Cook about 1—2 minutes or until set, being careful not to overbrown it. Serve immediately. Serves 4.

Serve as a dessert.

CHEESE

Many forget that cheese is actually concentrated milk and therefore holds all the food value of milk—calcium, riboflavin and protein. It is naturally an important source of energy for the body.

Italians not only favor cheese in cooking and baking, but a tray of assorted, tempting creamy cheeses and a bowl of fresh fruit are frequently served as dessert, as well. Unless you know the preference of your guests, it is wise to provide an assortment of cheeses. Some may prefer mild Bel Paese; others may like the robust flavors of provolone or Gorgonzola.

Most cheeses are served at room temperature to bring out their characteristic flavors and textures. Remove hard varieties from the refrigerator at least an hour before serving, but do not allow cut surfaces to dry out.

Remember that cut apples and pears you may be serving will darken unless dipped in lemon juice or other citrus fruit.

If you like, serve grissini or toasted slices of crusty Italian bread with the cheeses.

SUGGESTED CHEESE & FRUIT COMBINATIONS

Asiago (mild and smoky)
   (slices)   seedless grapes or pears

Bel Paese
   (slices, wedges)   McIntosh apples, seedless grapes or pears

Caciocavallo
   (slices, wedges)   seedless grapes, Sweet Bartlett pears

Gorgonzola
   (chunk served alone on tray with   apples or pears (especially Anjou and Bosc
      appropriate knives with which guests may cut)   pears)

Provolone
   (round slices, wedges)   seedless grapes, Sweet Bartlett pears

Taleggio (mellow and slightly piquant)
   (slices)   seedless grapes, pears

FONDUTA PIEMONTESE
Cheese Fondue, Piedmont Style

1 lb. diced Pastorella cheese (or any mild, soft
    cheese)
1 cup milk
1/4 cup butter
salt to taste

white pepper to taste
3 egg yolks
Italian bread cubes sautéed in butter
thinly sliced truffles (optional)

Allow cheese to soak in milk for 1 hour. Drain. Place in top of double boiler with butter, salt and
pepper. Cook over simmering water in bottom section of boiler, stirring constantly until cheese melts.
When mixture is smooth, beat in one egg yolk at a time. Stir constantly until thick. Pour into a hot
serving dish. Surround with sautéed cubes of bread which are speared with forks and dunked in
the fondue. If desired, top fondue with thinly sliced white truffles. Serves 4–6.

PASTICCINI DI FORMAGGIO
Cheese Cakes

2 tbs. butter
3 1/2 tbs. flour
4 tbs. grated Parmesan cheese

pinch of salt
few grains of cayenne
3 egg whites, stiffly beaten

Melt butter in a medium-size saucepan. Add flour and stir until well blended. Remove from heat.
Add cheese, salt and cayenne. Fold in egg whites. Drop 1/2 tablespoonfuls of mixture one inch apart
on a large well-greased baking sheet. Bake in a preheated oven at 350°F. for 12 minutes or until
golden. As soon as they are done, remove with a spatula. May be served with salads. Makes about 20.

MOZZARELLA IN CARROZZA
Fried Cheese Sandwiches

4 thin slices mozzarella affumicata (smoked
    mozzarella)
4 eggs
salt and pepper to taste

8 slices of bread
4 tbs. butter
minced fresh parsley

In a shallow dish, beat eggs well with salt and pepper. Dip bread slices in eggs. Heat butter in a
large skillet. Sauté slices on one side until golden. Turn 4 slices over. Place a mozzarella slice on
each of the 4 slices of bread. Sprinkle with some parsley. Top with the other slices of bread, cooked
sides down. When golden, turn and cook other side of sandwich. Serves 4.

FRITTATINE IMBOTTITE CON RICOTTA
Italian Cheese Stuffed Pancakes

Batter:

3 medium eggs

7 generous tbs. flour

1 1/2 heaping tbs. grated Parmesan cheese

1 1/8 cups milk

2 tsp. melted butter

1/8 tsp. salt

1/2 tsp. butter

In a medium-size bowl, beat eggs lightly. Add flour, cheese, milk, melted butter and salt. Beat well. In a small cast-iron skillet (6 1/4") melt 1/2 tsp. butter over low flame. Pour in exactly two tablespoons of batter and quickly tip and swirl pan to cover bottom with a thin layer. When set on edges and golden, turn carefully with spatula, being careful not to pierce pancake. Using fingers helps to avoid this. Cook other side until golden. It is not necessary to butter the pan again. Continue process until all of the batter has been used. Allow to cool.

Filling:

1 1/2 lbs. well-drained ricotta *or* mild creamed cottage cheese with tiny, soft curds

3 slices chopped Virginia ham

3 tbs. grated Parmesan cheese

2 tbs. minced fresh parsley *or* 1 1/4 tsp. dry parsley

salt and pepper to taste

If using cottage cheese, put it through a fine sieve. Mix filling ingredients well. Fill each center of pancakes with 2 rounded tablespoonfuls of filling. Roll up each pancake. In a shallow 12"x16" greased baking tin, place pancakes, folded-over sides down, in a single layer side by side. Bake in a preheated oven at 350°F. for 12–15 minutes or until browned. Makes 16–18.

Unfilled pancakes may be prepared hours ahead, cooled, wrapped and refrigerated. They may also be frozen. Thaw completely before filling.

CALZONE FONDUTA
Calzone Fondue

1 lb. sweet Italian sausage

1 tbs. olive oil *or* corn oil

8 oz. can pizza sauce

3/4 lb. drained ricotta

12 slices enriched bread

4 eggs

2 cups milk

1/2 tsp. salt

1/2 cup grated Parmesan cheese

Remove casing from sausage. Break meat into 3/4-inch pieces. Cook in a large skillet in olive oil, turning to brown all sides. Remove from heat. Add pizza sauce. Shred ricotta with a fork. Stir into sausage mixture.

Arrange four slices of bread in the bottom of a greased 8" or 9" square baking dish. (Crusts may be trimmed off, if desired.) Spread half the sausage mixture over bread. Place four more bread slices over sausage mixture. Spread remaining sausage mixture over bread and top with remaining bread slices.

Beat eggs, milk and salt together. Pour over sandwiches in baking dish. Sprinkle Parmesan cheese over top. Bake in a slow oven (preheated to 325°F.) for 40–45 minutes or until set. Serves 8.

BASTONCINI DI MOZZARELLA FRITTI
Deep-Fried Mozzarella Sticks

1 lb. mozzarella

flour

1 beaten egg

bread crumbs

vegetable oil for deep frying

Cut mozzarella into 2-inch squares. Roll mozzarella in flour, then in egg, then in bread crumbs. Roll a second time in egg and bread crumbs. In deep, hot vegetable oil, fry a few at a time for 2 minutes or until golden. Serve hot. (Can be prepared ahead of time and refrigerated until ready to be fried.) Serves 4–6.

May also be served as an antipasto.

DESSERTS
in the old tradition

10

Now the dessert! The course which ties up the loose ends of the "story of a meal." The final revelation that is earnestly anticipated.

As far as we know from written accounts, ice cream, a favorite dessert with Italians, had its start during the reign of Emperor Nero in 62 A.D. He delighted in magnificent dishes of snow flavored with nectar, fruit pulps and honey brought by fast runners from the Appenines.

We next hear of Marco Polo who brought a recipe for sherbets to Europe from the Far East.

When Catherine de Medici became queen of France, she brought the recipe for Italian sherbet with her from her homeland.

Almost everyone envies the knack and wisdom that go into a perfect cake, cookie or soufflé. If you enjoy desserts, most likely you have an appreciation for that "by eye" prudence the Italian *nonna* (grandmother) has. Some of that knowledge is included here, in this chapter.

These recipes are delicacies that Italians wouldn't do without on holidays and special occasions. But they may also serve as delightful snacks or themes at coffee klatsches, if you like.

SOME THINGS TO REMEMBER

All-purpose, presifted unbleached flour is recommended for all cakes, pastries and dough except in recipes which suggest cake flour. Resift presifted flour.

Flour, baking powder, sugar, milk and butter should be at normal room temperature. Remove eggs from refrigerator at least 1 hour before using to allow them greater volume when beaten. If desired, margarine may be substituted for butter.

A flour sifter obtains a finer dough or batter. If you have a flour bin, leave the sifter in it after using. If not, dry-wipe the sifter and place in a plastic bag to keep clean. Always use standard measuring cups and spoons.

For successful cake making, always read recipe carefully. Have the size pan the recipe recommends.

A well-shaped cake always makes a fine impression on family and friends. To avoid that terrible hump in the middle of one, after pouring batter into proper pan, with the back of a spoon gently push batter from the center to the outside edges, meanwhile turning pan slowly with other hand. Repeat procedure until you've made a full turn. If done correctly, a nicely shaped cake is assured every time.

Rolling out dough is not difficult, if one remembers to follow a few simple rules.

First, always place your dough on a floured surface. It is important to flour your rolling pin. When rolling dough, always roll from the center out in all directions until you have arrived at your desired thinness and measurement.

You will sometimes find that the edges stick to the surface. If so, take a dull knife with a rounded edge (such as a butter knife) and gently release dough by lifting from surface on all sides.

To lift pastry into desired pan, just place your rolling pin at the top of dough and gently lift it up over rolling pin. Keep rolling gently toward you until all of the dough has been collected. Then place on edge of pan and unroll gently. Fit dough to pan nicely, but not taut. Trim edges, roll under and flute if suggested.

A fluted pastry wheel is a handy tool for cutting dough besides giving it an attractive and decorative edge. Wash and dry immediately after every use. A small, sharp knife is needed to make clean cuts and edges.

When folding in egg whites, do not stir or beat. Fold by moving the spoon down through the mixture to the bottom, then up toward you in an overlapping motion until ingredients are well blended.

Yeast must never be dissolved in cold or hot water. The temperature should be lukewarm for moist yeast and warm for dry yeast.

Before whipping heavy cream, place bowl, hand beater or electric beaters in refrigerator about half an hour. If desired, add 1 teaspoon or more sugar to 1/2 pint of cream.

To blanch nuts or fruit, soak in boiling water 2 minutes or until skins soften for easy removal.

After lemon rind has been grated or peeled, wrap the lemons tightly in plastic wrap and refrigerate.

When deep frying, use enough oil to allow food to float freely. A good way to test proper temperature of oil is to brown a 1-inch bread cube in 60 seconds.

Preheat oven for 10 minutes before baking desserts.

Cakes are done when cake tester or toothpick inserted in center of cake comes out clean and when cake shrinks from edges of pan. Cookies are baked when they spring back from the touch of a finger and are brown.

Place cake on rack and let cool for 5 minutes. Then turn out. For a sponge type, turn pan upside down on rack and let cool.

MAKING CAKES AT HIGH ALTITUDES

Most cake recipes need adjustments for success at high altitudes. As a rule, up to 2500 or 3000 feet, little adjustment is needed. But above that, it is often necessary to reduce the leavening and sugar, or in very rich cakes, the shortening. For sponge cakes, the eggs may have to be increased at very high altitudes.

Since cakes differ in richness and balance of ingredients, no set rule of adjustments can be made. However, here is a guide or starting point that may help in adjusting your sea-level recipes.

RECIPE GUIDE FOR HIGH ALTITUDES

	3000 feet	5000 feet	7000 feet
Reduce baking powder:			
For each teaspoon, decrease	1/8 tsp.	1/8 to 1/4 tsp.	1/4 tsp.
Reduce sugar:			
For each cup, decrease	1 tbs.	1 to 2 tbs.	2 to 3 tbs.
Increase liquid:			
For each cup, add	1 to 2 tbs.	2 to 4 tbs.	3 to 4 tbs.

NOTE: When two amounts are given, try the smaller adjustment first. If cake still needs improvement, use larger adjustment next time. There will always be exceptions to these adjustments, so use them only as a guide. Only repeated experiments with each will determine the most successful proportions.

BISCOTTI REGINA
Sesame Seed Cookies

4 cups sifted flour
2 tbs. baking powder
1 cup sugar
pinch of salt
1 cup shortening

2 eggs
3/4 cup milk
2 tsp. vanilla extract
1 1/4 cups sesame seeds*
1 tbs. milk or more

In a large bowl, blend flour, baking powder, sugar and salt. Add shortening and blend by rubbing mixture between palms of hands until texture is fine. In a medium-size bowl, beat eggs thoroughly. Add milk and vanilla extract. Mix. Gradually add to flour mixture and blend well after each addition. On a lightly floured board, knead dough until smooth. Place in a large bowl. Cover. Let stand for 30 minutes.

Just before rolling dough, place sesame seeds in a shallow dish and moisten with milk by mixing with fingers. Take medium-size pieces of dough. On a lightly floured board, roll into long cords the thickness of the middle finger. Cut into pieces 3" long. Roll cookies in moistened sesame seeds. Add more milk if seeds become dry. Place cookies on large greased cookie sheets 1 1/2" apart. Taper ends and round off. Flatten cookies slightly. Bake in a preheated oven at 375°F. for 30 minutes or until golden brown. Makes about 7 dozen.

*Fresh sesame seeds can be purchased by the pound or less in Italian bakeries. If an Italian bakery is not accessible, they can be obtained at the supermarket.

GOCCI DI CIOCCOLATA
Chocolate Spice Drops

2 cups sifted flour
1/2 cup shortening
1 cup sugar
1/2 tsp. cloves
1/2 tsp. nutmeg
1 tsp. cinnamon

3/4 tsp. baking powder
3/4 tsp. baking soda
1/4 cup cocoa
1/4 cup ground nuts
1 cup milk
confettini (tiny candy sprinkles)

In a large bowl, place flour and shortening. Cut in shortening with a knife. Add sugar, cloves, nutmeg, cinnamon, baking powder, baking soda, cocoa and nuts. Mix. Add milk gradually, mixing thoroughly. On a large greased cookie sheet, drop 1 tsp. of dough at a time, 1 1/2 inches apart. Bake in a preheated oven at 350°F. for 8–10 minutes or until done. If oven becomes overheated, after each batch is done, leave oven door open while placing more cookies on greased tin. Remove from oven. Let cookies cool. Meanwhile, make this frosting:

Frosting:
2 cups confectioners' sugar (sifted)
3/4 tsp. shortening
3 tbs. evaporated milk

2 tbs. warm water
1/4 tsp. almond *or* vanilla extract

Mix frosting ingredients until smooth. Frost cooled chocolate drops. Sprinkle tops with confettini. Makes 9–10 dozen.

The daughter of a Roman hotel cook gave me this recipe. They were a frequent dessert included in her mother's storehouse of treasured formulas.

BISCOTTI AL' ANICI
Anise Slices

1 lb. sifted flour
2 1/2 tbs. baking powder
1/2 tsp. salt
1/3 cup combined butter and shortening

6 eggs
1 cup sugar
1 1/2 tsp. anise extract

On a wooden board, combine flour, baking powder, salt and butter with shortening by rubbing mixture between palms of hands until texture is fine. In a large bowl, beat eggs well. Combine with sugar. Blend in anise extract. Make a well in dough and pour in egg mixture. Knead until smooth. If sticky, add a small amount of flour.

On large greased cookie sheets, shape dough into oblong loaves 5 inches wide and 3/4 inch thick, making sure that loaves are at least 2 inches away from all edges of pans (one loaf for each pan). Bake in a preheated oven at 350°F. for 20 minutes or until light brown. Remove from oven and cut diagonally into 1-inch wide slices. Cut longer slices in half diagonally. Turn slices on sides. Let bake for 10 minutes more (5 minutes on each side or until golden brown). Makes slightly more than 3 dozen.

Anise Slices, sometimes called "Anisette Toast," are a Venetian creation both Northern and Southern Italians enjoy.

BISCOTTI D' ASSUNTA
Susan's Cookies

4 tbs. butter
1 tbs. shortening
1 1/4 cups sugar
4 eggs

1 lb. sifted flour
2 tsp. baking powder
grated rind of 1/2 large lemon
pinch of salt

Glaze:
1 egg
1 tbs. milk

In a large bowl, cream the butter with shortening. Add sugar and eggs. Beat thoroughly. In another large bowl, blend flour, baking powder, rind and salt. Add gradually to butter and shortening, mixing well each time. On a lightly floured board, knead dough until smooth. Roll medium pieces of dough into long cords 1/2 inch thick. Cut into pieces 3 1/2" long. Form into "U" or "S" shapes. Place cookies an inch apart on large greased cookie sheets. To glaze: Beat egg with milk and brush tops of cookies. Bake in a preheated oven at 375°F. for about 12–15 minutes or until golden brown. Makes about 7 dozen.

BISCOTTI DI CILIEGIE
Cherry Slices

1 cup sugar
8 tbs. creamed butter
6 beaten eggs
4 1/2 cups sifted flour
4 tsp. baking powder

1/2 tsp. salt
8 oz. jar maraschino cherries, chopped (reserve
    liquid)
3 oz. coarsely chopped almonds

In a large bowl, mix sugar with butter. Add eggs, flour, baking powder, salt, cherries, cherry liquid and almonds. Beat well until batter is smooth. Divide batter into 4 equal sections. On large greased cookie sheets, spoon and shape batter into oblong loaves 5 inches wide and 3/4 inch thick,

(Continued on following page.)

making sure that loaves are at least 2 inches away from all edges of sheets (one loaf for each pan).

Bake in a preheated oven at 350°F. for 15 minutes or until light brown. Remove from oven and cut into 1-inch wide slices diagonally. If some slices are too long, cut diagonally in half. Turn slices on sides. Let bake for 10 minutes more (5 minutes on each side or until golden brown). Makes about 5 dozen.

PORCELLATE SICILIANI
Sicilian Fruit-Filled Cookies

3 1/2 cups sifted flour
3 tsp. baking powder
1/3 tsp. salt
1/2 cup sugar
3/4 cup shortening

2 beaten eggs
1/2 cup lukewarm water
2 tsp. vanilla extract
confettini *or* sifted confectioners' sugar

Filling:

3 cups ground dry figs
1 1/2 cups ground raisins
1 1/4 cups water
1 cup chopped roasted almonds

4 tsp. grated orange rind
6 oz. plum *or* grape preserves (at room temperature)
1 tsp. cinnamon

Glaze:

1 egg
1 tsp. milk

On a large wooden board, combine flour, baking powder, salt, sugar and shortening. Blend by rubbing mixture between palms of hands until texture is fine. Make a well. Add 2 beaten eggs, water and vanilla extract. Blend. Knead until smooth. Let stand covered for 30 minutes.

Meanwhile, prepare filling: Before grinding figs, remove stems and cut figs in small pieces. Place ground figs, raisins and water in a large, heavy aluminum saucepan over low flame. After water simmers, cook for 5 minutes, stirring constantly with a wooden spoon. Remove from heat. Add almonds, orange rind, plum or grape preserves and cinnamon. Cool.

Divide dough into two parts. Roll out 1/8 inch thick. Cut out into 3-1/2-inch squares. Fill centers and length of squares with 2 heaping teaspoons of fruit filling. Fold and press edges down well. Form into horseshoe or "S" shapes.

When making horseshoe shapes, the folded edge should be on top. Flatten top slightly. If when shaping, the folded edge appears to open slightly, that's alright. The filling is sticky enough to assure good adhesion to dough. Then take a small knife and tap the top lightly with the blade to create a textured look.

However, when making "S" shapes, close edges as above; only this time, roll filled cookie lightly to look like a small sausage. Place on large cookie sheets, seam sides down, an inch and a half apart. Flatten tops. Form into "S" shapes. With blade of knife, tap tops lightly to give a textured look.

In a small bowl, beat egg with milk. Brush tops with mixture and sprinkle each with confettini. Bake in a preheated oven at 375°F. until golden. Cool.

If confettini topping is not desired, just brush cookies with egg mixture and bake as directed above. When cool, dust with sifted confectioners' sugar. Makes about 3 1/2 dozen. Store in large cookie jars, cookie tins or on large trays covered tightly with plastic wrap, then aluminum foil.

In Ciminna, these cookies were given the affectionate provincial name of *Porcellate,* literally meaning "stuffed little pigs" which seem hardly to contain themselves. They are a traditional Christmas dessert, but excellent anytime.

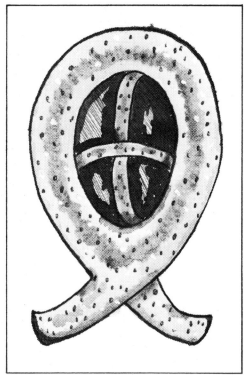

Drawing: Rose Barrese

MAMA'S POOPI CON UOVA
Mama's Sweet Easter Egg Nests

3 1/2 cups sifted flour
3/4 tbs. baking powder
pinch of salt
3/4 cup sugar
6 tbs. shortening
2 beaten eggs

1 tsp. vanilla extract
3/4 cup milk
6 hard-boiled eggs (in shells, cold)
1 beaten egg white (frothy)
confettini (tiny candy sprinkles)

On a wooden board, blend flour, baking powder, salt and sugar. Add shortening and work in by rubbing mixture between palms of hands until texture is fine. Make a well. Beat eggs with vanilla extract. Pour in well and blend into mixture. Add milk gradually. Blend. Knead until smooth. Place in a bowl. Cover. Set aside for 30 minutes.

Color cold hard-boiled eggs with desired Easter vegetable colors. Divide dough into seven portions. With hand, roll 6 pieces of dough like bread sticks 11 1/2 inches long. Form into an ℓ shape or loop. Place hard-boiled egg in loop. With hand, roll short, very thin pieces of dough from remaining portion of dough. Form a cross (+) over each egg. Press ends of the cross down well into loop of dough. Brush dough with beaten egg white. Sprinkle with confettini. Place on a cookie tin. Place in highest point of oven. Bake in preheated oven at 350°F. for 25 minutes or until golden brown. Makes 6.

These make a delightful Easter morning dessert! Each region of Italy has its own version of this recipe made in various and interesting shapes and sizes.

In the province of Brindisi, they prepare sweet breads at Eastertime with one or more eggs that harden during baking. They are called *Puddriche cu l'eu* and *Cudrure cull'ove* there. The eggs are a symbol of life and birth. **(See drawing above.)**

CASSATELLE ALLA SICILIANA
Sicilian Cream Tartlets

Dough:

2 cups sifted flour

1/4 tsp. baking powder

pinch of salt

1/2 cup butter

1/2 cup hot milk

1/2 tsp. vanilla extract

2 small egg yolks

sifted confectioners' sugar

Filling:

1 lb. drained ricotta *or* mild, creamed, small-curd
    cottage cheese (sieved)

1 oz. chopped sweet chocolate

1/4 tsp. cinnamon

3 heaping tbs. sugar

sifted confectioners' sugar

In a small bowl, combine flour, baking powder and salt. Place butter in a large bowl. Add milk and vanilla extract. Beat until well blended. Beat in egg yolks. Add flour mixture gradually. Beat until smooth. Cover. Chill about half an hour. Then roll out 1/8 inch thick on a lightly floured board. With a 2-3/4-inch cookie cutter, cut out disks. Place on cookie sheets, one inch apart. Bake in a preheated oven at 450°F. for 8–10 minutes or until golden brown. Cool.

In a medium-size bowl, mix filling ingredients until smooth. Refrigerate until ready to use. Before serving, spread about a tablespoonful of filling on a disk. Top with another disk. Repeat process until all ingredients are used. Sprinkle tartlets with sifted confectioners' sugar. Makes about 2 dozen.

There are several ways to make Cassatelle, one of which is deep-frying small filled pillows of dough. But I found that doing them this other way keeps the ricotta moist and from becoming discolored by melted chocolate, therefore light and creamy.

TORTA D'ARANCIO E UVA SECCA
Orange Raisin Cake

1/2 cup butter

3/4 cup sugar

2 eggs (at room temperature)

1 tsp. grated orange rind

juice of 1 orange (at room temperature)

milk (at room temperature)

2 cups sifted flour

2 tbs. baking powder

pinch of salt

1 cup seedless raisins

sifted confectioners' sugar (optional)

In a large bowl cream the butter with sugar. Add eggs. Beat. Place orange juice in a cup. Fill with milk until it measures 1 cup. Add milk, orange juice and rind to mixture. Beat until smooth.

In a medium-size bowl, blend flour, baking powder, salt and raisins. Add gradually to butter mixture. Beat until smooth. Pour in a greased 9"x9"x2" baking pan. Bake in preheated oven at 375°F. for 30 minutes or until golden brown. Cool. If desired, sprinkle with confectioners' sugar.

When we were children (seven of us), Mother occasionally surprised us after school with an enormous version of this cake which vanished in no time.

SAVOIARDI DILETTO
Ladyfinger Delight

25 ladyfingers
1/4 cup flour
5 tbs. sugar
1/8 tsp. salt
2 egg yolks
2 cups milk
2 tsp. butter

1 tsp. vanilla extract
sweet rum
1 lb. can sliced peaches, drained
sweet vermouth
maraschino cherries, drained on absorbent
paper

To make custard: Combine flour, sugar and salt. In a medium-size bowl, beat egg yolks. Combine with milk. Add to flour mixture gradually and stir. Cook in double boiler over simmering water. Stir constantly over low flame until thick. Add butter and vanilla extract. Cool.

Split ladyfingers in half and line bottom of an 8"x8"x2" baking dish with 15 ladyfinger halves (split side facing down). With fingers, sprinkle lightly with sweet rum (too much may cause a bitter taste). Cover with some custard and then peach slices. Add a second layer of ladyfinger halves. Sprinkle lightly with vermouth. Cover with some custard and more peach slices. Third layer of ladyfinger halves should be sprinkled lightly with rum. Press down slightly with hand to make layers more compact. Cover with remaining custard. Top off with peach slices and a few maraschino cherries. Refrigerate for at least 5 hours before serving. Serves 9 or more.

PANETTONE
Fruit Bread

4 cups sifted flour
5 tbs. sugar
1 pkg. dry yeast (dissolved in 1/4 cup warm
    water)
3/4 tbs. corn oil
1/4 cup melted butter (salted)

1/2 cup scalded milk (cooled)
3 beaten eggs (at room temperature)
1 tsp. vanilla extract
1 1/4 cups seedless raisins (if too dry, soften
    with warm water)
1/2 cup chopped dried citron

Place flour and sugar on board. Blend. Make a well. Add dissolved yeast. Blend by rubbing mixture between palms of hands until texture is fine. Add corn oil and butter, blending in the same manner. Make a well. Add milk, eggs and vanilla extract. Work in the same manner. Knead until smooth. If sticky, sprinkle some flour on board. Place dough in a large bowl. Cover. Set aside in a warm place. Allow to rise about 1 1/2 hours or until double in bulk. Then punch down. On board, add and work in raisins and citron, a small amount at a time. Knead until fruit is evenly distributed. Divide dough in half. Knead each portion for 30 seconds. Place in 2 greased high molds (preferably empty 2 lb. coffee tins). Cover. Let rise again until double in bulk.

Preheat oven to 350°F. and place molds on grating in middle of the lower part of the oven. Bake for 15 minutes. Lower temperature to 325°. Cover tops of each panettone with brown paper. Continue baking for another 20 minutes or until golden brown or gives a hollow sound when thumped. Cool and unmold.

In Milan, panettone is the "king of cakes," and some are shaped to resemble the Lombard church domes. It is the custom to serve it at the end of a Christmas dinner, but as everywhere else in Italy, it is popular at all times.

TORTA DI RICOTTA CLASSICO
Classic Italian Cheese Cake

Dough:

1 1/4 cups sifted flour
1/4 cup sugar
1/2 tsp. salt
1/2 tsp. lemon peel, grated

1/2 cup sweet butter
1 egg yolk
2 tbs. Liquore Galliano

Mix flour, sugar, salt and lemon peel in a bowl. Cut in butter until mixture resembles coarse meal. Mix in egg yolk and Galliano until pastry is blended. Press pastry over bottom and up sides (1 3/4 inches) of 9-inch spring-form pan. Bake in a preheated oven at 350°F. for 15 minutes, until dry, but not browned.

Filling:

30 oz. ricotta *or* mild, creamed cottage cheese
    with tiny, soft curds
4 eggs
1/2 cup sugar
1/4 cup flour

1/4 cup Liquore Galliano
2 tbs. golden raisins
2 tbs. finely chopped candied orange *or*
    lemon peel

If using cottage cheese, put through a fine sieve. Blend cheese, eggs, sugar and flour in a bowl. Stir in Galliano, raisins and peel. Pour cheese filling into crust in pan. Bake in a preheated oven at 325°F. for 1 hour or until golden brown. Release cake from spring-form and cool on a rack. Makes a 9-inch cake.

Recipe courtesy of McKesson Wine & Spirits Co.

GATO DI NOCE
Nut Torte

3 eggs
1 cup sugar
3 tbs. water
2 tbs. fine bread crumbs

2 tsp. baking powder
1 cup chopped nuts
1/2 pt. heavy cream
sugar to taste

In a large bowl, beat eggs well until they turn light yellow and thicken. In a small bowl, mix sugar and water. Add to eggs in small amounts, beating well after each addition. Combine bread crumbs, baking powder and nuts. Add to egg mixture gradually, beating well after each addition.

Line two 8" round cake pans with wax paper. Divide mixture evenly into pans. Bake in a preheated oven at 350°F. for 20–25 minutes or until done. Remove from pans and let cool on a wire rack.

Whip half of cream with sugar to taste until thick. Spread one layer of cake with half of cream. Cover with the other layer and refrigerate. Just before serving, whip other half of cream with sugar to taste and spread on top.

PASTA MARGHERITA
Margherita Cake

6 eggs, separated
1/2 cup sugar
juice of 1 lemon

1 cup potato flour
3/4 tsp. vanilla extract
sifted confectioners' sugar

In a large bowl, beat egg yolks well. Add sugar gradually. Beat thoroughly for about 2 minutes. Add lemon juice. Beat for 10 minutes. Fold in flour gradually. Beat egg whites until stiff. Fold into mixture. Transfer to a 9"x9"x2" greased baking pan which has been powdered with confectioners' sugar. Bake in a preheated oven at 375°F. for 20–25 minutes or until golden brown. When cool, sprinkle with vanilla extract and confectioners' sugar.

I'm not sure why this cake is called "Margherita." But it may be because it's light and delicate as a daisy which Italians call *margherita*. The sugar on top is like white petals.

To give the cake an airy look, form a design by placing a large paper doily on top and sprinkle with sifted confectioners' sugar. Hold doily tautly at both sides and carefully lift straight up to keep the sugar from smudging.

PANE DI SPAGNA CON CAFFE
Hot Coffee Spongecake

4 eggs, separated
1 cup sugar
6 1/2 tbs. hot black coffee (*caffè espresso*)

1 cup sifted flour
1 1/2 tsp. baking powder
1/2 tsp. salt

In a large bowl, beat eggs until thick and lemon colored. Add sugar gradually, beating constantly. Add hot black coffee about 2 tbs. at a time, beating well after each addition. Beat egg whites stiff, but not dry. Fold into egg mixture.

In a small bowl, combine sifted flour, baking powder and salt. Fold into egg mixture gradually until well blended. Pour into two 8" greased layer pans. Bake in a preheated oven at 350°F. for 20–25 minutes or until golden brown. Allow to cool. Meanwhile, prepare filling.

Lemon Custard Filling:
2 tbs. flour
2 1/2 tbs. sugar
1/16 tsp. salt
1 cup milk
1 beaten egg yolk

1 tbs. lemon juice
1 tsp. grated lemon peel
1 tsp. butter
2 tbs. blanched chopped hazelnuts

sifted confectioners' sugar

Combine flour, sugar and salt. Combine milk with egg yolk and add gradually to dry mixture. Cook in top of double boiler over simmering water. Stir constantly, over low flame, until thick and smooth. Add lemon juice, peel and butter. Cool. Add chopped hazelnuts. Spread between spongecake layers. Sprinkle top of cake with confectioners' sugar. Serves 6–8.

Serve with steaming *caffè espresso*.

ZUPPA AL' INGLESE
Italian Rum Cake

1 8-inch spongecake
sweet rum
sweet Marsala
7 tbs. strawberry jam (at room temperature)

1/2 pt. heavy cream
1 tsp. sugar
1/2 tsp. almond extract
4 tbs. mixed candied fruit, chopped

Follow same directions for Hot Coffee Spongecake (without filling), except substitute hot milk for black coffee and add 1 tsp. vanilla extract. Cool. Slice spongecake vertically into 1-inch-wide slices. Spread out slices and divide into three equal portions. With fingers, sprinkle two portions of cake lightly on one side with sweet rum (too much may cause a bitter taste) and the third with Marsala.

In an 8-inch-square baking dish, arrange a layer of rum-sprinkled slices (sprinkled side up). Spread with strawberry jam. Arrange a layer of Marsala-sprinkled slices (sprinkled side up). Whip half of the heavy cream with 1/2 tsp. sugar and 1/4 tsp. almond extract. Combine with half of the candied fruit. Spread layer with mixture. Arrange another layer of rum-sprinkled slices. Keep cake in refrigerator for at least 5 hours before serving. Just before serving, top with remaining cream whipped with 1/2 tsp. sugar and 1/4 tsp. almond extract. Sprinkle with balance of candied fruit. Serves 6—8.

Legend says this dessert was fashioned after the famed English trifle.

TORTA CON MARASCHINO
Maraschino Cake

1 plain round pound cake (2 lbs.)
Maraschino liqueur
1 pt. heavy cream

2 tsp. sugar
maraschino cherries (drained on absorbent
　　paper)

Slice pound cake in three layers. Sprinkle one side of each with Maraschino liqueur. Whip 1 1/3 cups heavy cream with 1 1/3 tsp. sugar. Spread each layer except the top with whipped cream. Place cake in refrigerator for at least 5 hours before serving. When ready to serve, whip remaining cream with 2/3 tsp. of sugar and spread on top. Slice sufficient amount of cherries in half to top cake. Serves 10—12.

CASSATA ALLA SICILIANA
Sicilian Cream Tart

Spongecake:

2 cups sifted cake flour	1 1/2 tsp. vanilla extract
3 tsp. baking powder	1 1/3 cups sugar
1/2 tsp. salt	2/3 cup boiling water
8 egg yolks (2/3 cup)	

In a medium-size bowl, sift together flour, baking powder and salt. Set aside. In a large bowl, beat egg yolks with vanilla extract until thick and light in color. Gradually add sugar and beat until very thick. Slowly beat in boiling water. Fold in flour mixture. Turn into two greased and wax-paper-lined 9-inch layer cake pans. Bake in a preheated oven at 350°F. 20–25 minutes. Cool on cake racks, loosen with spatula, turn out of pans and remove paper. With serrated knife, split cake layers to make four thin layers.

Ricotta Filling:

15 oz. *or* 1 lb. ricotta *or* mild, creamed cottage cheese with tiny soft curds	1 tbs. milk
	1 tsp. vanilla extract
1/4 cup sugar	1/4 tsp. almond extract
1/4 tsp. salt	1/3 cup finely chopped mixed candied fruit
3 tbs. orange liqueur	2 oz. semi-sweet chocolate, chopped

If using cottage cheese, press through a sieve. Drain ricotta. Combine ricotta, sugar, salt, liqueur, milk, vanilla and almond extract in small bowl of electric mixer. Beat until smooth and creamy. Stir in candied fruit and chocolate. Chill. Stack split cake layers, spreading ricotta mixture over first three layers and topping with a plain layer. Chill 1 hour or longer before frosting.

Chocolate Butter Cream:

1 cup sugar	2 squares (2 oz.) unsweetened chocolate
1/4 cup flour	1 cup soft butter
1/4 tsp. salt	2 tbs. orange liqueur
1 cup milk	2 tsp. vanilla extract

Mix sugar, flour and salt in a small saucepan. Gradually stir in milk. Add chocolate. Cook, stirring constantly, over moderate heat for 8–10 minutes until chocolate melts and mixture thickens. Cool to room temperature.

Cream butter. Gradually beat in chocolate mixture. Add orange liqueur and vanilla. Generously frost side and top of cake, reserving 1/2 cup butter cream. Chill cake and reserved butter cream.

Put reserved butter cream in pastry tube with fluted tip. Make rosettes around top edge of cake. Chill overnight before serving. Makes a 9-inch cake.

Cassata is traditionally served at Italian feasts and holidays. It may also be included in a wedding menu. For such an occasion, exclude unsweetened chocolate from Chocolate Butter Cream and proceed as directed. Decorate top with crystallized violets and silver candies, if desired.

The wedding cake probably originated in early Roman days when the bride and groom ate a traditional cake made of flour, salt and water. They ate it together and feasted the guests. Eventually the cake was broken over the bride's head as a symbol of plentifulness and each guest took a piece of the broken cake away with him to ensure plentifulness for himself also.

The old custom of giving confetti (not colored paper, but sugared Jordan almonds) in small boxes to guests is still observed at Italian weddings. It is a survival of the pagan custom of throwing nuts at a wedding.

SPHINGI DI RICOTTA
Italian Cheese Puffs

3 eggs, slightly beaten
2 tbs. sugar
1 lb. ricotta *or* mild, creamed cottage cheese
    with tiny, soft curds (drained)
1 cup sifted flour

4 tbs. baking powder
1/2 tsp. salt
2 tbs. rum, brandy *or* sweet Marsala
corn oil and shortening for deep frying
sifted confectioners' sugar

If using cottage cheese, put through a fine sieve.

In a large bowl, combine eggs, sugar and ricotta. Beat thoroughly. Add flour, baking powder, salt and rum. Blend well. Cover. Let stand for 1 hour.

Heat corn oil and shortening over low flame in a deep saucepan or deep fryer. Drop in batter by teaspoonfuls. Fry until golden on all sides. Do not overbrown. Remove and drain on absorbent paper. When cool, sprinkle with confectioners' sugar. Serve immediately. Makes about 3 1/2 dozen.

ZEPPOLI ALLA SICILIANA
Sicilian Raisin Puffs

2 lbs. sifted flour
1/2 cup shortening
1/4 tsp. salt
2 heaping tbs. sugar
1 cake moist yeast (dissolved in 1/2 cup
    lukewarm water)
2 beaten eggs

1/2 cup seedless raisins (if dry, soften in warm
    water and drain)
3 cups lukewarm water
2 tsp. vanilla extract
corn oil and shortening for deep frying
sifted confectioners' sugar

In a 14-quart kettle, place flour, shortening and salt. Blend by rubbing mixture between palms of hands until fine. Add sugar, yeast, eggs, raisins, water and vanilla extract. Beat very well until batter hangs stiffly from a long-handled wooden spoon. Cover. Keep in a warm place. Allow to rise for about 2 hours or until bubbles appear on top.

Heat corn oil and shortening over low flame in a deep skillet or deep fryer. Drop in batter by heaping tablespoonfuls. Cook a few at a time, until golden on both sides, being careful not to overbrown them. Remove with perforated spoon. Drain on absorbent paper. When cool, sprinkle with confectioners' sugar. Serve immediately. Makes 6 dozen or more.

This is a highly favored dessert for Christmas Eve or March 19, St. Joseph's Day.

Zeppoli are really a Calabrian creation containing a plain mixture of flour, water, yeast and salt. But Mother used her Sicilian ingenuity to enrich these wonderfully airy puffs.

STRUFOLI
Honey Balls

3 large eggs
1 tbs. creamed salted butter
1/2 tbs. sugar
1/2 tsp. vanilla extract
2 cups sifted flour

1/2 tsp. baking powder
8 oz. jar honey
corn oil and shortening for deep frying
confettini (tiny candy sprinkles)

In a large bowl, beat eggs well. Add and mix in butter, sugar, and vanilla extract. In a small bowl, combine flour and baking powder. Add gradually to egg mixture. Knead until smooth on a large, lightly floured board. Cover. Let stand for 30 minutes.

Taking medium-size amounts of dough at a time on board, roll under palm of hand until rope-like or the width of a finger. Then cut into 1/2-inch pieces. Toss pieces in flour.

Meanwhile, in a deep fryer with wire basket, heat corn oil and shortening over low flame. Gradually and gently add a handful of pieces. Do not crowd pan. Stir constantly to avoid sticking. If sticking does occur, break apart gently with a fork. Turn them with a slotted spoon occasionally and cook until golden brown on all sides, being careful not to overbrown.

Cut only enough dough to cook at one time. Repeat process until all dough has been used. When done, lift wire basket. Drain pieces on absorbent paper.

Melt honey in a deep, heavy aluminum pan over low flame. Add balls. Mix constantly with a long-handled wooden spoon just until balls hold honey and are well coated (3 to 3 1/2 minutes—no longer or honey will carmelize). Transfer to doilied platters. Form honey balls into mounds. While hot, sprinkle generously with confettini. Serve cool. Makes 2 large platters.

This is a delicious Christmas, New Year and Easter treat.

FARFALLETTE DOLCE
Sweet Bowknots

2 egg yolks
4 1/2 tbs. sugar
1/2 tbs. white vinegar
1/4 cup milk
1/2 jigger whiskey

1/2 tbs. melted butter
1 1/2 cups sifted flour
corn oil and shortening for deep frying
sifted confectioners' sugar

In a large bowl, beat egg yolks well. Mix in sugar. Add vinegar, milk, whiskey, and butter. Gradually add flour, mixing well after each addition. On a floured board, knead dough until smooth. Let stand covered for 30 minutes. Then roll out dough until very thin. With pastry cutter, cut dough into strips 6 inches long and 3/4 inch wide. Tie in individual bows.

Heat corn oil and shortening over low flame in a deep fryer. Fry bows until golden, being careful not to crowd pan or overbrown. Remove with perforated spoon. Drain on absorbent paper. Cool. Place on a platter. Sprinkle with sifted confectioners' sugar. Makes about 2 platters.

A favorite Christmas or New Year's dessert, but can be enjoyed anytime. If serving for these holidays, place paper doilies on platters under bowknots.

MELE IN PASTELLA
Apples in Batter

4 medium apples (cooking variety)
corn oil for deep frying

Batter:

1 egg yolk
1 cup sifted flour
1 tbs. melted butter
1 tbs. sweet rum *or* whiskey

pinch of salt
1 cup cold water
1 stiffly beaten egg white

sifted confectioners' sugar

Beat egg yolk. Add flour, butter, rum, salt and water. Beat thoroughly. Allow to stand covered for 2–3 hours. Peel, core and slice apples about 1/2 inch thick. Fold in stiffly beaten egg white in batter. Dip apple slices in batter.

Heat corn oil over low flame in a deep fryer. Fry apple slices until golden on both sides. Remove with a perforated spoon. Drain on absorbent paper. Sprinkle with confectioners' sugar. Serve warm. Serves 6.

If desired, other fruits such as peeled sliced fresh peaches and bananas may be used instead of apples.

DITI DI RISO
Rice Fingers

1 cup rice
1 1/4 cups milk
1/2 cup sugar
2 eggs

1/2 tsp. vanilla extract
flour
corn oil for deep frying
sifted confectioners' sugar

In a heavy, medium-size saucepan, cook rice in salted, boiling water until half done (about 15 minutes). Drain. Add milk and sugar. Continue cooking for 10 minutes more or until tender, stirring frequently. Place in a medium-size bowl and allow to cool. Add eggs and vanilla extract. Mix well. Place rice mixture on board. Shape into "fingers" about 3 inches long and 1 inch wide. Dredge in flour.

Heat corn oil in a skillet over low flame. Using spatula, gently place rice fingers in oil. Cook until golden on both sides. Remove carefully with a perforated spoon. Drain on absorbent paper. When cool, sprinkle with confectioners' sugar. Makes about 2 dozen.

DONZELLINE
Sweet Little Damsels

1 cup sifted flour
1 tbs. butter
pinch of salt
4 tbs. milk

corn oil and shortening for deep frying
combined confectioners' sugar and cinnamon
    (sifted) *or* sifted confectioners' sugar

On a large wooden board, combine flour, salt and butter by working mixture between palms of hands. Add milk gradually to make a rather stiff dough. If too sticky, add more flour. Then roll into a thin sheet. Cut into 1-inch squares, diamonds or triangles. Cook pieces in deep, hot corn oil and shortening, over low flame, until golden. Do not overbrown. Remove them with a perforated spoon. Drain on absorbent paper. When cool, sprinkle with combined confectioners' sugar and cinnamon, or sifted confectioners' sugar.

PASTIERA DI RICOTTA
Italian Cheese Pie

Pasta Frolla (Flaky Sweet Pastry):
2 cups sifted flour
1 tbs. baking powder
pinch of salt
1/3 cup sugar

1/2 cup shortening
1 egg
1 tsp. vanilla extract
1/4 cup milk or more

Filling:
1 1/2 lbs. drained ricotta *or* mild creamed cottage
    cheese with tiny soft curds
2 eggs

5 tbs. sugar
1 oz. semi-sweet chocolate, cut into bits
2 tbs. Maraschino liqueur

sifted confectioners' sugar

On a wooden board, combine flour, baking powder, salt and sugar. Add shortening. Blend by rubbing mixture between palms of hands until fine. Make a well. In a small bowl, beat egg. Add vanilla extract. Add to well. Blend in the same manner until texture is fairly fine. Gradually add milk. Add more milk if necessary. Work in same manner. Knead until smooth. Cut away 3/4 of dough. Roll out on floured board until thin.

Line a greased 9-inch piepan with dough (leaving 1 inch of pastry overlapping edge of pan to roll under later).

In a large bowl, beat ricotta until very smooth. If using cottage cheese, put through a fine sieve. Beat in eggs. Add sugar, chocolate and Maraschino liqueur. Mix well. Add ricotta filling to pieshell. Roll out remaining smaller portion of dough and cut out strips 1/2-inch wide. Place strips over filling in lattice design. Roll edges of strips and dough under together.

Bake in a preheated oven at 375°F. for 30 minutes or until pastry is golden brown and filling is firm in center. Remove from oven. Cool. Sprinkle with confectioners' sugar before serving.

If this pie is not eaten the same day it's baked, it keeps nicely for a few days in the refrigerator. As it mellows, the filling acquires a creamy taste similar to ice cream.

TORTA DI MELE ALLA CONTADINA
Apple Pie, Farmer's Style

Filling:
8 medium cooking apples, sliced
1 tsp. cinnamon
2 tbs. sugar

Pastry:

2 cups sifted flour
1 level tbs. baking powder
1 tbs. sugar
1/8 tsp. salt

3 heaping tbs. shortening
8 tbs. cold water
1 tsp. vanilla extract
milk

In a large bowl, combine apples, cinnamon and sugar. Set aside. On a board, combine flour, baking powder, sugar and salt. Add shortening. Rub mixture between palms of hands until texture is very fine. Gradually add water and vanilla extract. Then knead dough well until smooth. Divide dough in half. Roll out both pieces to fit pan. Line greased 9-inch piepan with one piece, leaving 1 inch of pastry overlapping edge of pan to flute later. Fill with apples. Cover with top piece of pastry. Make a few slits in center of top pastry. Turn edges under and flute. Brush top with milk. Bake in a preheated oven at 375°F. for 40 minutes or until golden brown.

This pie is Mother's and has a real homespun quality because of its bread-like crust. Its simplicity is the secret to its charm.

TORTA DI ZUCCA
Pumpkin Pie

Pasta Frolla (Flaky Sweet Pastry):
2 cups sifted flour
pinch of salt
2 tbs. sugar
small amount of beaten egg white

2 beaten egg yolks
1/2 cup butter
4 tbs. milk

Place flour, salt and sugar on board. Mix. Make a well. Add egg yolks and butter. Rub mixture between palms of hands until fine. Add 1 tbs. of milk at a time. Knead until smooth. Wrap in wax paper. Chill for 45 minutes. Cut away 3/4 of dough. Roll out until thin. Then do same to remaining smaller portion of dough to use as strips for top. Cut 1/2-inch-wide strips with a pastry wheel.

Filling:
2 heaping cups fresh pumpkin, cubed
milk
2 eggs, separated
1 tbs. fine bread crumbs
1/8 tsp. salt

1 tsp. cinnamon
1/4 tsp. nutmeg
3 1/2 tbs. finely chopped blanched almonds
2/3 cup sugar

In a medium-size saucepan, cook fresh pumpkin in milk to cover until tender. Then put through a sieve over a medium-size bowl. Add egg yolks, bread crumbs, salt, cinnamon, nutmeg, almonds and sugar. Mix. In a small bowl, beat egg whites until stiff, not dry. Fold into pumpkin mixture.
Line an 8-inch buttered piepan with 3/4 of pastry, leaving 1 inch of pastry overlapping the

edge. Brush bottom with egg white. Add pumpkin filling. Arrange strips on filling in lattice design. Roll edges of strips and dough under together. Bake in a preheated oven at 450°F. for 10 minutes. Reduce temperature to 325°. Bake for 20 minutes more or until golden brown and firm. Makes one 8-inch pie. Serves 6–8.

PASTIERA DI GRANO
Easter Wheat Pie

1/2 lb. dry wheat
10 cups water

Pasta Frolla (Flaky Sweet Pastry):

2 cups sifted flour	1/3 cup butter
pinch of salt	3 egg yolks
1/2 cup sugar	3 tbs. milk

small amount of beaten egg white

Filling:

1 1/2 lbs. well-drained ricotta *or* mild creamed cottage cheese with tiny, soft curds	1 tsp. vanilla extract
	grated rind of 1 large lemon
1 1/4 cups sugar	1/2 cup chopped dried citron and orange peel
6 beaten egg yolks	6 stiffly beaten egg whites

Purchase dry wheat without husks. Wash. In a large pot, soak wheat overnight in 10 cups of water. Then bring to a boil over high flame. Lower flame. Cover. Cook for 1 1/2 hours or until soft. If too much water evaporates, add more. Stir frequently to prevent sticking. Allow to cool. Place wheat in a colander. Run under clear, cool water to remove starchiness. Drain well.

To make pastry: Combine flour, salt and sugar. Add butter. Blend by rubbing mixture between palms of hands. Add egg yolks, one at a time. Blend in the same way. Add milk. Knead until smooth. Form into a ball. Cover with wax paper. Chill for 30 minutes. Then take 3/4 of dough and roll out 1/8-inch thick. Line an 11-inch piepan or a round 9"x2" baking pan with dough, allowing one inch of dough to lap over edge. Brush bottom of pieshell with small amount of beaten egg white.

To make filling: In a large bowl, beat well-drained ricotta* until very smooth. If using cottage cheese, put through a fine sieve. Add sugar and egg yolks. Beat until well blended. Add vanilla extract, lemon rind, mixed dried fruit and wheat. Mix well. Fold in stiffly beaten egg whites.

Pour filling into pieshell. With remaining dough, cut out 1-inch wide strips with a pastry wheel. Arrange strips in lattice design on filling. With overlapping dough, turn edges under and flatten slightly. Bake in a preheated oven at 350°F. (in lowest point of oven) for 50 minutes or until center is firm and pie is golden brown. Serves about 20.

This is a deliciously rich traditional Easter dessert.

Uncooked dry wheat can be bought at most Italian bakeries and grocery stores, but other ethnic groceries may carry it too. I purchase mine at a Greek grocery on Ninth Avenue in New York City. Already-cooked wheat is often available in Italian pastry shops during Easter week.

*Most ricotta does not have to be drained. However, if much liquid is present, place a piece of clean muslin in a large strainer to drain well.

SOUFFLE DI RISO
Rice Soufflé

1/2 cup rice
2 1/2 cups milk
1 1/2 tbs. butter
1/3 cup sugar

1 tsp. vanilla extract
1 tbs. sweet rum
4 eggs, separated (at room temperature)
sifted confectioners' sugar

In top of double boiler with boiling water in bottom section, cook rice in milk until tender. Stir frequently. Shortly before removing from heat, add butter, sugar, vanilla extract and rum. Set aside to cool. Beat egg yolks and add to mixture. Beat egg whites until stiff (not dry) and fold in. Pour into a buttered 8"x8"x2" baking dish. Bake in a preheated oven at 325°F. for 25 minutes or until golden brown. Do not open oven door while baking. Sprinkle with confectioners' sugar. Serve immediately. Serves 6.

SOUFFLE DI FARINA DI PATATE
Potato Flour Soufflé

2 1/2 tbs. potato flour
1/2 cup sugar
1 1/4 cups milk
2 tbs. melted butter

grated peel of 1 lemon
3 eggs, separated (at room temperature)
sifted confectioners' sugar

Place flour and sugar in a medium-size pot. Gradually add milk mixed with butter to this mixture. Warm over low flame, but do not boil. Stir. Remove from flame. Add lemon peel. Beat in egg yolks, one at a time. Beat egg whites until stiff, not dry. Fold in. Pour into a greased 2-quart baking dish and bake in a preheated oven at 325°F. for 25 minutes or until golden brown. Do not open oven door while baking. Sprinkle with sifted confectioners' sugar. Serve immediately. Serves 6.

SOUFFLE DI CASTAGNE
Chestnut Soufflé

1/3 lb. chestnuts
1 1/2 cups milk
1/2 cup sugar
3 tbs. melted butter

2 tbs. Maraschino liqueur
1 tsp. vanilla extract
5 eggs, separated (at room temperature)
sifted confectioners' sugar

Cut a crisscross on pointed end of chestnuts. In water to cover, cook them for 15 minutes or enough to make them easy to peel. Remove inner skin. Then in a saucepan cook chestnuts and milk over low flame for 45 minutes or until tender. Put through sieve over a large bowl. Add sugar, butter, Maraschino liqueur and vanilla extract. Mix. Add egg yolks one at a time, beating well after each addition. Beat egg whites until stiff, not dry, and fold in. Pour mixture into greased 2-quart baking dish. Bake in a preheated oven at 325°F. for 25 minutes or until golden brown. Do not open oven door while baking. Sprinkle with confectioners' sugar. Serve at once. Serves 6.

GHIACCIATA DI MELE
Apple Ice

2 lbs. cooking apples, peeled, cored and sliced
3 tbs. water
2 tbs. sugar
3 tbs. seedless raisins
grated peel of half a lemon

pinch of cinnamon
heavy cream (whipped with sugar to taste)
8 toasted hazelnuts, blanched and finely
    chopped

Put apples and water in a large pot. Cover. Cook, over low flame, until tender. Put the apples through a sieve. Then add sugar, raisins, lemon peel and cinnamon. Bring to the boiling point. Lower flame and cook gently 5–6 minutes, stirring constantly. Cool completely.

Put apple mixture in refrigerator for 2 hours. Divide into 4 servings. Put in dessert cups. Top each with whipped cream. Sprinkle with toasted chopped hazelnuts. Serves 4.

DOLCE TORINO
Torino Dessert

1/4 lb. ladyfingers
cognac *or* sweet rum
1/4 lb. sweet butter (without salt) (1/2 cup)
1/2 tsp. confectioners' sugar *or* extra fine sugar
1 egg yolk

1/4 lb. sweet chocolate
2 tbs. cream *or* milk
2 or 3 drops vanilla extract
1/4 cup blanched, lightly toasted almonds*,
    cut in half

Split ladyfingers in half. Sprinkle them lightly on split sides with cognac or sweet rum (too much may cause a bitter taste). In a medium-size bowl, cream butter with sugar and egg yolk.

Cut chocolate into small pieces. In a small saucepan, place chocolate in the cream or milk. Over very low flame, stir until chocolate melts. Remove from flame. Pour melted chocolate over butter, sugar and egg yolk mixture and add vanilla extract. Mix well until it forms a smooth cream.

Place a layer of ladyfinger halves in a dish, split sides down (about 5 across in 2 rows), and spread with a small amount of chocolate cream. Cover with another layer of ladyfingers, spreading more cream on top. Repeat with another layer. Pat layers down lightly to make more compact. Be sure all sides are aligned. Cover top and sides with chocolate cream. Sprinkle with toasted almonds. Refrigerate at least 5 hours before serving. Serves 4.

*To toast almonds: Place blanched almonds on a cookie sheet in a preheated oven at 300°F. for 10–15 minutes or until lightly toasted. Stir occasionally.

PRUGNE CON VINO D'OPORTO
Prunes with Port

1 lb. dry jumbo prunes (pitted)
sugar
Port wine

drop of vanilla extract
dollops of sweetened, whipped heavy cream
tea biscuits

Wash and drain prunes. Place in a medium-size bowl. Sprinkle with sugar. Cover with port. Add vanilla. Mix. Cover. Place in refrigerator and allow to marinate for 12 hours.

Place prunes and mixture in a medium-size saucepan over low flame. Cook until tender. Remove to bowl. Place in refrigerator to chill. Then place in a crystal or serving bowl. Garnish with dollops of sweetened whipped heavy cream. Serve with tea biscuits. Serves 4.

FRAGOLE DAMA BIANCA
Strawberries with Meringue

1 qt. ripe strawberries
1/2 cup sugar
1/4 cup Curacao *or* other liqueur

2 egg whites
3/4 cup heavy cream

Wash strawberries. Hull and dry. Place in a serving bowl and sprinkle strawberries with 2 tbs. of sugar and liqueur. Cover and refrigerate if not serving immediately.

Thirty minutes before serving, beat egg whites until peaks form. Then gradually beat in the remaining sugar until egg whites are stiff. Whip the cream and fold into meringue. Spoon over the berries and chill. Serves 6–8.

DOLCE ALLE PERE DI PAOLA
Paula's Pear Dessert

1 lb. 14 oz. can of halved pears
1/4 cup blanched almonds, toasted and chopped
8 oz. jar maraschino cherries (reserve syrup)

2 tbs. cornstarch
1/4 tsp. cinnamon
3/4 tbs. grated lemon peel

Drain pears and reserve the syrup. Place pears in a baking pan. Fill cavities with chopped almonds. Drain maraschino cherries. Reserve syrup and place in a measuring cup. Add enough pear syrup to cherry syrup to equal 3/4 of a cup. Then mix in cornstarch and cinnamon. Let cook over low flame, stirring for 15 minutes or until syrup starts to boil. Remove from heat. Add cherries and lemon peel. Pour all over pears. Bake in a 12"x16" shallow baking pan in a preheated oven at 350°F. for 15 minutes. Serve either hot or cold. Serves 6.

PESCHE RIPIENE
Stuffed Peaches

6 large firm, fresh peaches
3 peach kernels, chopped*
2 oz. ground blanched almonds (4 tbs.)

6 tbs. sugar
5 ladyfingers, crumbled
1 tbs. finely chopped candied fruit

Wash peaches and cut in half. Remove pits and enlarge cavity enough for filling. Use a nut-cracker to extract kernels from peach seeds. Or use a heavy hammer: Place pits inside a cloth, ends closed, and strike with hammer.

Mix peach pulp, kernels, almonds, 5 tbs. sugar, ladyfingers and candied fruit. Then fill each peach with a spoonful of mixture. Place the 12 halves in a greased, shallow 12"x16" baking pan (filled part facing up). Sprinkle with remaining sugar. Bake in a preheated oven at 350°F. for 10 minutes or until peaches are cooked through. Serve warm. Serves 6.

STREGA MACEDONIA
Strega Fruit Cup

12 fresh ripe apricots
4 jiggers Strega (orange liqueur)
1/2 pt. heavy cream, whipped with sugar to taste

4—6 maraschino cherries (drained on absorbent paper)
vanilla wafers

Peel apricots by placing them in boiling water for 1—2 minutes or until skins can be easily removed. Slice. Place in a large bowl. Pour Strega over them. Cover and let marinate for 1 hour. Fold in whipped cream. Place in dessert cups. Top each with a maraschino cherry. Chill thoroughly. Serve with vanilla wafers. Serves 4—6.

Other fruits such as sliced ripe bananas, pineapple, peaches or cherries may also be prepared this way.

MELE AL FORNO
Baked Apples

6 large baking apples
6 tbs. sweet butter
6 tbs. sugar
1 tsp. cinnamon

grated rind of 1 lemon
1 cup sweet Marsala
granulated sugar
light cream

Wash apples and dry. Core apples. Let butter soften at room temperature. In a small bowl, mix butter, sugar, cinnamon and lemon rind. Fill apple cavities with mixture.

Pour Marsala in bottom of a 7"x11" baking pan. Place apples in pan. Sprinkle top of each with sugar. Bake in a preheated oven at 375°F. for 30 minutes or until tender. Do not overcook. Serve with cream. May be served hot or cold. Serves 6.

BUDINO DI RISO
Rice Pudding

2 cups milk
1/2 cup rice
1/4 cup sugar
1/4 cup seedless raisins
2 tbs. finely chopped candied fruit or peel
pinch of salt

3 tbs. heavy cream
2 beaten egg yolks
1 1/2 tsp. vanilla extract
1 stiffly beaten egg white
fine bread crumbs
whipped heavy cream (optional)

Put milk in top section of a double boiler. Place over boiling water. Over high flame, allow milk to come to a boil. Lower flame. Add rice. Cook for about 45 minutes or until milk is absorbed. Stir frequently. Remove from heat. Add sugar, raisins, candied fruit or peel, salt, heavy cream, egg yolks and vanilla extract. Mix well. Then fold in stiffly beaten egg white.

Sprinkle some bread crumbs on the bottom of a greased 8"x8"x2" baking dish. Transfer rice mixture to dish. Sprinkle top with more bread crumbs. Bake in a preheated oven at 350°F. about 15 minutes or until golden brown. Serve cold. Serves 4.

If desired, serve cold, topped with sweetened whipped cream.

ZABAGLIONE STREGA
Strega Custard

6 egg yolks
1/2 cup sugar

2/3 cup Strega (orange liqueur)
ladyfingers

In top of a glass or enamel double boiler, beat egg yolks and sugar with a wire whisk until thick and pale in color. Gradually beat in Strega. Place over boiling water. Over low flame, continue to beat until mixture begins to thicken and froth. Do not boil. Remove from flame and immediately strain into sherbet glasses lined with ladyfingers. Serve hot. Serves 6.

DOLCE DI RISO E CACAO
Rice and Cocoa Dessert

1/2 cup raw rice
1 qt. milk
5 tbs. sugar
pinch of salt
4 tbs. butter
peel of 1 lemon (whole, not grated)

1 tsp. vanilla extract
3 eggs, separated
1/2 cup cocoa
very fine dry bread crumbs
sifted confectioners' sugar

In a medium-size saucepan over low flame, cook rice with milk, sugar, salt, butter, lemon peel and vanilla extract. Cook for 30 minutes or until tender, stirring frequently. Remove from flame. Discard lemon peel. Beat in egg yolks and set aside.

In a small saucepan over low flame, put cocoa and a small amount of water (just enough to dissolve cocoa). When well blended, remove from flame, add to rice and mix well. In a medium-size bowl, beat egg whites until stiff and fold into rice.

Butter a 1-quart mold and sprinkle with bread crumbs. Pour rice mixture into mold. May be served cool or cold. Right before serving, sprinkle with sifted confectioners' sugar. Serves 4—6.

TORRONE
Brown Nougat

8 oz. jar honey
1/2 lb. sugar (1 cup)
5 tbs. water

5   5-1/2-oz. bags shelled almonds
confettini (tiny candy sprinkles)

Melt honey over low flame in a heavy medium-size aluminum pan. Set aside. Place sugar and water in a small pan. Heat and stir over low flame until sugar melts. Add to honey. Add almonds. Mix. Stir constantly with a wooden spoon over low flame for about 30 minutes or until almonds are toasted and syrup is darkened and somewhat thick.

When done, pour into a well-buttered baking tin (12"x16"). Smooth and flatten with a wooden spoon. Sprinkle generously with confettini. Allow to set for about 8 minutes. If too soft, let stand for a few more minutes, but do not allow to harden as cutting will be difficult. Cut nougat into 2-inch squares. Use spatula to make removal easier. Cool. Serve in a crystal candy dish at Christmas or anytime. To store, place in an airtight jar. Do not refrigerate.

GELATO ALLA MARSALA
Ice Cream Marsala

1/2 lb. macaroons
sweet Marsala
vanilla ice cream

Crush macaroons in a medium-size bowl and blend with Marsala until pasty. Put 1 1/2 tbs. of mixture in dessert dishes. Top with vanilla ice cream. Serves 3–4.

GELATO DI MARASCHINO
Maraschino Ice Cream

2 egg yolks
4 tbs. sugar
1 tbs. Maraschino liqueur

9 maraschino cherries (quartered and drained on absorbent paper)
1/2 pint heavy cream

In a medium-size bowl, place eggs, sugar and Maraschino liqueur. Using an electric mixer, beat at medium speed for 15 minutes. Then add maraschino cherries and mix with a spoon. In a chilled bowl, beat cream until thick. Then add to egg yolk mixture by folding very delicately.

Place in a dry ice cube tray (10 1/2"x4"x1 1/2"). Place in freezer. Leave cold control at moderate and let stand for 1 3/4 hours. Then without removing ice cream from tray, turn it with a spoon, mixing slightly. Smooth out with back of spoon. Return to freezer. Let stand for 2 1/2 hours more. Then raise cold control to coldest position. Let freeze for 1 hour. Serves 6.

If desired, top each serving with a whole drained maraschino cherry. To keep ice cream in freezer, cover tray tightly with aluminum foil.

Ice cream was once called the "dessert of kings" because only royalty could afford it. Thirteenth century Venetians called it "delicious," but only the wealthy there could enjoy it because the freezing process was so difficult and costly. Actually, the art of making ice cream has changed very little since then.

GELATO DI VANIGLIA CON SALSA DI FRAGOLE
Vanilla Ice Cream with Strawberry Sauce

1 qt. vanilla ice cream
4 cups ripe strawberries

2 tbs. sugar
1/2 cup sweet vermouth

Wash strawberries. Hull and dry. Slice. Place in a bowl. Sprinkle with sugar. Pour sweet vermouth over strawberries. Mix and chill. Spoon over servings of ice cream. Serves 6 or more.

ANGEL TORTONI

1 egg, separated
1 cup prepared eggnog
1/4 tsp. salt
1/4 tsp. vanilla extract
1/4 tsp. almond extract
1 1/2 cups angelfood cake crumbs, toasted

1/3 cup finely chopped toasted almonds
1/3 cup toasted coconut flakes
2 tbs. sugar
1/2 cup heavy cream, whipped
8—10 red maraschino cherries
8—10 small pieces green candied cherries

In a small bowl, beat egg yolk. Combine with eggnog and salt in a small saucepan. Cook over low heat until mixture thickens, stirring constantly. Chill. Stir in vanilla and almond extracts, toasted cake crumbs, almonds and coconut. Beat egg white until frothy. Gradually add sugar and continue beating until stiff and shiny. Fold into chilled eggnog mixture. Then fold in whipped cream. Place about 1/3 cup of mixture into each of ten fluted paper baking cups set into a muffin pan. Freeze until firm (at least 4 hours).

To serve: Peel off paper cups. Make "flowers" for garnish by slashing cherries to resemble poinsettias and draining them on absorbent paper. Place one "flower" shiny side up on each serving. Insert a piece of candied green cherry in the center of each "flower." Serves 8—10. **(See photo on opposite page.)**

GELATO DI VANIGLIA CON SALSA DI LAMPONI
Vanilla Ice Cream with Raspberry Sauce

2 10-oz. pkgs. frozen raspberries (thawed)
1 1/2 tbs. sugar *or* sugar to taste

2 tbs. Curacao (or other preferred liqueur)

Put raspberries through a sieve into a medium-size bowl. Add sugar and Curacao. Mix and chill. If thicker sauce is desired, place mixture in a small saucepan. Stir over low flame until thicker. Cool and chill. Serve over ice cream. Serve with vanilla wafers. Serves 6 or more.

Angel Tortoni. See recipe on opposite page.

Photo courtesy of American Institute of Baking.

The Italian expression, *Pronto!* (Ready!) can sometimes be the coffee bell ringing in the aroma of freshly brewed black coffee to the table—a wonderful climax to a delicious *pranzo* (meal)!

The gleaming silver coffee service is set down. And much to the extreme pleasure of everyone, steaming *caffè espresso* is poured into fine china demitasse cups or clear coffee glasses. For the purist, the coffee must be "as is," without sugar or trimmings, but the beverage laced with liqueur or topped with thick whipping cream holds a special charm for others.

The Italian buys coffee immediately after the bean has been roasted and ground to the texture of granulated sugar. This is because coffee loses its flavor with time. In 15 days, nearly twice as much coffee would be necessary to get a cup worthy to be spoken of. So, a small amount is bought so it will be consumed at least within a week, being kept refrigerated, meanwhile, in a tightly closed jar.

A sparkling clean *caffettiera* or *macchineta* is used to brew it—a coffee maker that can be purchased in aluminum or copper in department or hardware stores. Two, four, six and eight-cup coffee makers are available.

CAFFE ESPRESSO
Coffee, Italian Style

4 tbs. Italian roasted ground coffee	**sugar to taste (optional)**
4 cups water	**lemon peel**

The *caffettiera* or *macchineta* has two cylinders, one with an inverted spout and another with a strainer part that holds the coffee. Put coffee in strainer part. Screw back top. Pour water in bottom section. Replace strainer part. Cover with top cylinder with inverted spout.

Place over heat. When a generous amount of steam escapes bottom section, remove from flame. Very carefully turn *caffettiera* upside down (by holding handles firmly together). The boiling water will drip down into the lower section. When water is completely in lower section, the coffee is ready to be served in demitasse cups or coffee glasses. Serve with sugar and a twist of lemon peel. Serves 8.

CAFFE CAPPUCCINO
Sweet Italian Coffee

Add 1 tbs. of frothy, very hot milk to every 3/4 cup of *caffè espresso*. Stir in sugar to taste. Sprinkle lightly with cinnamon.

OR

Stir in sugar to taste in every cup of *caffè espresso*. Top each with whipped heavy cream and sprinkle lightly with cinnamon.

Caffè Espresso

CAFFE REALE
Royal Italian Coffee

Fill demitasse cups 3/4 full with *caffè espresso*. Add a dash of cognac and sugar to taste. In place of cognac, you may add a dash of either anisette, rum, white creme de menthe, curacao, or Cointreau.

CAFFE LUNGO
Diluted Italian Coffee

To every 1/2 cup of hot *caffè espresso*, add 1/2 cup of boiling water (for those who desire weak black coffee). Serve with sugar and lemon peel.

CAFFE SANTO
Health Coffee

To every cup of *caffè espresso* add a few drops of Fernet-Branca (stomachic bitters). Add sugar to taste. Recommended for easier digestion.

ESPRESSO BY THE CUPFUL

If an Italian coffee maker cannot be obtained, there is another way to enjoy this beverage. Into each demitasse or espresso cup, measure 2 teaspoonfuls of Medaglia D'Oro freeze-dried espresso. Fill with 3/8 cup (3 oz.) of boiling water and stir. Serve with a twist of lemon peel and sugar if desired.

CAFFE GELIDO
Iced Espresso

Into a tall 10-ounce glass, measure 2 level teaspoons of freeze-dried espresso. Add 1/4 cup cold water and stir. Add 4 ice cubes and fill glass with more cold water, stirring. If desired, add super-fine sugar.

ITALIAN AFTER-DINNER GUESSING GAMES

After dinner while everyone is still sitting around the table, having spoken of a diversity of things, Grandmother starts some guessing games to which the grandchildren are all ears, searching for answers with a giggle . . .

Dopo del pranzo che ancora tutti rimancono atorno la tavola e si parla di diversi discorsi, alloro all'ultimo la nonna incomincia a dire qualche indovinello quale tutti i inpotini attentamente cercano di rispondere e indovinare . . .

On the mountain of Becafu
there is something that goes,
"Fu, fu!"
It is not a monk, but has a beard!
It is not a sheep, but has horns!
    What is it?

*Sopra la montagna
di Becafu
ce una cosa che fa, "Fu, fu!"
Non a monaco ma ciava la barba,
non e un pecoro ma ciava le corna!
    Cosa è?*

In a garden,
I entered and found
some lovely ladies
dressed in violet,
with hats of green!
    What are they?

*In un giardino entrai
belle donne che trovai
vestite violace
col cappelli verdi in testa!
    Che sono?*

White mountain;
black seed.
The man who sows it
always thinks.
    Who is he?

*Bianca montagna;
nera e la semenza.
L'uomo che semina,
sempre pensa.
    Chie lui?*

It is round and more round;
and looks like a glass without a bottom.
But—a glass it is not!
    What is it?

*Tanto rotondo
bicchiere senza fondo
Bicchiere non è
Indovina cosa è?*

ANSWERS:

1. a snail   2. eggplants   3. a writer putting his words down on white paper   4. a ring.

RISPOSTE:

1. un lumaca 2. melanzane 3. l'uomo che scrive sopra carta bianca 4. anello

Excerpted from "Southern Italian Folklore in New York" by Pauline Barrese, originally published in the *New York Folklore Quarterly*, New York Folklore Society, c/o Farmers' Museum, Cooperstown, New York.

213

INVITATION TO DINNER IN OLD CIMINNA

In Mother's kitchen in Ciminna, Sicily, copper pots hung against a whitewashed wall like burnished soldiers waiting to be marched to the stone stove. As always, the stove was gorged with such kindling as dead sumac roots and olive branches gathered by Mother's father, Nonno (grandfather).

In the corner of the room patiently stood *le quartari*, large terra-cotta jugs holding water drawn by Mother and her mother Nonna (grandmother) from a fountain in the piazza.

This evening, Zia Anna and Zio Filippo (Aunt Anna and Uncle Philip) were coming to dinner. So Mother and Nonna industriously prepared dinner together. Flushed with pleasure, Mother chopped onion for the special-occasion meat sauce that was to bubble until its fragrance filled every nook of the house. She chatted with Nonna as she placed bread in the hot oven and then inserted a small iron door called *balata* in its entrance. Drawing some water from a *quartara* with a white ceramic pitcher, she wet some rags to tuck tightly around the door's edges, making the chamber air-tight.

Dear Zia Anna and Zio Filippo would soon arrive to kiss Mother, her small brother Guiseppe and Nonna affectionately. They spoke about little things and then sat around the great linen-covered oak table to share a pasta and meat meal destined to be completely at the mercy of Zia Anna's raves.

Meanwhile, Zio Filippo's appreciative sighs could be heard with every sip of Nonno's home-made wine poured from a brown jug, until his lips turned as red as rubies.

Relishing fresh figs and a variety of nuts after dinner, the men then went off to play *Scuppa* in an adjoining room with a gray billow of pipe smoke about their heads. It was a card game their great-grandfathers also enjoyed for incalculable hours.

Nonna ground the roasted coffee beans to brew *caffè* on the stove in a small clay pot of boiling water which would later be strained.

As soon as everyone gathered once more to delight in the steaming black beverage, Mother was to remind Nonna to start some *indovinelli* (guessing games). And when Zia Anna couldn't guess one, she threw back her dark head and laughed heartily, only to be joined by the others.

After an evening of lightheartedness and fun, company too soon departed. Mother helped Nonna return the rinsed dishes and pewterware to the deep cupboard. And rehung the copper pots scoured with white sand and lemon juice until they scintillated like the sun.

Later that night, Mother and her family went upstairs to bed, their way lighted by the glow of an oil lamp. Content with tradition, they were to dream of not another or better life in Ciminna.

PLANNING A DO-AHEAD BUFFET

The secret to unfrazzled nerves in serving an Italian buffet is to plan a do-ahead menu. This includes doing shopping several days before, cooking and refrigerating certain items a day ahead so you have very little to prepare the same day of the occasion.

BUFFET MENU
Chilled Vermouth with Lemon Peel
*Roast Leg of Lamb with Rosemary
*Garden Fresh Potato Salad
*Tomato Slices with Basil
*Stuffed Eggs with Pimiento
*Rolled Fillets of Anchovies with Capers
*Sardines with Green Olives
Sweet Red Peppers in Vinegar
Valpolicella Wine
Black Queen Olives
*Sicilian Rolls
*Anise Slices
*Ice Cream Marsala
*Caffè Espresso
Sweet Sherry (optional)

*Recipes included in this book. See index. Increase amounts of ingredients in recipes as necessary.

DAY BEFORE BUFFET

Early in the Day
Take out all dishes, platters, trays, silverware, glasses, napkins, tablecloth, caffettiera, demi-tasse cups, centerpiece, etc. to be used. Place in a handy closet space. Choice should have a coordinated color scheme, e.g., red, white and blue.

Roast leg of lamb. Let cool quickly. Cover with plastic wrap and place in refrigerator.

While lamb is cooking, prepare dough for bread rolls. When dough is ready, bake rolls. Let cool completely. Place in plastic bags. Tie and place in refrigerator to keep fresh.

Cook potatoes for salad and boil eggs. Prepare potato salad and place in a large bowl. Pack salad in bowl with a wooden spoon to mold. Cover and refrigerate.

Place boiled eggs under cool water and shell carefully. Prepare except for pimiento garnish. Place on serving platter. Wrap and refrigerate.

In the Afternoon:
Bake anise slices. Cool completely. Keep in a tight container.

Roll anchovies with capers. Place on a serving platter large enough to later place sardines, olives and sweet red peppers in vinegar cut in thick strips. Cover. Refrigerate.

Wash tomatoes. Dry. Refrigerate.

DAY OF BUFFET

Early in the Day
Set buffet table attractively with centerpiece. Place dishes, silverware, glassware, napkins, demi-tasse cups, salt and pepper shakers, and unchilled wines on the table. These may be placed on one end of the table. Cover all with a large table-cloth or plastic cover to keep dust-free.

Remove bread rolls from refrigerator. Cut almost in half. Return to plastic bags. Leave at room temperature. If preferred, place in bread baskets or trays and wrap.

About Two Hours before Buffet
Remove roast leg of lamb from refrigerator. Remove fell (skin). With a sharp knife, cut fairly

thin slices. Place on a serving platter. Mince fresh parsley and sprinkle over lamb slices. Wrap and refrigerate.

Then unmold potato salad on bed of crisp lettuce leaves in center of serving platter or tray. Remove tomatoes from refrigerator. Slice and prepare according to recipe. Surround potato mold with tomato slices overlapping each other. Wrap loosely and return to refrigerator.

Prepare sardines according to recipe except for olive garnish. Cover and refrigerate. Slice stuffed green olives and place in a separate dish. Cover and refrigerate. Slice pimiento strips. Wrap and refrigerate.

Remove rolled anchovies from refrigerator. Attractively arrange olives and strips of red peppers in vinegar on same platter. If you want the olives to look shiny, dry them and then roll them lightly in oil. Leave space on platter for sardines to be placed later. Refrigerate.

About One Hour before Buffet

Prepare Ice Cream Marsala except for ice cream. Place in dessert dishes in refrigerator.

Chill vermouth. Valpolicella and sweet sherry may be served at room temperature. If preferred, sweet sherry may also be chilled.

About One-Half Hour before Buffet*

Remove leg of lamb, potato salad with tomatoes, stuffed eggs, rolled anchovies with capers

and sardines from refrigerator. If desired, run tines of fork lengthwise along length of filling for fancier looking eggs. Garnish with pimiento.

On same platter with anchovies, sweet red peppers and black olives, place sardines. Garnish sardines with sliced stuffed olives.

Cut strips of lemon peel 2 inches long and 1/4 inch wide. Place on small dishes to accompany appetizer wine and *caffè espresso*, if desired.

Fill coffee maker with proper amount of ground coffee.

Place all foods, including bread rolls and anise slices, in an interesting arrangement on buffet table. Place proper serving utensils alongside foods. (A nice way to serve anise slices is to place them on a pedestaled cake dish.)

At Buffet Time

When guests arrive, serve chilled sweet vermouth with lemon peel.

After buffet, remove dessert dishes from the refrigerator and add ice cream to macaroon and Marsala mixture. Serve.

Meanwhile, make *caffè espresso*. Serve coffee with anise slices.

Serve sweet sherry, if desired.

*If buffet is given on a warm day, foods should be kept in refrigerator until a few minutes before serving to avoid spoilage.

BUFFET MENUS

Chilled Dry Sherry
*Miniature Veal Rolls, Sicilian Style
Genoa Salami

*Potato Salad

Provolone
*Fried Eggplant

*Sicilian Rolls

Black and Green Olives   Pickles
*Black Coffee   *Maraschino Cake

*Sliced Roast Turkey
*Miniature Meatballs
Capocollo

Bel Paese Cheese
*Tomato Slices with Basil

Peperonicini al'Aceto
Cantaloupe Slices

Chilled Marsala   *Roast Leg of Lamb with Rosemary
*Grilled Sausages   Mortadella
                          Anchovies
*Potato Croquettes   *Eggplant and Pimiento Salad
*Celery Stuffed with Gorgonzola   Provola
Olives   Pickles
Grissini (Bread Sticks)   *Sicilian Rolls
*Black Coffee   Fresh Sugared Strawberries
                    *Sicilian Cream Tartlets

Chilled Dry Sherry   Proscuitto
*Tuna Foam   Capocollo
*Sautéed Breaded Celery   *Tomato Slices with Basil
                      *Marinated Vegetables
Provolone   Bel Paese or Fontina Cheese
                          Pickles
                  Green and Black Olives
                      *Sicilian Rolls
*Black Coffee   *Ladyfinger Delight   Assorted Nuts

Chilled Dry Vermouth   Capocollo
Sicilian Salami   Zampino
*Salad with Mayonnaise   *Roasted Peppers
Bel Paese Cheese   Provola
*Caponatina   Pickles   Black Olives
                      *Sicilian Rolls
                  *Hot Coffee Spongecake
*Black Coffee   Assorted Fruits and Nuts

---

*Recipes included in this book. See index. Increase amounts of ingredients in recipes as necessary.

PLANNING A DO-AHEAD DINNER

The number of courses served at an Italian dinner depends on the occasion or lack of it. Holidays and special occasions call for five-course meals while everyday menus include two or three.

Having guests to dinner becomes a festive time and much interest is devoted to the preparation of an impressive menu. The following is a dinner menu for guests and a guide for preparing it ahead which I hope will help you economize your time and enjoy the occasion as much as your guests will.

DINNER MENU

Chilled Dry Sherry
*Antipasto (Celery Stuffed with Gorgonzola,
Rolled Salami Slices)
*Rice Dumplings in Broth
*Breaded Chicken Breasts
*Potatoes with Cream
*Buttered Carrots
*Mixed Salad
Well Chilled Soave or White Chianti
Assorted Fruit in Season
Assorted Nuts
*Torino Dessert
*Caffè Espresso
Brandy

*Recipes included in this book. See index. Increase amounts of ingredients in recipes as necessary.

THE DAY BEFORE

Early in the Day
Take out all dishes, silverware, glassware, bowls, platters, tablecloth, napkins, caffettiera, etc. to be used. Place in a handy closet space.

Prepare chicken broth. Cool quickly. Place in refrigerator.

Prepare antipasto. Cut celery sticks and stuff with Gorgonzola. Place on a serving platter. Cover with plastic wrap. Slice salami and wrap also. Refrigerate.

Put first four ingredients of Mixed Salad in a bowl. Cover, wrap and refrigerate.

In the Afternoon:
Flatten chicken breasts. Cover and refrigerate.

Boil carrots. Drain. Cut in fine slices. Cover and refrigerate.

Wash fruit. Dry. Place in a fruit bowl in the refrigerator.

Place assorted nuts in bowls with picks and nutcrackers.

SAME DAY OF DINNER

Early in the Day
Set table with soup bowls on dinner plates, soup spoons, dinner and salad forks, dinner knives, napkins, water and wine glasses, salt and pepper shakers. Cover with a tablecloth or plastic cover to keep dust-free.

Prepare Torino Dessert and place in refrigerator to set.

Bread chicken breasts. Cover. Return to refrigerator.

Three Hours before Dinner
Prepare rice balls for broth. Cook. Place in a bowl. Cover and keep in a cool place.

Strain broth. Cover and place in refrigerator.

One Hour before Dinner
Chill wines.

About 40 Minutes before Dinner
Boil potatoes.

Fill coffee container with proper amount of ground coffee.

Remove chicken broth from refrigerator. Remove fat from top. Place in a pot. Cover and set aside.

About 30 Minutes before Dinner
Prepare two skillets with butter for chicken breasts. While chicken is cooking, prepare garnishes and warm serving platter for chicken and bowl for potatoes. When chicken and potatoes are done, arrange on platter and bowl, cover, and place in a warmer.

Remove antipasto from refrigerator and place in center of dinner table. Roll salami slices and secure each with a toothpick.

Remove carrots from refrigerator.

About 20 Minutes before Dinner
Put hot water in bottom section of double boiler and bring to a boil. Place carrots in top section and heat thoroughly. Prepare. Place in a

warm bowl. Cover and keep in a warmer.

Dinner Time

When guests arrive, serve appetizer wine with antipasto. Meanwhile, start heating broth. When antipasto course is done, remove tray or platter. Remove dinner wine from refrigerator and place on dinner table.

Place hot broth in tureen in center of table. Place rice balls in soup bowls. Ladle broth over them.

After each course, remove dishes and course utensils.

For the salad course, which is served immediately after the main course, remove salad from refrigerator. Toss lightly with salad dressing.

After dinner, remove all dishes, utensils and water glasses from table. Place bowls of fruit and nuts on table to be served with dinner wine. After completion, remove all.

For the dessert course, set demitasse cups, dessert dishes, coffee and dessert spoons at each place.

Meanwhile, make *caffè espresso*. Pour. Serve with dessert. Serve brandy afterwards in attractive glasses.

SPECIAL HOLIDAY MENUS

CONFIRMATION MENU

Chilled Dry Sherry
*Beef Broth
*Stuffed Capon
*Roast Potatoes
*Fried Eggplant
*Mixed Salad
Soave
*Italian Cheese Pie
Sliced Peaches
*Black Coffee
Moscato

BAPTISM MENU

Chilled Marsala
Mafalde with *Sauce with Meatballs
and *Beef Roll
*Chicken with Sage
*Steamed Carrots
Lettuce Salad with *Basil Dressing
Red Chianti
Fresh Fruit
Assorted Nuts
*Cherry Slices
*Sesame Seed Cookies
*Anise Slices
*Black Coffee
Anisette

CHRISTMAS EVE MENU

Chilled Dry Vermouth
Antipasto
*Cream of Mushroom Soup
*Stuffed Shrimp with Italian Ham
*Artichoke Hearts with White Wine
*Red Pepper Salad
White Chianti
Fruit
*Sicilian Raisin Puffs
*Black Coffee
Maraschino

CHRISTMAS MENU

Chilled Marsala
*Clear Chicken Broth
*Lasagne
*Roast Turkey
*Fried Sausages
*Stuffed Mushrooms with Purée of Peas
Escarole Salad with *Italian Dressing
Soave
*Roasted Chestnuts
Prickly Pears
*Sicilian Fruit-Filled Cookies
Assorted Nuts
*Black Coffee
Cognac

Photo courtesy of Western Growers Association.

NEW YEAR'S EVE MENU

Chilled Dry Sherry
Antipasto
*Onion Soup
*Roast Beef
*Fried Sausages
*Hot Whipped Potatoes
*Sautéed Broccoli
*Tomato and Onion Salad
Red Chianti
Fruit
Assorted Nuts
*Honey Balls
*Black Coffee
Asti Spumante

NEW YEAR'S MENU

Chilled Dry Vermouth
*Manicotti
*Deviled Chicken
*Veal Rolls, Sicilian Style
*Stuffed Artichokes Neapolitan
*Steamed Mushrooms
*Red Pepper Salad
White Chianti
Assorted Nuts
Fresh Fruit
*Italian Rum Cake
*Black Coffee
Cognac

EASTER MENU

Chilled Marsala
*Antipasto (Stuffed Eggs with Pimiento,
Rolled Salami Slices)
*Clear Chicken Broth
*Spring Lamb
*Potato Croquettes
*Steamed Asparagus
*Steamed Carrots
Green Salad with *Italian Dressing
Valpolicella Wine
Assorted Nuts
Fresh Fruit
*Easter Wheat Pie
*Black Coffee
Strega

BIRTHDAY MENU

Chilled Sweet Vermouth with Lemon Peel
*Clear Chicken Broth
Farfalette with *Italian Tomato Sauce
*Braised Chicken with Sherry
*Peas with Asparagus
*Mixed Salad
Soave
Grapes (served on crushed ice)
*Sicilian Cream Tart
*Black Coffee
Maraschino

ENGAGEMENT MENU

Asti Spumante
Antipasto
*Clear Chicken Broth
*Chicken Breasts with Parsley
*Stuffed Orange Balls
*Sautéed Broccoli
*Steamed Carrots
*Mixed Salad
Soave
Cantaloupe Slices
*Classic Italian Cheese Cake
*Black Coffee
Liquore Galliano

WEDDING MENU

Asti Spumante
Antipasto
*Manicotti
*Rolled Stuffed Veal Roast
*Sautéed Breaded Mushrooms
*Peas with Asparagus
*Mixed Salad
Bardolino Wine
Fruit in Season
Confetti (sugar-coated Jordan almonds)
*Sicilian Cream Tart
*Sesame Seed Cookies
*Cherry Slices
*Anise Slices
*Black Coffee
Chilled Sweet Sherry

BRIDAL SHOWER BUFFET MENU

Asti Spumante
*Roast Turkey
*Veal Rolls, Roman Style
Sardines
*Grilled Sausages
*Salad with Mayonnaise
Provolone
Bel Paese Cheese
*Broccoli with Lemon
Pickles
*Roasted Peppers
Black Olives
*Sicilian Rolls
Red Chianti
*Cherry Slices
*Sesame Seed Cookies
*Black Coffee
*Strawberries with Meringue
Cognac

*Recipes included in this book. See index.

COOKING TERMS

Appetizer (*Antipasto*)—a relish served before a meal. Anything that sharpens the appetite, such as fish, meats, cheese, pickles, etc.

Bake (*Infornare*)—to cook by dry heat in an oven.

Baste (*Innumidire*)—to moisten roasted meat or fowl at intervals with melted butter, oil, pan drippings, etc.

Beat (*Sbattere*)—to whip with a fork, spoon or beater.

Black Coffee (*Caffè Espresso*)—a strong, black beverage.

Blanch (*Scottare*)—to scald or steep nuts, fruits, etc. in boiling water to remove skins.

Blend (*Mischiare*)—to mix or mingle ingredients.

Bread Crumbs (*Bricioli di Pane*)—hard bread grated to a fine consistency or bread broken up to be used in meat loaves, meatballs, stuffings or sprinkled *au gratin.*

Bread Sticks (*Grissini*)—crisp, long, slender sticks of bread usually eaten as antipasto.

Capers (*Capperi*)—young, green pickled berries used in sauces, etc.

Capon (*Capone*)—fowl emasculated for tenderness and increased size.

Cayenne—powdered pod and seeds yielding a very hot, pungent flavor. Used as a condiment in sauces, meat and chicken dishes.

Chicory (*Cicoria*)—a dark green European and American plant grown for its roots and as a salad green.

Chop (*Tagliare*)—to cut into small pieces.

Cloves (*Chiodi di Garofano*)—dried tropical flower bud used as a spice in cakes or cookies.

Cinnamon (*Cannella*)—an aromatic reddish-brown spice used as a flavoring in desserts. Cinnamon sticks are used in black coffee.

Citron (*Cedro*)—a fruit similar to a lemon, but larger and less acid. The thick yellow rind of the citron is candied for use in fruit cakes and puddings, etc.

Cognac—a superior French brandy. Used also as a flavoring in desserts and black coffee.

Combine (*Combinare*)—to blend and mix ingredients.

Confettini—tiny multicolored candies used to sprinkle on desserts.

Cover Partially (*Copri Parzialmente*)—to place a lid loosely over a pot (about 1/2" from edge).

Crushed Red Pepper Seeds (*Pepe Forte*)—a hot, pungent spice used lightly on fish, vegetables, and other foods.

Dredge (*Infarinare*)—to coat with flour or bread crumbs.

Honeydew (*Melone*)—a sweet, smooth white variety of muskmelon. Eaten as a dessert or appetizer.

Italian Green Pepper—a conical-shaped, mild, light green pepper, thinner-skinned and milder than the bell pepper.

Mash (*Ridurre in Polpa*)—to reduce to a soft, pulpy state by pressure with a fork, spoon or pestle.

Medium-Cooked (*Al Dente*)—expression to describe cooked macaroni which is neither soft nor hard.

Mince (*Tritare*)—to cut or chop in very small pieces, as onions or garlic.

Pasta—dough which contains flour, fat and water for the crust of pies as well as bread and macaroni.

Pepper (*Pepe*)—a pungent East Indian spice. Dried berries yield black pepper. Dried ripe seeds yield white pepper.

Perforated Spoon (*Cucchiaio Perforata*)—a spoon with small holes through which oil or any other liquid can be released from cooked foods while being removed from cooking utensil.

Roll Out (*Rotolare*)—to press or level out dough with a roller.

Rum—an alcoholic drink distilled from fermented cane juice and molasses. It is sometimes used as an essence in baking.

Sauté (*Trifolare*)—to cook in a small amount of fat or butter.

Scallion (*Cipollina*)—a kind of onion, only more delicate.

Sesame Seeds (*Semi di Sesame*)—an East Indian seed used on breads and cookies.

Sherry—a wine of various colors used as an appetizer, dessert or cooking wine.

Simmer (*Bollire a Fuoco Lento*)—to boil very gently.

Skin (*Pelare*)—to strip the skin of fruit, nuts, etc.

Sliver (*Tagliato Allungo*)—to cut into long, slender pieces.

Steam (*Cuocere a Vapore*)—to cook foods surrounded by water vapor in a covered container.

Stuff (*Imbottire*)—to fill food with seasoned bread, meat, rice, etc.

Tomato Paste (*Salsina*)—tomatoes processed into a thick, concentrated form.

Toss (*Scuotere*)—to stir up with a quick, light motion.

Truffle (*Tartufo*)—an edible, blackish fungus that grows beneath the soil. Used sliced on cheese fondue.

PURCHASING GUIDE

VEGETABLES

Artichokes—should be plump and have no brown color. Look for fleshy leaves with fresh green color.

Asparagus—medium-thick, tender stalks with good green color are best. Should not be wilted.

Broccoli—fresh, tight, dark green heads are desirable. Stems should be crisp.

Cabbage—select fresh, firm, well-shaped heads. Avoid those with decay and yellow leaves.

Carrots—avoid large, cracked, or withered carrots. Should be firm and have some green at the top.

Cauliflower—tight, white firm heads are desirable. Look for fresh leaves.

Celery—healthy stalks are crisp and break with a snap. The heart should be clear of any brown spots.

Cucumbers—medium-sized, dark green and firm ones are best. Avoid those with soft tips.

Escarole—should be tender, fresh and crisp.

Eggplant—should be heavy and firm. Softness and dark spots are bad signs.

Green Peas—should be bright green, have good shape and freshness. Yellow shells indicate hardness. Look for full shells.

Lettuce—head should be firm and fresh.

Mushrooms—select firm ones with no soft spots.

Onions—look for those with no soft spots or sprouts.

Peppers—should be firm, thick-skinned and crisp. Softness and limpness are bad signs.

Potatoes—select clean, smooth ones. Avoid those with decaying spots.

Spinach—fresh, clean, dark green leaves are desirable. Avoid decay.

String Beans—do not select those with hard and dry skins where the beans show. Tender ones are desirable.

Tomatoes—should be firm and plump. Avoid ones with soft, decaying spots.

Turnips—smooth, heavy ones are best. A few deep leaf scars around the crown are a good sign.

Zucchini—avoid large or wilted ones. Select the small type.

FISH

There is a great variety of fresh fish on the market. But certain important qualities should be looked for in all:

→ In whole fish, eyes should be bright, clear and not sunken.

→ Gills should be red. When stale, they are grayish.

→ Flesh should be firm and fresh looking.

→ Should have a fresh odor, especially around the gills.

→ Shellfish (clams, mussels) should be tightly closed.

→ Smaller lobsters are best for tenderness.

→ Fillets should be fresh and sweet-smelling.

MEAT

Beef—should have rich, red color. Firmness and good texture are important. Old beef is dark, limp and has a rough texture. Fat indicates tenderness and flavor.

Lamb—flesh should be firm and have a good pink color.

Liver—fine liver has a fresh, red-brown color.

Pork—select pork with fresh, pink-gray color. Firmness is essential. Fat should be white, not yellow.

Veal—flesh should not be limp. Look for pink-brown color. Fat on veal is an indication of quality.

POULTRY

Most consumers today buy poultry already cleaned and packaged. But if you are interested in buying a fresh-killed fryer, broiler or roaster from the chicken market, the following qualities should be looked for:
- → Flesh should be whitish in color. Too much yellow indicates excessive fat.
- → Sturdy, firm breast.
- → Evidence of fat on breast and thighs.
- → In young fowl, skin should not be rough. Look for sharp claws and short hairs. In old fowl, look for the opposite.
- → Enough flesh on body.
- → Should have no unpleasant odor under the wings.

FRUITS

Apples—must have good color and firmness. Avoid ones with soft, brown spots.
Apricots—should be firm, golden yellow and not shriveled or have signs of rot.
Fresh Figs—should be ripe, soft and without sour odor.
Grapes—select firm, fresh, good-colored ones that stick to stem. Mold indicates decay.
Honeydew—select ones that are grayish in color, have a sweet smell, and are soft at blossom ends. Avoid those with dark, deep, soft spots.
Lemons—choose firm, smooth, bright yellow ones.
Oranges—should be heavy, firm and smooth.
Peaches—avoid those with decayed spots or bruises, also wormy and uneven shaped ones.
Strawberries—select fresh, well-shaped, bright red berries. Green caps should be attached.

EGGS

When purchasing eggs, shape and color do not indicate quality. Whether white, cream-colored or brown eggs, the nutritional value in all is similar—much to the surprise of those who believe brown eggs have more value. Color only indicates the breed of chicken it came from.

The quality of an egg is generally the result of food given to the chickens and care exercised in the handling of the eggs. A deep-colored yolk means the chicken was fed some green food and is a sign of quality.

Eggs should always be purchased refrigerated and stored likewise at home.

FROZEN FOOD GUIDE

Food	Months Storage Period	Food	Months Storage Period
Beef	10 to 12	Eggs	6 to 8
Bread (unbaked)	1/2 to 2	Fruits	12
Bread (baked)	12	Fatty Fish	3
Cakes (unbaked)	2 to 3	Ground Beef	6 to 8
Cakes (baked)	4 to 8	Lamb	10 to 12
Cheese	3 to 4	Pork	4 to 6
Cooked Meats	3 to 8	Poultry	6 to 8
Cream	4 to 6	Sausage	1 to 3
Cookies (unbaked)	6 to 9	Veal	10 to 12
Cookies (baked)	12	Vegetables	12

NOTE: Cool cooked foods to room temperature before freezing. Wrap all foods tightly in moisture-resistant wrap.

TABLE OF EQUIVALENTS

pinch or dash	less than 1/8 tsp.
3 tsp.	1 tbs.
2 tbs.	1 liquid ounce of fat
4 tbs.	1/4 cup
16 tbs.	1 cup or 8 ounces
2 cups	1 pint
2 pints	1 quart
4 quarts	1 gallon
16 ounces	1 pound
1 stick of butter	1/2 cup or 1/4 lb.
1/4 lb. of butter	8 tbs. butter
1 1/4 lb. all-purpose flour, sifted	4 cups all-purpose flour, sifted
1 lb. rice	2 1/3 cups raw rice
1 lb. rice	about 8 cups cooked rice
1 lb. broken macaroni	about 12 cups cooked macaroni
1 lb. grated cheese	about 5 cups grated cheese
1 bouillon cube	1 tsp. beef extract
1 cup granulated sugar	1 cup brown sugar, well packed
2 cups granulated sugar (about)	1 lb. sugar
2 1/2 cups confectioners' sugar (about)	1 lb. confectioners' sugar
1 cup sifted all-purpose flour	1 cup sifted cake flour + 2 tbs. all-purpose flour
juice of 1 lemon	3 to 4 tbs. juice
1 sq. unsweetened chocolate	1 oz. unsweetened chocolate
1 large onion, chopped	about 1 cup chopped onion
1/2 tsp. onion powder	1 tbs. chopped raw onion
1/8 tsp. minced garlic or garlic powder	1 clove fresh garlic

SEASONAL BUYING GUIDE

In order to serve the very best vegetables, it is important to know their peak seasons. This seasonal guide will help you choose vegetables of high quality.

VEGETABLE	SEASON
Artichokes	Peak: March, April, October, November.
Asparagus	Peak: March, April.
Beans, Green	All year. Peak: summer months.
Beets	All year. Peak: June and July.
Broccoli	All year. Peak: March.
Cabbage, Green	All year.
Carrots	All year.
Cauliflower	All year. Peak: March.
Celery	All year.
Cucumbers	All year. Peak: May, June, July.
Eggplant	All year. Peak: July, August, September.
Endive, Escarole	All year.
Greens (chicory, dandelion, spinach, etc.)	All year.
Green Onions	All year. Peak: May through August.
Dry Onions	All year.
Parsley	All year.
Green Peas	All year. Peak: March, April, May, June.
Green or Bell Peppers	May to December. Peak: October.
Salad Vegetables	All year, but grown in limited quantities in winter months.

To insure ultimate quality in fresh fish, it is advisable to purchase it in the proper season. The following guide includes most of the fish used in the recipes in this book.

FISH	SEASON
Bass (striped)	All year.
Clams	All year.
Crabs	All year.
Cod	All year.
Eel	All year.
Flounder	All year.
Haddock	All year.
Lobster	All year.
Mackerel	April to November.
Salmon	Summer, Fall.
Shrimp	Spring, Fall.
Sole	All year.
Tuna	Spring, Summer, Fall.

INDEX

Pauline Barrese was born in Greenwich Village, New York. Her early childhood years were spent on Leroy Street adjoining the famed St. Luke's Place which once housed Mayor Jimmy Walker and such eminent writers as Sherwood Anderson and Theodore Dreiser. Growing up in the Village encouraged her deep appreciation of poetry and art. Educated in New York schools, she went on to write poetry, short stories, articles and nonfiction books for both adults and young people. She also paints.

Pauline's poetry has appeared in national magazines, journals and anthologies including the *Chicago Tribune Magazine, America, New York Herald Tribune, Maine Sunday Telegram, Oyez, DeKalb Literary Arts Journal, Epos* and *Steppenwolf.* Her poems have also been broadcast on radio under the auspices of the University of Wisconsin, on WEFG-FM in Winchester, Virginia, and on other stations in New York, Pennsylvania and Maryland.

Her father's Italian ghost tales entranced her as a child and Sicilian and Calabrian folklore have been subjects of several articles of hers published in the *New York Folklore Quarterly.*

She has written a column for *The Writer's Voice* for several years. Interviews by her have appeared in *Downbeat Magazine* and have been syndicated worldwide.

Pauline's love for cooking has long been competing with her writing. She has now combined the two arts in the writing of this cookbook.

Pauline sees similarities in the elements of poetry, art, and cooking—balance, rhythm, and imagery. "Like a poet or artist," she says, "the cook presents a product which expresses her individual feelings."

Pauline Barrese